Cruelly Murdered

Other Books by Keven McQueen:

Cassius M. Clay, Freedom's Champion

Offbeat Kentuckians: Legends to Lunatics

More Offbeat Kentuckians

Murder in Old Kentucky: True Crime Stories from the Bluegrass

The Kentucky Book of the Dead

KEVEN MCQUEEN

Cruelly Murdered

The Murder of Mary Magdalene Pitts
and Other Kentucky
True Crime Stories

Jesse Stuart Foundation
Ashland, Kentucky
2008

Dedicated to many aunts and uncles:
Glenn ("Doc") and the late Mildred Casteel,
Howard and Curtie McQueen, Glenwood and Mildred McQueen,
Jesse Lee and Patti Casteel, Kenneth and Nadine Moore,
Sherill and Wavelene Lakes.

ISBN# 1-931672-49-0

FIRST EDITION

Cover and Book Design by Brett Nance

Published By:
Jesse Stuart Foundation
1645 Winchester Avenue
Ashland, KY 41101
(606) 326-1667 • JSFBOOKS.com

Contents

We all within our graves shall sleep
A hundred years to come;
No living soul for us shall weep
A hundred years to come;
But other men our land will till,
And others then our streets will fill,
And others' words will sing as gay,
And bright the sun shine as to-day,
A hundred years from now!

        --Coz, "A Hundred Years to Come," 1870.

How Isaac Desha
Escaped the Noose Five Times

Richard Dogget was the proprietor of a tavern on the Fleming County border back in the days when Kentucky's highways were traveled by rough characters such as trappers and backwoodsmen—perhaps even the occasional outlaw seeking to dodge a posse. On the first day of November 1824, however, Dogget had a celebrity among his guests: twenty-two-year-old Isaac Bledsoe Desha, son of Governor Joseph Desha, who had been elected in 1823.

The Deshas lived in Mason County. Isaac was practically a newlywed, having married Miss Cornelia Pickett on January 28, 1823, or November 28, depending on which account is correct. The marriage was troubled, if we believe one authority who states that one day, Cornelia "was so terrified at [her husband's] manner and appearance that she left him the next morning and she refused to live with him again." (They had a daughter anyway: Margaret, born around 1824.) Perhaps it was because of domestic infelicity that Isaac Desha was staying at the inn.

A second guest of note arrived at Dogget's tavern the next morning, on November 2: Francis Baker, a newspaperman who had been plying his trade in Natchez, MS, as editor of the *Mississippian*. He was picking his slow way to Trenton, N.J., where he planned to marry his longtime fiancée. Baker is described as being short, bespectacled, heavyset, and bald—though he was only thirty-one. Baker may have lacked physical charms, but he rode a grey mare of singular beauty. No doubt, tavern keeper Dogget was pleased to have such refined, genteel guests instead of roughnecks and murderers.

Baker arrived just in time for breakfast and ate a leisurely meal with several men, including Isaac Desha. Baker intended to hit the road after he rested up, but first he wanted to visit an acquaintance who lived in the area: Captain John Bickley. Desha offered to lead Baker to Bickley's home. Witnesses saw the two riding their horses in the direction of Maysville. Baker's grey mare was adorned with saddlebags; Desha's bay horse had none. The time was eight a.m.

Two hours later, Milton Ball, who lived near the governor's house, saw a rider-less grey mare wandering aimlessly on the highway. It wore a saddle and bridle, but its owner was nowhere to be seen. Ball caught the mare and rode it with the intention of finding her owner. After Ball had traveled a few hundred yards another rider-less horse came his way—a bay that he knew belonged to Isaac Desha. Ball noticed that the horse had a saddle but no bridle. Milton's brother, Elizmon, caught the second horse and rode it to the Desha residence as a neighborly gesture.

As Milton Ball rode in search of the mare's owner, he encountered Isaac Desha on foot and carrying two saddlebags. Desha claimed the grey mare was his property. After Isaac and Milton caught up with Elizmon, Desha parted company with the brothers and took the horses home.

Not long afterwards, two hunters found the empty, discarded saddlebags. Yet Francis Baker seemed to have disappeared. People had their suspicions, but they tended to keep their theories to themselves since Isaac Desha was the governor's son.

Within a week, the suspicions were hidden no longer. On November 8, Milton and Elizmon Ball found the body of Francis Baker hidden behind a fallen tree beside the highway on the border of Fleming and Mason Counties, close to where Milton had seen Isaac Desha carrying the saddlebags. Baker had been partially stripped of his fine clothing and clubbed with a blunt object. A bridle and fragments of a whip were found near the crime scene; when Desha's bay horse had wandered the highway, its bridle was missing. It was not lost on citizens that Isaac Desha, the last man to see Baker alive, owned a loaded riding whip that could have inflicted the blunt force injuries evident on the corpse. No one had seen Desha's whip since the disappearance of Baker. The murderer had also cut Baker's throat and stabbed him in the arm, shoulder, and chest with a dirk of an odd "four-square" shape. Isaac Desha owned a custom-made dirk that precisely fit the holes in Baker's shirt.

Furthermore, it was found that Desha possessed the dead man's grey mare, his gold watch, and the money and clothing that had been packed in Baker's saddlebags. Desha explained that he had met "two men in the road," conveniently unnamed, who had sold him the mare— which he did not recognize as stolen property even though he had just been out riding with its owner. He was not able to produce the two strangers, nor did he even try to account for his possession of Baker's watch, saddle, bridle, and the contents of his saddlebags. Francis Baker was buried in the Methodist churchyard at Shannon, near May's Lick; his suspected killer was arrested and sent to the Flemingsburg jail.

It is not every day that a governor's son is accused of murder, so the arrest of Isaac Desha was a sensation. The Kentucky Legislature granted a change of venue to Cynthiana, Harrison County, on the excuse that Desha could not get a fair trial in Fleming and Mason Counties. The governor could afford a number of top defense attorneys, including senior counsel Judge John Rowan. The prosecution was equally well staffed and included Commonwealth's Attorney William Wall. Judge George "Peg Leg" Shannon presided. The late Francis Baker's brother traveled a long distance to witness the proceedings.

The trial began on January 18, 1825, and ended on January 31 after the jury had heard from twenty prosecution witnesses and twenty-seven defense witnesses. It took the jury only an hour to reach a guilty verdict and recommend that the governor's son be executed by hanging. Desha's defense attorneys were not about to let such a thing happen without a protracted fight. John Rowan filed a motion for a new trial. He claimed that several persons, including the sheriff, had improperly remained with the jury to deliberate after the members had retired. Some jury members had been allowed to enter and leave the courthouse as they pleased. Also, a couple of jurors were cowed by anonymous threatening letters they had received, including one that read: "If the jury do not bring in a verdict against the prisoner, they will be hung in effigy and burnt." This must be one of the all-time wimpiest attempts at intimidation, as the writer did not vow to hang and burn the jury for real, but only in effigy. Rowan probably would have complained if the sheriff had *not* remained with the jury in light of the fact that they had received threatening letters. Most relevantly, Rowan objected that there was not enough solid proof to justify his client's conviction.

To the astonishment of many, Judge Shannon agreed, or at least pretended to, and granted a new trial scheduled for June 1825. The *Kentucky Reporter* editorialized: "[W]e believe nine-tenths of the [legal] profession are against the Judge. Indeed, this decision has produced a very general sentiment of disapprobation, if not disgust, among candid men of all parties."

The second trial was delayed until September. This time a Judge Brown presided. On the twenty-fourth day of that month a second jury found Desha guilty "notwithstanding the patronage of his father...and the supple pliancy of a subservient Legislature," in the spiteful words of the *Kentucky Reporter*. But this would not do, so the attorneys appealed on the grounds that the prosecution had not proved the murder took place in Fleming County, as specified in the indictment. A correspondent in Cynthiana wrote, "[I]t is believed that if this hole had not been found, another would, and that there was to be a new trial, any how—for he is the governor's son, and he is to be allowed to murder and rob upon the public highway—and is neither to be sentenced, nor hanged." The Desha-friendly court agreed and ruled that the prisoner would be tried a third time. The *Kentucky Reporter* referred to the trial as a "farce" and a "mockery." A paper titled the *National Advertiser* asked, "How long will the arm of Justice be stayed?"

The public grew angry and restless because it sensed, rightly or wrongly, that a murderer was being given special treatment due to his family connections. The *Reporter* caught the mood of many when it sarcastically referred to Joseph Desha as "Joseph I" as though he fancied himself a king rather than a governor: "And is that man fit to govern the people of this Commonwealth, who upon his oath is charged with a faithful administration of the laws of his country—and will pardon his son, and refuse it to others, under the same or even lighter circumstances?" Similarly, from the *Winchester Gazette*: "It would seem that justice has either bade adieu to Kentucky, or that her judges are the most corrupt and desperate men living."

Though it is impossible to prove at a distance of nearly two centuries, it does seem to the disinterested observer that some political back-scratching was going on. The *Paris Citizen* complained that the Legislature had performed an act of "extraordinary interference" when it passed a special measure to grant Isaac Desha a change of venue to Harrison County. It was probably not a coincidence that one member of the Legislature happened to be Judge Brown, who had presided over the second trial. The evidence against Isaac Desha was so compelling that a guilty verdict was practically a no-brainer; after all, he was in possession of the dead man's effects and was the last person seen with him—and no other viable suspects had turned up. Yet, two judges overturned two juries' verdicts and ordered new trials. Both judges were close friends of the governor's, making the fact that they presided over the trials a seeming conflict of interest.

However, while it may appear that Isaac Desha was a spoiled child of privilege, the fact that he was the governor's son was a double-edged sword. It is true that he probably received considerations that no ordinary man in such an unpromising predicament would have received. On the other hand, his father's enemies turned the judges' decisions into a political controversy by suggesting that the junior Desha's kid-gloves treatment was symptomatic of the corruption in the reigning Jeffersonian Republican party. This kind of thing wouldn't be happening, they implied, if only the Democratic Republicans or the National Republicans (Whigs) were in power!

After more of the usual and expected legal delays, Desha's third trial began in February 1826. The venue, Cynthiana, was the same; the evidence and witnesses were the same; and though the judge and jury were different, the verdict was the same the third time around:

guilty with the recommendation of the death penalty.

We may deduce Isaac Desha's frame of mind after this setback by the fact that he tried and failed several times to procure the narcotic laudanum and a pistol. Around July 8, 1826, he cut his throat in his jail cell—not an act one would expect of an innocent man. A surgeon from Lexington performed emergency measures and rescued him from the threshold of death. For what little time that remained in his life, Desha had to wear a silver tube in his windpipe which permitted him to breathe and speak in a whisper. The *Frankfort Argus* said of the pipe: "It has to be frequently changed or cleaned. When it is removed, he struggles, and were it not replaced, would soon suffocate. Whether guilty or innocent he has suffered worse than the pains of death and will carry with him to the grave a mark which nothing can efface."

For some reason, Desha was not speedily hanged as the jury prescribed. There probably was additional legal wrangling, given that it would make Kentucky a laughingstock—more so, that is—if her governor's son were executed for being a murderer and a common highwayman. In addition, Desha's near-suicide left him weak and in ill health for some time. He was released on bail after physicians declared that confinement would endanger his life.

By now, it seemed clear to even the most generous spectator that certain elements within the Kentucky legal system were determined to try Desha over and over until a verdict of "not guilty" was reached. His attorneys tried to have the case dismissed "on the ground of the unconstitutionality of the venue law," whatever that could mean. The motion was overruled in March 1827. Although most accounts claim that Desha was tried twice, he appeared before the Harrison County Circuit Court for the fourth time the following June. Defense attorneys had filed a motion to have the case discharged since there was difficulty obtaining a jury, but again they were overruled. Worse, doctors testified that Desha was now strong enough to withstand the rigors of prison life, and the new judge, a less sympathetic soul than the previous ones, ordered that he be remanded to jail.

It has been said that Governor Desha feared that Isaac might die if he were sent back to prison. On June 18, the same day the judge issued his order, the concerned father performed the most controversial act of an already troubled governorship: he granted his son an unconditional pardon. The news was greeted with howls of contempt from the governor's political enemies and even some of his supporters. The residents of other states read about it in their papers and thought that the pardon confirmed something they had already suspected: that life was considered a cheap commodity in a barbarous state like Kentucky. Governor Desha faced such a cyclone of criticism that, according to legend, he resigned from office. In actuality, he limply finished out his term.

Isaac B. Desha was a free man, but he did not have long to enjoy his liberty. He was the subject of many legends. Some claimed he moved to Mexico; others said he lived in Honduras; still others maintained that he had been seen in New York City and California. The most exotic yarn was that he went to Hawaii and had a number of children by a native woman. The following story appears to be the truth.

After he was pardoned, Desha changed his name to John Parker and joined Stephen Austin's Texas colony, San Felipe de Austin. He had learned absolutely nothing from his close shaves with the law. In May 1828 he rode to San Antonio with a wealthy Ohio horse trader named Tom Early, but he returned to San Felipe noticeably richer and without Early. Not long afterwards, Early's body was found east of Gonzales. The mayor of San Felipe happened to be from Washington, KY, and it did not take him long to figure out that the "John Parker" with the distinctive silver breathing tube was really the notorious Isaac Desha. He was arrested and charged with committing his second murder, suggesting that the Kentucky juries who had convicted him earlier were correct in their judgment.

This time around, Desha had no influential father to rely upon; it looked like he would at last receive the fate that he had previously escaped several times. One version of events has him committing suicide in prison, but in fact he died of a fever on August 13, the day before he was to stand trial. Lucky guy. Before he passed on to a better world—or a far worse one—he confessed that he had murdered and robbed Francis Baker and Tom Early and had planned to kill a couple of other members of the San Felipe colony as well. It would be interesting to know what Desha's former defense attorneys and the softhearted judges back in Kentucky thought when it became manifest that their efforts to thwart justice had kept a murderer free to kill again.

Governor Desha's popularity had been on the wane even before his son was arrested; afterwards, his career was all but over. After leaving office more or less in disgrace, Desha retired from politics in 1828 and moved to a farm in Harrison County. He died on October 12, 1842, and was buried in Georgetown Cemetery. The Kentucky Legislature eventually coughed up the money to buy a monument for his grave.

There is one final anecdote to tell concerning this notorious murder from early Kentucky history. It will be remembered that Francis Baker was about to marry his girlfriend before his path crossed that of Isaac Desha, who had other plans. The grief-stricken woman never recovered and never married. One version of events claims that she died in an insane asylum. Another version states that around 1878 or 1879, she made her first and only pilgrimage from New Jersey to Shannon, KY, in order to visit Baker's grave. She stayed in town for several days and each day brought a fresh bouquet to the tomb of the fiancé she had lost due to another man's avarice more than a half century before.

Adventures of a Busy Young Man

Kindly, well-intentioned souls who oppose the death penalty on principle sometimes lecture the rest of us barbarians with reasons why a certain murderer should not meet the same fate he doled out to some hapless person (or people, if said killer was industrious). Many of the humanitarians' arguments amount to this: circumstances beyond their control cause murderers to annihilate others. Poverty, bad parental role models, lack of education and privilege, lack of societal acceptance, insanity—any or all of these things can turn a man into a murderer, so the argument goes, and therefore we should consider criminals to be victims themselves and not hold them responsible for their actions. Any punishment they do incur should be "humane"— for example, jail time, community service, plea-bargaining for lesser sentences, or mandatory psychiatric counseling. The idea that some people are just naturally evil is denounced as being unfashionable, judgmental, simplistic, and cruel.

Yet, every now and then, a puzzling figure such as Edward W. Hawkins will come along and send the philanthropists scrambling for new theories. Hawkins was a man who "had it all," and therefore, by their reasoning, no convenient excuses can be made to explain his actions. He was born into affluence rather than poverty. His parents were solid citizens, though his father had an intriguing eccentricity, which shall be described momentarily. His mother was, if anything, overprotective rather than neglectful. Hawkins received a good education in an era when most young men received rudimentary schooling at best and lived out their years toiling on farms. The literary quality of his jailhouse memoirs attests that he was neither insane nor stupid. He grew up in the country—a fact that will dismay those who believe rural life inspires virtue while city life is a certain breeder of vice and wicked behavior. Rather than being a social outcast, Hawkins was popular and had—what may be called with laughable understatement—a way with women. In later years, his half-brother remembered him as having "the reputation of being the handsomest man in the county, having a perfect physique." Despite all of these advantages, Hawkins blossomed into one of the liveliest villains who ever trod the soil of this proud old Commonwealth.

Edward Hawkins's life story is so laden with preposterous-but-true incidents and bizarre details that it almost sounds like a surrealistic novel. For starters, Hawkins was born a triplet on Woodward Creek, Estill County, on July 11, 1836; the other two birth siblings were girls. Edward was one of the thirty-seven children of John W. Hawkins. The elder Hawkins had managed this prodigious feat by having twenty-two children by his first wife, Mary Barnes, and fifteen by his second, Polly Smith. Very interestingly, in the light of Edward's later adventures, despite the elder Hawkins's repute in the community he might have been a bigamist. There is no documentation that he divorced his first wife and the two women lived in separate cabins with their children on the Hawkins farm. They dwelt "in perfect harmony," according to one account. Although he had his son Edward by his first wife in 1836, he had married his second wife in 1824—meaning either that the elder Hawkins was a bigamist, the divorce records from those days are spotty, or Polly Smith was a *very* indulgent and understanding second wife.

Those with a sympathetic attitude toward criminals would claim that Edward Hawkins "learned" his womanizing ways from his father's example. Probably true, but it does not explain the predilection for murdering and thieving that sent him to the gallows. Perhaps the best explanation for the way he turned out was offered by his half-brother nearly fifty years after Edward's death: "I now attribute his downfall, in a great degree, to his excessive vanity." Edward himself admitted that he was bad from the cradle: "The first acts of my life, which I now can remember, were mischievous and evil disposed. My great evil trait in infancy was a reckless disobedience of my parents." Mr. Hawkins tried to punish his son for his misdeeds, but the boy's pious mother sheltered him and attempted to correct her son only through tearful but ineffectual pleadings. He was spoiled and had to have his way all of the time. He managed to avoid punishment for the petty crimes of his youth—such as stealing fishhooks, penknives and watermelons—and later acknowledged that his success hardened him and paved the way to perpetrating larger crimes for greater thrills. At a tender age, he also learned the delights of gambling with cards. A few conscientiously applied paddlings early in life might have done the lad a world of good and also saved the lives of five men, including Edward himself.

In 1849, when he was only thirteen years old, Hawkins abandoned the farm after two years of practice at stealing from friends and neighbors. In Lexington, a man identified only as "W. R." took the boy under his wing and educated him in the more subtle methods of theft: cheating at cards and passing counterfeit money. Hawkins found in Louisville a criminal mentor who instructed him in picking pockets, just as Fagan taught Oliver Twist. After making money through forgery, stealing horses, and by joining a band of professional thieves in Hazel Green, Wolfe County, he was finally arrested for breaking into a store in Pleasant Valley. He spent a year in the penitentiary. After he was released on April 10, 1855, he returned home to his parents and three dozen siblings, unrepentant and well schooled in the arts of crime. He found that his mother had gone blind and was "almost distracted at the news of [his] misfortune and bad conduct." Hawkins felt badly, but not enough to stop what he was doing.

A few weeks after his homecoming, nineteen-year-old Hawkins decided to do some traveling out of fear that the many forgeries he had committed would catch up with him. He always had a problem with women; he was obsessed with them, admitting in his autobiography that his chief motive for going to school was to flirt with the girls. Women found the rascally fellow attractive, with predictable results. He journeyed to Madison County, where he married seventeen-year-old Elizabeth Gabbard on May 17 after a brief courtship during which he told her a thousand lies, including assurances that he was the son of a wealthy man and was due to receive a vast inheritance when he turned twenty-one. He tried to support his unwitting bride in high style by "robbing night and day," as he put it.

Perhaps Hawkins did not enjoy connubial bliss very much; perhaps he found maintaining a wife through larceny too expensive or too hazardous; or perhaps Elizabeth discovered that he had been lying about his background. Whatever the reason, only one month into their marriage (one month and two days, to be fair) he abandoned his bride, went to Lexington, and joined the Army. They shipped him off to Fort Leavenworth in the Kansas Territory, where he commenced robbing the quartermaster of supplies. He enjoyed military life about as much as he enjoyed domestic life; after serving only seven months of his five-year enlistment, he deserted. He later claimed to have murdered a commanding officer, but this was never confirmed.

The girls in the Kansas-Missouri region were good-looking and ripe for the plucking, so he elected to stay in the area. Posing as an Army recruiter, he courted a girl known as "Miss S. S." in Liberty, MO. He married her on January 27, 1856, without having first troubled to divorce Elizabeth Gabbard. Within a week, he had the burning urge to go to Lexington, MO. He started the journey with his second wife, but ditched her in Camden. He arrived in Lexington on February 2, where he immediately started dating "Miss M. M." He married her on February 7, only five days after he first arrived in town, although he was still married to his first and second wives. His lies had grown in ambition; he had told his second fiancée that he was an Army recruiter, but he told the third one that he was an Army officer.

A mere twenty days later, Hawkins fled back to Leavenworth—a bold move indeed for a deserter to return to the military city from which he deserted. There he got a crush on "Miss C. R.," his landlord's daughter. He posed as a man named Anders and claimed to be the editor of the *American Eagle*. Strange to say, it appears that he did not marry her. While in town, Hawkins pulled off several high-risk con jobs and his first documented murder.

One of Hawkins's lowlife friends had passed counterfeit greenbacks and had been so careless as to leave a witness.

Hawkins took care of this by going to Jackson, MO, and tracking down the witness, a man probably named William Jones. ("This, I think, was his name," wrote Hawkins.) He sportingly attempted first to bribe the man not to testify against his friend. Jones refused. Hawkins resorted to threats. When Jones still refused Hawkins shot him near the left eye. Displaying precocity and sophistication, he ran over the corpse's head with a wagon to make it seem as if he had been killed in an accident. The authorities suspected nothing. Hawkins wrote that his conscience bothered him, but only for a little while.

Perhaps because he was nervous about the murder, soon afterward Hawkins pulled up stakes and moved to Glasgow, MO. It was not long before he was smitten by "Miss M. F.," a child of only thirteen summers. One might expect him to have won her favor by masquerading as a salesman of lollypops or dollhouse furniture, but instead he passed himself off as a lawyer named Andrews. Hawkins married the girl on May 25. She was the third bride he had taken since the beginning of 1856 and the year wasn't even half over yet. He took to his heels on June 3, abandoning his blushing bride, but taking with him money the girl's father had given him for purchasing a house.

In Elkhorn, Hawkins "borrowed" a horse, which he rode to Topeka in the Kansas Territory. He sold the beast there for $135. We find him next in the town of Easton, where in the guise of being a dentist he met, courted, and married "Miss C. W." on June 18. He accomplished all of this in fewer than nine days, still without having divorced wives one through four. Hawkins must have found the charms of number five hard to resist, for he remained with her a whole three weeks before he left for Boonville, MO, where he sold a horse and buggy—hired by his latest father-in-law—for $300.

When Hawkins judged it was safe, he sneaked back to Kansas. Over the next three weeks, he indulged in so many crimes major and minor that I pass over them for fear it would tax the reader's patience to read about them all. He celebrated his birthday on July 11, 1856 by putting on a disguise and going to a town called Lexington, whether in Missouri or Kansas he does not say, to witness a public hanging. As Hawkins took in the spectacle, he was unaware that the same fate would be his before his next birthday came.

Things got too warm for Hawkins in the Midwest, so he hurried back to Kentucky in August. He soon continued doing business at the old stand; on August 28, while in Shelby County, the accomplished seducer met the fifteen-year-old daughter of a man whose initials were H. D. Posterity does not record what false occupation Hawkins claimed when he met this unfortunate. Although she was engaged to another man, she became Hawkins's sixth concurrent wife on September 1. Their matrimonial heaven lasted until October 24. On that day, an acquaintance embarrassed Edward to no small degree by innocuously bringing up, in the presence of Mrs. Hawkins number six, details about his past that he preferred her not to know. The resulting domestic disharmony filled Edward with the spirit of vengeance. He tracked the unwitting tattletale all the way to Dayton, OH. Under the guise of friendliness, he got the man drunk and then deliberately picked a fight with him in front of several witnesses. When the dust cleared, Hawkins had avenged himself with a four-pound knife and his opponent had paid dearly for having told the truth. Because Hawkins cleverly made it look like a case of self-defense, he was acquitted at his trial. He returned to Shelby County covered in glory, but when his wife found out that he had killed a man in a fight, she was overcome with shame and hanged herself.

After this event, Hawkins hastened to his birthplace in Estill County. He doesn't say so in his memoirs, but I suspect the Shelby Countians wanted to stick his head on a pole. When he got home, he discovered that his mother had died while he had been gallivanting about the country causing trouble. His father had packed up and moved to Ohio.

Perhaps the suicide of his last wife and the death of his mother caused Edward Hawkins some uncomfortable moments, but he soon consoled himself by getting engaged for the seventh time after a three-day courtship, this time to "Miss B." The date of the wedding was set for August 25, 1857, and it was number seven's good fortune that circumstances to be described below prevented the nuptials.

Hawkins left Estill County on November 10 to visit his father's new home in Ohio: "There I found plenty of pretty girls that suited me." After a courtship that lasted all of one day, an all-time speed record even by Hawkins's brisk standards, he became engaged to "Miss E. J. A." on Christmas Day—I suppose as insurance in case things didn't work out with number seven. Of course, he kept knowledge of the other wives and brides-to-be away from his latest fiancée, who in only a week became his penultimate fiancée. On New Year's Day 1857, Hawkins started dating girl number nine, whom he had stolen away from his brother Thomas. He proposed to her the very next day and set a wedding date for January 15, only two weeks away. It is a good policy to pay everyone a sincere compliment, so let it be said of Edward Hawkins that at least he wasn't lazy.

While in a nostalgic mood, Hawkins visited fiancées number seven and eight, and then went back to Estill County, possibly itching to find number ten. He didn't stay long for fear of being arrested on those old charges of counterfeiting and forgery. He went to Madison County on March 9 to visit Elizabeth Gabbard, his very first (and only legal) wife and was astonished when she wanted nothing to do with him: "I told her that I still loved her dearly, and would take her and take care of her, but I had deceived her so badly at first that she could not confide in me."

To prevent his visit to Madison County from being a total loss, two days after Elizabeth spurned him, Hawkins stole a mare and rode back to Estill County. While on the way, our restless villain visited the town of Proctor (then in Owsley County, now in Lee). Nobody knew him there, so he felt confident in once again pretending to be an Army recruiter. He almost became engaged for the tenth time to a "Miss D." He had progressed so far as to convince the girl to run off to the Kansas Territory with him when the law caught up at last on

March 25 and interfered with his plans for seduction.

On that day, Sheriff James Land and Deputy Jesse Arvine arrested Hawkins for having stolen the horse in Madison County. The lawmen started for the Irvine jail with their prisoner that afternoon, but they made two grave mistakes: they failed to tie Hawkins's hands and they did not watch him as closely as they would a coiled rattlesnake. Deputy Arvine and Hawkins were riding on the same horse between two landmarks: the Contrary Hill and the Winding Stairs Hill. At some point, Arvine decided to get off and walk so as not to fatigue the horse. Hawkins's practiced eye noticed that Sheriff Land carried his pistol in the breast pocket of his coat. Hawkins managed to pull his horse up close to Land without exciting the sheriff's suspicion. In a flash, Hawkins had the sheriff's gun and fatally shot the deputy walking behind. Almost simultaneously, Hawkins pulled Sheriff Land off his horse. The lawman hit the ground and begged for mercy. Hawkins personally liked the sheriff; in his memoirs he noted that Land "had treated me with so much kindness." However, this was no time for sentimentality. He shot Land through the right eye and made a quick escape.

Hawkins spent a few days on the run and hiding in such exotic locations as a coal shanty and a cave. Five days after murdering the lawmen, he crossed the river into Ohio. As he rode toward Manchester on April 2, he suddenly became aware that an armed posse was right behind him. Hawkins chose to play it cool. He rode ahead of them as casually as he could manage and after a while he dismounted and started working on a rail fence as if he were a farmer. As the posse rode by, they realized that he was the man they were looking for, but decided not to challenge him. However, they did correctly guess his destination. On April 5, a posse invidiously described by Hawkins as "a set of fools and cowards" surprised him in the woods near his father's house. They captured him and sent him back to Irvine.

The law acted with the same admirable speed Hawkins himself had displayed during his amorous escapades. He stood trial less than a week after his arrest, was found guilty, and sentenced to hang at the end of May. His unpopularity was such that the press reported erroneously that he was taken from the jail and lynched.

Hawkins, realizing that he was going to die, spent his last month of life writing a jailhouse autobiography: *The Confession of Edward W. Hawkins*. It is a well-written document, but the florid, melodramatic touches reflect the literary style of its era. The author mourns over his wasted life and offers his wretched example as a warning to young men everywhere to follow the laws of God. It is difficult to tell whether his tone is genuinely contrite or whether there is a note of boastfulness that lies just below the surface—particularly when he describes his romantic conquests. In one interesting section, Hawkins writes: "I would greatly prefer my present [death] sentence to a lifetime in the penitentiary." No doubt this sentiment will greatly surprise those who oppose capital punishment for humanitarian reasons.

The biggest event in Edward Hawkins's life came on May 29, 1857. The record does not state whether any of his plethora of wives and fiancées attended the hanging. He rode to the gallows sitting on his own coffin—a cavalier touch. At the gallows, he delivered a pretty speech in which he warned young men not to keep bad company and cautioned women not to be led down the primrose path of surfeited folly by deceitful men. His words were taken seriously, as he was considered something of an expert on both subjects.

The gallows was not the traditional sort, that is, an elevated platform with a trapdoor. It was a long upright pole with a crossbeam sticking out at a right angle. The rope was tied to the crossbeam and Hawkins was to stand on a wagon parked beside the pole with the rope tied around his neck. When the sheriff gave the signal, the wagon would drive away and Hawkins was to be left dangling. That was the plan, anyway. The condemned man was willful to the end: when the sheriff ordered the driver to take off, Hawkins, perhaps fearing slow strangulation, deliberately jumped from the wagon. He chose wisely, if that was his intention, because his neck broke instantly and he passed away like a summer's eve. The attentive reader will have noticed that Hawkins managed to accomplish his many triumphs, including his own hanging, before he reached his twenty-first birthday.

After the execution, Hawkins's relatives carried away his body. He did not get a cemetery burial and a grave marker. Instead, he was planted under a persimmon tree 300 feet from the family's house on Cressy Road. For many generations, his only monument was the initials "E.H." carved into the tree. In 1966, some of his relatives erected a gravestone at his burial spot.

Hawkins's confession was considered such an effective cautionary tale that it was still in print as late as 1907 when a Winchester newspaper published it in its entirety. The publisher, R. R. Perry, stated in the preface: "I give [the confession] currency with the hope that it will be a warning to young men and women to avoid that which is evil." The booklet included bonuses: a photo of the gallows pole which was still in existence in 1907, a letter written from Hawkins to his father, and a transcription of his gallows speech.

There was also an afterward written in October 1906 by Hawkins's only surviving sibling: half-brother G. B. Hawkins of Irvine. "I can remember very clearly his mean and overbearing nature," the old man wrote. "Notwithstanding his criminal inclinations and his malicious and treacherous nature, he was a favorite with the entire family and all the neighbors."

Gore in Garrard

"When sorrows come, they come not single spies, but in battalions," said King Claudius to Queen Gertrude in *Hamlet*. The citizens of Garrard County must have felt the same way, though they might have phrased it differently, when two bloody incidents took place in their community within a few days in January 1882. The cause of the first tragedy was as unfathomable as insanity, but the cause for the second was all too pedestrian.

About two and a half miles from Lancaster, near the Danville Pike, lived a farmer named James R. Wilmot—hardworking, well-respected, and about sixty. He had a 250-acre farm located on a high bluff with a scenic view of the Dix River. His house was a two-story log cabin, estimated to be a century old. With him lived his ninety-year-old mother Elizabeth; his wife, fifty-five, also named Elizabeth; two teenage daughters—Mattie, eighteen, and Mary, fourteen; and his sons James I., Jr., twenty-one, and Benny, ten. Also present in the Wilmot household was a girl named Alice Colvin, who worked for the farmer and had sleeping quarters upstairs. Wilmot was noted for the kindness he showed his family.

Rabelais once remarked that the greatest of all blessings was to be in debt, for then you knew that your creditors would earnestly pray that you would enjoy a long and prosperous life. That isn't how Wilmot felt about it. He had owed a security debt of $450 which he had signed on behalf of a brother-in-law. After making payments for some time, he finally managed to reduce the debt to $180. Although well-to-do for the era—he was worth an estimated $8,000 to $10,000—for some reason, the relatively trifling $180 debt preyed on his mind. He became irrational and then completely insane, though the symptoms were not obvious enough to arouse alarm until it was too late. In retrospect, people found strange his frequent remark that his livestock and his family were destined to starve. Wilmot was determined not to let them die in such a horrible way. A quick death, that was the answer! The only way out was to perform what his diseased mind considered a mission of mercy.

The sequence of the following appalling events was pieced together by the coroner based on eyewitness testimony and the condition of the corpses.

The night of January 17, 1882, seemed ordinary; the family stayed up late sitting by the fire and enjoying cheerful conversation. Despite this heartwarming scene, early in the morning of January 18, Wilmot procured a sharp new ax and went to the bedroom where his two daughters slept and killed them instantly with blows to the neck and chest. Mrs. Wilmot must have been awakened, for her body was found facedown on the floor and bore four wounds in the head and back. Wilmot tried to kill his boy Benny, but the child avoided the ax by ducking under a table and the distracted father moved on to other matters by visiting his mother's room.

Around 5 a.m., Alice Colvin, the servant girl, heard the sound of Mr. Wilmot walking out of his mother's bedroom after having killed her with a single deep cut in the chest. Investigating, Colvin noticed that Wilmot was carrying a long object in the gloomy hallway. She asked what he was doing and he replied: "I have killed my family and I am going to kill myself." Terrified, Alice ran to the nearby house of neighbor Enoch Parks, grabbing young Benny as she fled. As she was leaving, the other son, James Jr., came downstairs to see what all the noise was about. When he saw that his father was holding a shotgun and intended to use it, James Jr. wrestled with him, fortuitously managing to strike the barrel just as the older man fired, forcing the bullet upwards into the ceiling. Like Alice Colvin, young Wilmot ran to the neighbors. We can only wonder if the elder Wilmot walked through the house surveying his handiwork before he placed the shotgun on the table, hid the ax behind a door, and walked to his barn.

Neighbors quickly arrived at the farm, but were afraid to go inside the house until the light of dawn revealed the body of James R. Wilmot dangling in the barn. He had hanged himself with a plow line.

The next day, a large crowd accompanied the five bodies to the family cemetery only a few hundred yards away from the scene of the massacre. It was the talk of the community for a few days and then forgotten by everyone except those with the most direct connection to the bloodbath: the three traumatized survivors. The one with the shortest lifespan was Alice Colvin, who died only eight months later on September 23, 1882, at the age of twenty-one. I have been unable to find out the cause of her death, but witnessing the Wilmot massacre could not have been beneficial to her health. The youngest member of the family, Benny Wilmot, lived to the age of fifty-eight, dying in Boyd County on February 13, 1930, probably haunted to the last minute of his life by memories of the night his father snapped and killed almost his entire family. The final survivor of that awful night was James Isom Wilmot, Jr., who appears to have moved to Arizona and died in 1944. The house itself burned to the ground on the night of February 16, 1898.

The Garrard County coroner earned his pay in January 1882 because on the twentieth, only two days after the Wilmot massacre, came another shocking crime. At first, it seemed as if the latest murder were committed by a freelance maniac imitating the Wilmot crimes because the victim had been killed with three blows from an ax. She was eighty-year-old Elizabeth Bland, commonly called "Miss Betsy," who lived about two miles from Lancaster with her widowed brother Joseph. The man who found the body, and who also made the body, was the dead woman's twenty-three-year-old grandnephew, William Austin, fresh from a visit to a distillery. Staggering drunkenly out into the road, Austin told two passersby, Ambrose Bourne and the entertainingly named Bright Herring, that his aunt had been murdered most foully. Bourne and Herring had good reason to doubt Austin's claim, given the smell of alcohol on his breath, but he insisted they come to the house and look. They humored him and got the shock of their lives when they saw the bloody, battered corpse of Miss Betsy—who clearly had been surprised in the worst possible way as she tried to kindle a fire for cooking supper. Leaving Austin behind, Bourne and Herring rode to Lancaster, where they found the dead woman's brother Joseph and Town Marshal Singleton. The group hurried back to the house to look for clues. The murderous ax had been left behind and Joseph Bland identified it as his property.

Some homicides take months, years, or even decades to solve. The murder of Miss Betsy took around thirty seconds. Something about William Austin's demeanor bothered Marshal Singleton and upon inspection, the lawman found blood on Austin's pants, boots, and face. The dead woman's face bore the clear imprint of a boot heel, which matched Austin's shoe. Austin had no convincing explanation, so he was arrested and faced a coroner's jury the very next day. He did not help his case by making conflicting statements during his testimony. He said that when he found his great-aunt's body he did not go near her, but instead immediately went on horseback to summon help from a neighbor. On the other hand, he contradictorily stated that she was not quite dead when he found her and that he got close enough for her to reach out and touch him, hence the blood on his clothes. The coroner noted that the poor woman's vertebra had been severed by the ax, causing instantaneous death. Austin's story about his dying great-aunt's fluttering hands was thus negated and he had to find another explanation for the blood found on his person.

Austin suddenly remembered that he had gone hunting earlier that day and, catching a rabbit, had crushed its head under his heel and pulled its head off. Perhaps he thought this barbaric explanation would charm the jury, but he was mistaken. It was pointed out that the gray hairs sticking to his bloody boot were from a human, not a rabbit, so if he had been stepping on the head of any of God's creatures, it was likely that of Betsy Bland. Though the evidence was circumstantial, it was sufficient for the jury to consider Austin guilty and deserving of a murder trial.

But if William Austin had murdered his great-aunt, why had he done so? The motive was not hard to discern: he wanted money. The old lady was known to keep forty or fifty dollars around the house, all of which was gone. Police noted that drawers had been rifled as though by a burglar. On the other hand, no money was found on Austin except for a silver quarter. The best explanation for the missing money is that Austin hid it just after committing the murder and never had a chance to retrieve it.

A *Courier-Journal* correspondent came calling when Austin was returned to his jail cell after the inquest and found the prisoner "cool and calm" and seemingly unworried. Austin put on his sad face and told the journalist that he was more heartbroken than anyone about the murder because Miss Betsy had been his best friend. She had paid some fines for him when he got in trouble, which seems to have been a pretty regular occurrence. Other relatives of Austin's were less willing than Aunt Betsy to jump through hoops for him; usually when a young thug gets into a scrape with the law, we hear touching stories about his father's unflinching support, including going into hock to buy the services of the finest lawyers and so on, but Austin's father was made of sterner stuff. He announced that he would not offer his son any assistance and stated that the law should take its course. If we read between the lines, it does not sound like he had much faith in his son's innocence.

There were the usual threats of lynching, but nothing came of them. The authorities did not so much as bother moving Austin to a jail in a neighboring county—the usual procedure in the event of an unusually heinous crime. Perhaps they secretly hoped he would get mobbed. The case of *The Commonwealth v. William Austin* commenced in Lancaster's Circuit Court in mid-February as torrential rains flooded the great outdoors. The state was represented by Commonwealth's Attorney Warren and George Denny, Jr., himself a former Commonwealth's Attorney. Austin's father must have had a change of heart because he attended every session and provided his son with three local defense attorneys: Burdett, Noel, and Walton.

Things got off to a bad start for Austin, who nevertheless seemed barely interested in the proceedings. Witnesses pointed out that the gray human hairs sticking to his boot were located on the heel, the section ground into the dead woman's face, and that the imprint of the tack-heads matched exactly the tack-heads on Austin's boot heel. In addition, gray hairs matching the ones found on the heel were found sticking to the bloody ax. Defense attorney Ben Burdett attempted to regain some ground with a four-hour speech pointing out that "the deceased woman's relatives would gain by her death, and that Austin could have no possible motive in committing the crime"—evidently forgetting that Austin numbered among "the deceased woman's relatives," as he was Betsy Bland's grandnephew. It was true that Austin had been living with the Blands for three months prior to the killing and that Miss Betsy had paid all his bills and otherwise spoiled him. Evidently, Austin had taken the fable of the goose that laid the golden egg to heart but had not learned its lesson. The defense also "undertook to show that threats had been made to take [Miss Betsy's] life." By whom, we are not privileged to know.

The trial lasted only four days. On February 17, the jury found Austin guilty and determined that capital punishment was the only appropriate way for him to pay for his unnecessary and brutal crime. All eyes were on Austin when the sentence was read and it was reported that "never was such perfect composure, under such trying circumstances, witnessed in the court-room." Even ex-Commonwealth's Attorney George Denny paid Austin's bravery a compliment, calling him "the nerviest man" he had ever encountered in all his years of legal practice. The prisoner smiled at reporters and said: "It's no use to get scared. I have only one thing to say. I want every man in that jury to come to my hanging. I want to talk to them." Exactly what he wanted to tell them was never divulged, but it is doubtful that he wanted to pay them compliments.

Two days later, Austin was officially sentenced to die on April 18, 1882. When Judge Michael Owsley asked him if he had anything to say, he replied: "Yes sir, I am not guilty." He said it with such calmness that many were convinced that he couldn't be lying. Then, as now, plenty of people are willing to believe any statement made by a convicted killer as long as it is made in a calm, measured tone. As he was led back to jail, Austin's only comment was made to Sheriff John Higginbotham: "Sheriff, this will give you a job." Once the trial was over, the police revealed that greed may not have been Austin's only motive for murdering his eighty-year-old great-aunt; the women who had dressed the body for burial noticed that "a nameless outrage had been committed on her person." When the word got out, idle threats of mobbing commenced anew. Garrard Countians seemed as proud of the fact that no lynching occurred as of the fact that the trial cost the state only $400.

As almost invariably happens to any convicted man, after William Austin was pronounced guilty, people began trying to pin all sorts of unsolved crimes on him. Some remembered that he had taken a trip to Texas with his cousin Sidney Vaughn, who allegedly had never been seen or heard from since. It was bruited about that Austin was the true identity of an unknown highwayman who recently had attempted to rob travelers on the Dix River Bridge between Lancaster and Danville. In addition, a couple of local blacks stated that the previous Christmas, Austin had unsuccessfully tried to inveigle them into helping rob a farmer named John Dunn of $15. They had been afraid to say anything about the incident until Austin was safely locked away. A person writing "in the name of justice to a legally-doomed man" wrote an indignant letter to the Courier-Journal clearing Austin of these unfounded charges. The author argued on Austin's behalf by offering convincing evidence that Sidney Vaughn was still alive; but the force of his other arguments was diminished by the fact that he wrote in anonymity and offered no proof to back up his claims.

Some argued, as did the bashful letter writer, that Austin had received a rushed trial. Considering the weight of evidence against him, one wonders how stretching out the length of the trial could have helped his case. At any rate, he did not meet his fate on the appointed day. On June 15, the Court of Appeals refused to overturn the verdict reached in

Garrard Circuit Court. "Many think that before the hangman's noose goes around [Austin's] neck he will make a full confession, while others say he will go through it all without acknowledging anything," a *Courier-Journal* correspondent had written a few months before. "It is quite likely that, should he finally conclude to talk, he will furnish some interesting things for the papers." And furnish interesting copy he did. On June 16, he elected to cheat the gallows and, in the process, cast further doubt on his innocence by attempting suicide—a pastime not usually undertaken by the wrongly convicted. Austin borrowed a razor from a fellow prisoner, saying that he wanted to shave. He shaved all right—down to the jugular. It turned out to be only a superficial wound. Soon, a heavily shackled Austin was boarding a train to the jail in Richmond, Madison County, for safekeeping. It is to be hoped that the jailers in Lancaster re-thought their liberal policy of allowing prisoners access to shaving razors.

The jail authorities in Richmond found their newest charge cheerful. The reason for Austin's optimism became evident when he granted an interview to a *Richmond Herald* reporter, telling him—of course—that he was as blameless as newborn triplets and that his innocence would someday be proved to the satisfaction of the entire world. He expressed the touching belief that any day he would receive from the governor a commutation to life in prison, if not an outright pardon with an abject official apology. The same assurances are given by about ninety-nine percent of the convicts on Death Row today—and just as sincerely and convincingly.

Yet, neither the commutation nor the pardon was forthcoming; on October 11, Austin was taken from Richmond to the noose waiting for him at Lancaster. "Austin's conviction was made upon a chain of circumstantial evidence strong as could be forged, but he has stoutly maintained his innocence, and as yet shows no sign of weakening," remarked a news report. When he arrived at the Lancaster jail, Austin impressed spectators by walking firmly with his head held high. He didn't even seem to be unnerved by the sight of the gallows. On his last day, he had many visitors, including some ministers and three of his brothers. His parents did not attend—not out of callousness but because Austin's mother was so prostrated with grief at the prospect of her son's hanging that it was feared a trip to the jail would kill her. Perhaps if those who lightly contemplate committing homicide would consider the effects their acts will have on their own families, there would be fewer murders.

Austin's attorneys Burdett and Noel told him that they had done all they could do for him and if he were guilty it would be good to confess. Again he maintained his innocence, but enigmatically told a minister that he would have something to say on the gallows, "but it would not be what people are expecting."

The next day was an unlucky Friday the thirteenth for William Austin. Back in Richmond, he had looked a minister of the Gospel right in the eye, had firmly taken said minister's hand, and had sworn that he was blameless. Now, having given up on getting that illusory pardon, and having only a couple hours before he was to be hanged, Austin spoke with another minister and this time admitted the truth: he was guilty. For months he had so convincingly spoken of his innocence that, had he not confessed, many of his supporters would have gone to their graves convinced a grotesque miscarriage of justice had occurred. Austin wrote a confession in which he blamed the whole sordid mess on whisky. He denied that he had taken any money from Betsy Bland. He claimed that he had murdered her simply because it had seemed like a good idea at the time: "...I had no motive in the world to kill her. I loved her as a mother.... When I got home from the still-house I saw the ax at the woodpile and then the awful thought came over me to take it and kill my great-aunt.... I want my fate to be a warning to all, all, young white and black." Like many a condemned man, Austin pathetically tried to add an ennobling gloss to his wasted life by convincing himself that his death would not be in vain if it prevented someone else from meeting the same fate: "I offer myself as a willing sacrifice on the gallows for the deed." He ended his confession by denying that he had murdered Sidney Vaughn or committed any crime other than the one he was being hanged for.

(This seems to indicate that the fate of the allegedly still-alive-and-accounted-for Sidney Vaughn was still undetermined.) He had time to also write a brief autobiography filled with regrets and tales of alcohol-influenced bad behavior.

In his cell, Austin heard a nearby mill blowing its noon lunch whistle. "Praise the Lord!" he cried. "I have only one more hour to live!" He celebrated this fact by smoking a cigar and listening to the advice of three ministers. At last, the fatal hour came and Sheriff Higginbotham took the prisoner away.

As he stood on the gallows—facing a crowd of two or three thousand who had come to see him pay the ultimate penalty for killing the woman upon whose charity he had been dependent—William Austin delivered an oration in which he admitted his guilt, declared that he loved everyone, and reiterated his warning about the deadly combination of whisky and bad company. After a round of handshaking, the legal procedures involving pinion, hood, and noose were completed. Austin was only twenty-five and left this world absolutely certain he would be meeting Miss Betsy in the next.

Death of an Artist

Fourth Avenue, Louisville, was not a place accustomed to murder. It was a genteel area of town and it was unthinkable that a couple of professional men would fight like street rowdies. On the morning of June 6, 1883, Mr. R. T. Fairman was privileged to witness the unthinkable at Dr. W. W. Barnes's dental office at 623 Fourth Avenue. As Mr. Fairman sat in a chair watching the dentist work on Fairman's sister's teeth, the office door opened and he saw Clarence Boyd—a noted young artist who was also Dr. Barnes's brother-in-law—standing in the hall. "I want to see you," he said angrily to the dentist. Barnes said he was too busy, but the painter insisted.

Putting aside his dental tools, Dr. Barnes stepped out into the hallway and Fairman heard the sounds of arguing and scuffling. He looked into the hall and saw Boyd attempting to throttle the dentist. Fairman tried to act as peacemaker, but Boyd declared that he had come to spill Dr. Barnes's blood and would not leave until either he or Barnes was dead. "When he said that he made a motion with his hand, as if at his hip-pocket," Fairman recounted in court that afternoon. The dentist drew his own pistol, firing two shots. One hit Boyd in the left arm. The other entered his back, near the spine, and passed through his abdomen. Immediately after being wounded, Boyd walked unaided out of the office. Having lost his hat in the fight and being the well-dressed gentleman of the period, he strolled into a millinery shop two doors below. "I am shot; let me lie down," he said to the shocked ladies in the store. They directed him to lie down on a divan in an inner room and sent for Drs. A. B. Cook and Hunt Stucky. After receiving treatment, Boyd was moved to his father's house at the corner of Third and Ormsby. I doubt that Boyd would have appreciated knowing that one of the bystanders who helped carry him home was employed at a coffin factory.

Courier-Journal typesetter V. D. Browne rented rooms in the same building housing the dental office and happened to be returning home just as the shooting occurred. Moments after hearing the shots, he entered the house and saw Dr. Barnes, pistol in hand. The dentist handed the pistol to Browne, stating that he shot Boyd in self-defense and would turn himself in. Dr. Barnes immediately strolled out onto the street, found a policeman, told his tale, and walked with the officer to the station. He paid $1,000 bail and was released.

Dr. Barnes refused to discuss the case with reporters except to confirm that the celebrated local artist Clarence Boyd had threatened him and had used opprobrious language before him. The wounded man's father, Robert Boyd, was more generous with details, speaking on behalf of his son who was "suffering too much to talk." The senior Boyd told a reporter that there had been bad blood between the combatants for some time. Dr. Barnes had been saying bad things about his wife Jessie, who was Boyd's sister, and Boyd had stormed over to the office seeking an explanation. The artist had not gone armed, said the wounded man's father, and the fact that Boyd had been shot in the back proved that he had been trying to get away when Dr. Barnes fired at him.

Just before leaving on his fatal mission, Boyd had left a note at his parents' home reading "Will return in a few minutes."

Clarence Boyd had been born in Ironton, OH, in 1855, the son of an iron merchant. The family moved to Louisville when Clarence was a boy. He had shown an aptitude for art early in life and attended the National Academy of Design in New York for two years, beginning in 1872. In 1874 he studied in Paris under the famous artists Leon Bonnat and Carolus-Duran. One of Boyd's classmates, portraitist John Singer

Sargent, would be recognized as a world-class artist. Around 1877, Boyd returned to Louisville and opened a studio on the second floor of the *Courier-Journal* building. There, he produced several works that gave him a reputation as a fine artist, perhaps even a genius. He produced well-received portraits, landscapes, and works with historical themes, including "Orlando Victorious," "The Laughing Fool," "Futurity," "The Touchstone," "Spring," "Ophelia," "In the Allegheny Mountains," "The Woodland Spring," "As You Like It," "The Wood-Cutters," and "For Lack of Gold." One painting, "Big Rock," was sold the day he was shot.

Dr. Barnes had married Boyd's sister, Jessie, in 1877, but the union was not happy. By 1883, Dr. and Mrs. Barnes had separated and were living in separate houses; he had custody of their son and she had their daughter. Around the time of their split, the dentist had begun publicly insulting his wife and her brother, sparking Clarence Boyd's temper and prompting his ill-fated visit to the dental office. When Boyd died of his injuries on June 8, the *Courier-Journal* eulogized him as a man who had "made a name for himself in the world of art....[whose] work has merited the recognition of the first cities in the land," and remarked that "few artists had a brighter prospect of ultimate fame." Yet for all his brilliance, here he lay, a corpse cooling in his father's mansion.

When Boyd died, Dr. Barnes was rearrested, this time on a charge of murder. Again he made bail and again he was released. While he was at it, the dentist had a warrant issued against Harry Boyd, Clarence's younger brother, who also had been threatening to kill him. Whatever Dr. Barnes had been saying about his wife and in-laws must have been *bad*.

The official coroner's inquest into Boyd's death was held on June 12. Little new information was unearthed, but five witnesses agreed that despite his threatening gesture during the fracas with Dr. Barnes, Boyd did not appear to have been armed. (Two of the witnesses, Mr. Fairman and his sister, had seen the actual shooting and the other three had given Boyd first aid.) The jury came to the foregone conclusion that the doctor did kill the artist with two pistol shots and should face Judge Thompson in the City Court.

During the latter hearing, the prosecution argued that Dr. Barnes should be charged with manslaughter. The defense intended to plead that it was an obvious case of self-defense, but Judge Thompson dismissed the warrant against Barnes on June 15, ruling that there wasn't enough evidence to try him. R. T. Fairman's eyewitness testimony made three things abundantly clear: Boyd had come to the dentist's office looking for trouble and explicitly threatening to kill Dr. Barnes—in fact, Barnes asked Boyd twice if he had come to murder him and twice Boyd answered in the affirmative; Barnes had asked him to leave; Boyd not only refused to go, but also had reached for his pocket as if to draw a gun. Dr. Barnes honestly had thought his life was in imminent danger and had taken desperate measures to save himself.

On June 27, scarcely a fortnight after Boyd's demise, forty-four of his paintings were put up for auction at Escott's Gallery. Many were unfinished, poignant reminders of their creator's untimely passing. Hundreds came to see and buy and some no doubt came simply to quench their morbid curiosity. "He has done nothing that isn't praiseworthy; he has done much that will keep his memory green," remarked a journalist.

It has often been said that nothing will give an artist's name a better chance at immortality than untimely death. This appears not to have been the case with Clarence Boyd. His reputation rose immediately after his death. For example, five months after the shooting, W. T. Price compared him favorably with renowned Kentucky artists such as painters Harvey Joiner, Matthew Jouett, Carl Brenner, and sculptress Enid Yandell: "He would have succeeded." In 1892, almost a decade after the artist's murder, the critics were calling Boyd "A Lost Leader" and "Louisville's Greatest Painter." Fellow artist Augustus Carl remarked that had he not died before he reached his prime, Boyd "by this time would…have been ranked among the very greatest American painters. Now he is forgotten by many people right here in his old home, but had it not been for his early death, the whole country would have been proud of him."

Despite the posthumous praise, modern works on Kentucky artists do not mention Boyd's name. Most of his canvases appear to have been lost over the decades, making a reevaluation of his work impossible. The University of Kentucky Art Museum owns one surviving Boyd painting, an unfinished work from around 1880 known both as "Indians Attacking" and "Pilgrims Attacked by Indians." The J. B. Speed Art Museum in Louisville possesses three Boyds, none of which is on display as of this writing: "Futurity" (1882), "A Girl I Know," and "Landscape with Figures" (dates unknown). Perhaps some of his paintings now sit neglected in secondhand stores or are family heirlooms, hanging on the dining-room walls of people who have never heard of the artist, let alone the dramatic story of his demise.

However, Clarence Boyd does have a unique claim to glory: he is likely the only painter in the annals of art to have been murdered by a dentist.

The Best-Looking Man Ever Hanged

In the mountains of eastern Wayne County, ten miles from Monticello, Jarvis Buck lived in a lonely cabin. His isolation was relieved when his sister Ellen and her ten-year-old son came to live with him. The Bucks eked out such a paltry existence that one might think they would never interest a man seeking to profit by committing murder. But a character of such low ambition lived only about five miles away. He was Granville ("Grand") Prewitt and like too many of his ilk before and since, he thought the way to conquer his poverty was not to work hard and to avoid bad habits, but rather to take the property of others. When Prewitt heard that Buck had recently sold a horse for eighty dollars, he schemed to get the money.

Prewitt put his plan, such as it was, into action on October 26, 1886. He went to the Bucks' cabin around suppertime. Though the family could barely feed itself, mountain hospitality required that the members provide sustenance for their unexpected guest. After the meal, Prewitt told Jarvis Buck that he knew a place where they could get a drink of whisky. The two rode away together, but only Prewitt returned. When Ellen inquired of her brother's whereabouts as she sat picking wool by the fire, Prewitt responded by beating her with a washboard. Her son ran for a neighbor's house and Prewitt, realizing he could not catch the child, thought it prudent to go into hiding. Before leaving, he looted the cabin for whatever he could take. The fruits of his murders amounted to $5.30 in cash, a pair of boots and some clothing.

When rescuers came to the cabin, they found Ellen dead: her throat was cut and her skull was fractured in three places. There was no trace of Jarvis Buck, but his body was found in the woods the next day. He had been slashed and nearly decapitated. Within a few hours, a posse found Granville Prewitt, who swore that he was as innocent as the angels. The ruse lasted about as long as it took to confront him with Ellen's orphaned son. Prewitt then declared that two locals, Jim Jones and Bill Simpson, had paid him to kill the Bucks. When he lured Jarvis Buck away from the cabin with a promise of whisky, he said, Jones and Simpson met them at a prearranged spot a hundred yards from the house. Prewitt killed Buck and Jones stole the dead man's money and clothes. Then Prewitt and Jones went to the cabin and killed poor Ellen. What exactly Bill Simpson was doing all this time, other than perhaps kibitzing, Prewitt did not make clear. Jones and Simpson were arrested, but Prewitt's confession turned out to be a lie. The boy had seen only Granville Prewitt attack his mother. Prewitt admitted that he had lied about Jones and Simpson's involvement; the two were set free.

The mountaineers of eastern Kentucky were not strangers to violence, as proven by the region's long and weary history of feuds and moonshining. Yet, one form of creative homicide was almost unknown in the mountains: lynching. It is a measure of Prewitt's unpopularity that he was threatened with mobbing. In fact, he had made up the story about Jones's and Simpson's involvement in the murders because he feared being lynched if he admitted being the sole perpetrator. The community calmed down when it was understood that the weight of the evidence against Prewitt all but guaranteed a conviction and a legal hanging.

The surefire conviction came in November. Despite an attorney's predictable claim that Prewitt was insane, the jury refused to be hoodwinked and found Prewitt guilty after two hours' deliberation. He was sentenced to be hanged in only two months.

It was initially planned that Prewitt would at least receive the dignity of a private execution to be viewed by only fifty witnesses who paid five dollars apiece for a ticket; as it turned out, the hanging was conducted on a gallows built on the rear lawn of the Wayne County courthouse. An enclosure was built around the gallows, but it fell far short of covering the platform. For all intents and purposes, Granville Prewitt's hanging would be as open to the public as a barn dance. When the big day came on January 12, 1887, the fifty witnesses had swelled to over 4,000—some coming from as far away as Tennessee. Treetops and rooftops were black with eager spectators, many no doubt cackling because they would be seeing for free a spectacle that some had paid as much as five dollars to observe.

Prewitt's execution was memorable for several odd remarks he made under the unpromising circumstances. He did not seem especially concerned about his imminent fate. While in jail awaiting his doom, Prewitt had been treated like a minor—very minor—celebrity. Sunday school students came to serenade him and the finest ladies of Monticello visited his cell in hopes that their proximity would improve his character. On his last morning, he was allowed a final talk with his wife, after which he was baptized. He kept a good appetite and informed a cellmate that he was "the best-looking man that was ever hanged." (The press disagreed with Prewitt's generous assessment of his own looks, calling him a "villainous-looking mountaineer.") When Prewitt's wife asked if their children could witness their father's hanging, he refused. Her droll reply: "You never did want your children to see anything!"

He walked to the gallows with a spring in his step and betrayed no outward signs of nervousness, telling those who tried to assist him: "I can make it; I'm not dead yet." When standing on the trapdoor, he put on a dainty pair of black gloves and complained when the guards strapped his arms and legs. Ellen Buck's son was present and some tasteless, unthinking person asked him to shake hands with his mother's murderer, which the boy refused to do. At last, Prewitt showed signs of agitation and delivered an oration on the dangers of alcohol and keeping bad company—in which he reasserted that he alone had committed the murders and expressed the wish that he might meet all the onlookers in Heaven. A couple of songs were sung at his request and then the hangman got down to the business of placing the black cap over his head and adjusting the rope around his neck. "I hate for you to do this," remarked Prewitt from under the cap. He murmured "Lord, have mercy on me" just as the trap opened.

Prewitt seemed to die instantly, for his body was motionless for twenty seconds. Then, suddenly he began convulsing and did not cease for a minute. This was a common, though eerie, phenomenon at hangings and as usual, it led people to speculate that Prewitt had strangled to death; but they were likely witnessing involuntary posthumous muscular spasms. When the body was removed from the gallows, Ellen Buck's son requested that the rope remain around his neck. Prewitt's friends took possession of the body and buried it near his former home. He had been only the fifth man to be executed in Wayne County's history—of the five, he was probably the most egotistical.

The Murdered Maid

O ver a century ago, a mansion at 1522 Brook Street, Louisville, belonged to A. Y. Johnson, Jr., a well-to-do bookkeeper at the firm of Barbee and Castleman. The residence was surrounded by pleasant open fields used for community functions such as baseball games and circus exhibitions. Across the street were an alley and an ice factory's warehouse. (The house no longer exists, but the Old Male High School is located opposite the location it once stood.)

It was both a status symbol and a necessity for a wealthy family in a large house to have domestic servants. The Johnsons had a maid named Jennie Bowman, a plasterer's daughter. By all accounts, they could not have made a happier choice. Jennie was twenty-three years old, hard-working, responsible, loyal, and, as circumstances would prove, uncommonly brave.

The chronology of the events that occurred on the morning of April 21, 1887, was later steeped in controversy and confusion. I have chosen to go by the timeline offered by the woman of the house, Mrs. Abbie Johnson, in the belief that she was in the best position to know what happened. At 9:30 a.m., according to Mrs. Johnson, she took her children to visit her nearby sister, Mrs. William R. Johnson, a walk of only two or three minutes. She left Jennie alone in charge of the house. When Abbie arrived, she realized that she had forgotten to bring a bundle of sewing, so Mrs. William Johnson sent her six-year-old son Alfred back to the house on Brook Street to retrieve it. The package was too heavy for the boy to carry alone, so Jennie Bowman accompanied him to the house of Mrs. William Johnson, then returned alone to her employer's house around 9:40 or 9:45 a.m.

Between ten and fifteen minutes later, Mrs. William Johnson sent her daughter Laura to 1522 Brook Street on a second errand to retrieve some buttons. The girl immediately knew something was amiss when she arrived, for the doors were locked and the maid did not answer the bell. She squeezed through a kitchen window and entered the silent mansion. In the dining room, she saw signs of a fierce fight: overturned chairs, scattered rugs, and broken glass. In the back hall, a large pool of congealing blood was on the floor. Blood was spattered and smeared on the stairwell wall. Worst of all, Jennie seemed to be missing. The terrified girl fled the house and hurried back to her mother.

Within minutes, Mrs. Abbie Johnson and several of her relatives and neighbors were at the scene. They heard groans issuing from the maid's apartment on the second floor over the kitchen. There they found Jennie lying unconscious on the floor in a pool of blood, her clothes torn and bloody, and her face battered beyond recognition. The *Courier-Journal* of April 22 features a sketch of Bowman wounded, a handkerchief supporting her jaw, and two gashes in her forehead. The gruesome drawing is not entirely accurate because the reporter described several injuries the artist chose not to depict:

A damp dish-rag that had been left on the dining room table was found drawn tightly about her throat....On either side of her neck the flesh was black and blue from finger imprints. On her head and forehead were seven cuts, evidently inflicted with some sharp instrument. The most serious of these were a gash extending from the crown down to the forehead, terminating just over the right eye, and a deep slash in the right temple. The skull had been fractured in no less than three places. One eye had been almost torn from the socket. The nose was flattened and the right jawbone was broken.

In addition, her lips were so swollen that she could barely speak and the left side of her body was paralyzed.

The crowd placed the maid on her cot and called for two doctors and the police. The doctors sewed up the gashes on Jennie's head, set her jawbone, and gave her opiates to make her more comfortable, but opined that her injuries were so severe that she had but a few hours to live. Even if she survived, they felt she would be partially paralyzed for life.

Because children had been sent to the house on two separate errands that morning, it was easy to recreate the circumstances of the crime. The police surmised that a burglar had been watching the house all morning, waiting for an opportunity to break in. Mr. Johnson left for work; later, Mrs. Johnson and the children went to visit the relative, leaving Jennie behind. Little Alfred returned on his errand and Jennie Bowman left with him to carry the parcel of cloth. At this point, the marauder must have broken in, believing the house would be empty for a while. He did not count on the maid's abrupt return and, when she surprised him, he panicked and attacked.

The criminal left behind the weapons: two fireplace pokers, one left upstairs and the other abandoned at the bottom of the stairs. The downstairs poker was over a foot long, weighed three pounds, and had a sharp hook at one end. It was sticky with blood and blonde hairs from Jennie Bowman's head clung to it. Of special interest was a broken water tumbler; fragments of glass had been found in the dining room, and detectives wondered whether she had injured the burglar.

The early stages of the police investigation were frustrating. Only seventy-five yards from the crime scene, workers were constructing a house but none had seen anything suspicious; nor had they heard anything amiss, a testament to the solid construction of the mansions of those lost days. An employee at the nearby ice factory reported seeing two white tramps in the neighborhood. Based on his description, the police searched at every train station in Louisville and at every road leading out of the city. Eight detectives went to check out the Indiana shore and others sailed the Ohio River in skiffs in case the criminals tried to escape in a boat. Before the day was over, seven men resembling the descriptions were arrested and held on suspicion.

Around 6:00 in the evening, Jennie returned to a faint, painful, and temporary consciousness. When an attending physician asked who struck her, she whispered: "It was a negro. I met him in the dining room, when he asked me if Mr. Johnson was at home. I said 'no,' when he seized me and struck me with a poker." She described her attacker and then fell unconscious again. Around midnight, she woke up for several minutes and provided more details. Jennie revealed that the burglar had not broken into the house in her absence, as had been surmised. She had just come home from the errand when she heard a knock on the side door. Opening it, she saw a large black man with a moustache and a long, dark coat. He asked if the family was home. When she replied that they were not, he grabbed her arm and demanded to know the whereabouts of the valuables. Jennie happened to be carrying a water tumbler, which she smashed over his head and raked across his face. Stunned, the burglar let go for a moment, then picked up the handiest weapon—the poker—and knocked her unconscious.

When she came to minutes later, she found that the burglar had carried her upstairs to the sewing room. Again, the large man demanded to know where the valuables were kept; again, she refused to tell him and again he clouted her with the poker. Jennie was strong and she fought as best she could. She fell to the floor half-conscious and watched as he ransacked the family's bureau drawers. As he looked for valuables, he heard young Laura Johnson trying to enter the house. The panicked burglars—for it soon became evident that there were actually two—hurried downstairs and escaped, probably leaving by the front door while the girl tried the back entrance. As the men fled the house, Jennie blacked out.

After telling this story to her caregivers, Jennie sank back into semi-consciousness, every now and then reflexively raising her arm in terror, as if warding off an attack. The authorities now had an excellent means of identifying one of the burglars: Jennie Bowman had slashed his face. Further encouraging news came three days after the assault, when it was reported that Jennie seemed to be recovering:

"[T]he wounded girl appears to realize there is hope. She was able to open one of her eyes yesterday, and looked appealingly at those around her."

At first, police thought that there had been only one intruder. Then Police Chief John H. Whallen noticed evidence that two men had attacked Jennie Bowman: smears of blood were on the walls on both sides of the stairs at the height of a man's waist, suggesting that Jennie had been carried upstairs by two men, one holding her torso and the other holding her legs. Had a single man carried her in his arms, the bloodstains would have been around shoulder height; had she been dragged upstairs the smears would have been low on the walls and close to the stairs. Days later, when Jennie's mind was clearer, she confirmed that she had seen a second burglar upstairs—a short black man in a short coat, who beat her with the second poker.

The fact that the victim was white did not bode well for race relations in the Falls City. There was open talk of lynching—not in rural areas, where it was no novelty, but in the midst of a major metropolis. A *Courier-Journal* reporter described the thirst for vengeance that had beset the town: "The murderous assault…has created more excitement and indignation throughout the entire city than any happening for many years, and, to judge by public opinion, if the perpetrator of the outrage could be discovered, he would never be allowed to appear before a bar of justice." Editorials urged that the law be allowed to fulfill its course.

At the same time, the paper understood why citizens were so frustrated with the law and sensibly argued that a few executions were needed to set examples for criminals of all races, who for too long had been given excessive latitude by the courts. The editorialists recalled recent cases of flagrant injustice. For example, James McCoy, an unoffending Louisville resident, had been murdered just feet from his home in winter 1886: "The murderer was found, tried and convicted; there was no excuse, no palliation, no indication of insanity, but he was sentenced to the penitentiary to stay until the memory of the deed has faded and some kind-hearted or 'genial' governor sets him free."

One McKeldin had shot a man to death and pleaded insanity though he actually had been drunk. The *Courier-Journal* complained that McKeldin should have been hanged or, at the very least, sent to an insane asylum. Instead, he got a mere three-year jail sentence. "The murderer is a privileged citizen," thundered the paper, "who confines his work to no hour and no locality. Gangs of idle and brutal men, white and black, infest the city, attack the women, rob our houses, and stand as a menace by every opened door. What happened to Jennie Bowman might have happened to anyone."

Governor Knott approved a $500 reward for the capture of the villain or villains and no one doubted that Bowman's primary attacker would soon be turned in by someone who took note of his highly publicized facial injuries. The police arrested several suspicious persons, including a man with cuts on his face. It turned out he had been thrown through a window during a fight and was able to prove it. However, a break in the case came on April 23, two days after the assault on Jennie Bowman.

Mrs. Mary Brannin was knocking on the doors of residences on Center Street. She was looking for her hired man, but did not know his exact address. Thus, she was compelled to try each house until she found him. When one particular door opened, the searcher's blood curdled because the man who answered resembled the reported description of the maid's attacker right down to the gashes in his face. History does not record what Mrs. Brannin said to the man—probably something along the lines of a faltering "Nice day, isn't it?" She bade the man farewell and he went back to his business, unaware that the lightning was gathering. Mrs. Brannin stopped the first policeman she could find, Officer Strohman, and related her suspicions. The policeman's superior officers thought her story good enough to check out and Officers Strohman and Stockwell went to see the man in person.

He turned out to be twenty-six-year-old Albert Turner, who did indeed have recent cuts to his face, throat, and right wrist—all caused by a jagged instrument such as broken glass rather than a straight blade. He had a local reputation as a gambler and a hoodlum with a partiality for beating women. The Miranda warning did not exist in 1887, and the officers simply arrested Turner and took him to the station without divulging their reasons. His wounds were examined—his increasing nervousness was clear to all observers—and when officers asked point blank how he got the cuts, he replied that he had been struck in the face with a stick while cutting wood. He denied knowing anything about the Bowman case until policemen entered the room carrying items stolen from the Johnson residence, all found in Turner's apartment. When he saw the items, he was overcome with terror and had to be restrained from fleeing the room. When he saw that all was lost, he cried: "I done it! But I couldn't help it! Only save me from the mob!"

Given the ugly mood rampant in the city, the officers realized that they would have to move Turner to a safer location before word of his arrest got out. Arrangements were made to send him to jail in Frankfort. Police Chief Whallen allegedly told Turner, "I will save your life, but upon one condition only, and that is that you make a confession of what you did at the Johnson house Thursday, and mind you tell the truth, or we will let them hang you." Later, under oath, Whallen denied having said it. Turner did more than confess. He named his accomplice.

At first, Turner claimed he had committed the crime by himself. Whallen told him of the blood evidence on the walls which indicated the presence of two men. Turner realized he had been caught in a lie and decided to come clean. He stated that on Thursday morning he had been walking by the Johnson house when he saw a black acquaintance named William Patterson sitting on the family's carriage mount. Patterson asked Turner if he would like to make some money by helping him burglarize the house. Patterson assured the reluctant Turner that he had seen everyone in the house leave. After the two broke into the mansion, Patterson looted the upstairs while Turner looked for valuables in the dining room. Soon, he encountered Jennie Bowman. In the fight that followed, she bit his thumb to the bone and slashed his face with the broken tumbler. In terror and rage, Turner beat her unconscious with the poker. When Patterson came downstairs to see what was going on, the two of them carried the maid upstairs to her quarters. (The police recreated this part of the story to test its validity. Two officers carried a girl of Bowman's size up the stairs in the fashion described by Turner and found that as they "carried the body up, every turn made in the stairs brought the girl's head against a blood spot.")

According to Turner, when they got Jennie upstairs, Patterson continued to beat the unconscious woman with the second poker and kicked her three times in the stomach, twice in the side, and twice in the head, breaking her jawbone. Patterson attempted to sexually assault the maid, thus soaking his underwear with her blood, but the already remorseful Turner stopped him. After the completion of the savage beating, the two sneaked out of the house and ran away in different directions. Turner admitted that he secretly had been relieved when the police arrested him, "for I hadn't closed my eyes and was frightened at every sound I heard."

There was no need to set up a dragnet to find William Patterson because he was already in jail. On April 23, the police had found the thirty-four-year-old man hiding in a dive on Green Street and picked him up for questioning. It did not escape their notice that he had some cuts on his face. Patterson seemed agreeable at first, but tried to run away when the police approached City Hall. Naturally, this reinforced the officers' suspicions and Patterson found himself spending a glum night in a jail cell. He was well known to the Louisville police, having previously committed crimes ranging from burglary and larceny to stealing cattle. A reporter described him as "one of the roughest characters in the city." On two occasions, he had attempted to stab policemen. While in the penitentiary for one of his sundry crimes, he had nearly killed a fellow convict by pounding his head with a sledgehammer—indicating that he was capable of violence such as was committed on Jennie Bowman.

Patterson was not thrilled when he learned that he had been

implicated by Albert Turner. He was taken aboard a train to join Turner in the relative safety of Frankfort and he spent the trip refusing to answer questions put to him by the police. When the train stopped briefly at LaGrange, Patterson requested that he be accompanied to the lavatory. Just before reaching the bathroom door, he bolted for the exit. An officer collared him and shackled him to a seat in the train. The incident did little to convince the authorities that Patterson was being truthful when he stated that he had never met Albert Turner in his entire life, "as God is my judge." (He was lying. It came out later that while he and Turner were not close friends, they had been acquaintances for years.)

Patterson's claim was further damaged at the Frankfort jail. He again maintained that he had never seen nor heard of Turner. To test his claim, the police put him in a line-up and brought out Turner, who immediately picked Patterson out of the group. Turner also told the police that if they examined Patterson's underclothes, they would find bloodstains. The officers did so and Turner's claim was verified: the clothes recently had been washed, but spots of blood were visible. Bloody thumbprints were also detected on his vest, coat, and the band of his hat, which Patterson had been very reluctant to hand over. These must have been Patterson's only clothes, since it was foolhardy in the extreme for him to wear such incriminating garments in public. In a fury, Patterson shouted, "Those white men put you up to telling these lies on me because there is money in it for them!" He did not reveal how the diabolically clever officers contrived to put bloody underclothes on him or how Turner possibly could have known he was wearing the same unless he had been at the scene of the crime. As though he had not already dug the hole sufficiently deep, Patterson said to Turner: "If I had something in my hand I would murder you for swearing away my life. Oh, I could kill you before these officers could get their hands upon me!" Then he lunged at Turner and tried to throttle him. It took six policemen to separate the men and lead them to separate cells.

The next day, Patterson provided a long, involved alibi concerning his wanderings about the city on the morning of April 21. He told his story with an attention to detail that would have been the envy of Dickens or Tolstoy, naming specific streets and times and the names of witnesses who saw him. He claimed he had spent his time from the morning to the late afternoon helping a woman move furniture from Twelfth to Eighteenth Street. He ended by saying, "I never saw Turner until last night, and though I've been in the penitentiary three times before, as God is my judge, I didn't have anything to do with this crime." His alibi lost credibility when an investigation revealed that he had helped the woman move on April 19, not April 21.

The most serious evidence against Patterson was his bloody undergarments. He tried to account for them by stating that the blood had come from a woman named Lizzie Caldwell, whom he had visited on the morning of the crime. He probably explained how so much of her blood got on his underwear, but the papers of that more demure era did not elaborate. The police located Lizzie Caldwell, who confirmed that she had seen Patterson on April 21—but at 5:00 p.m., several hours after Jennie Bowman's beating, and he did not venture past her front gate. She stated that she barely knew Patterson and had never been intimate with him.

The community continued to show much concern for "the child of poverty" who had bravely risked her life at her employer's house. The influential *Courier-Journal* took up a subscription for Bowman and encouraged readers to contribute. As of May 1, the amount collected was $643.25 and would eventually reach almost a thousand dollars. An organization called the Old Hickory Musical and Dramatic Club held a benefit in May, all proceeds to go to Jennie. Newspaper readers from across the country, including children, sent in sums. An Indiana flour company sent a barrel of its best product to the city in order to be auctioned off for Jennie's fund. (This had been a tried-and-true method of raising money for troops during the Civil War, then only slightly over twenty years in the past.)

Turner and Patterson had been taken to Frankfort for their safety, but when the particulars of their crime were revealed, they faced the distinct possibility of being lynched in Kentucky's lovely capitol city. Large, angry crowds gathered outside the poorly guarded jail and rumor held that some potential mob leaders had already selected a specific tree. Albert Turner was so certain that he was not long for this world that when he saw Mr. Duff, driver of the Louisville patrol wagon that had brought him to the city, the prisoner beseeched him to serve as his executor, telling him which of his possessions he wanted to go to specific relatives.

The *Courier-Journal* continued to plead with citizens: "Let the law take its course.... The people look to the law for protection, and not to a mob. Their confidence has been shaken by the many perversions of justice with which we are familiar.... Hanging without a trial is not punishment, it is another murder, and this is not a community of criminals. We want crime punished, and the law vindicated, and it can only be done by a fair and impartial trial and a prompt execution." The thirst for revenge sometimes crossed racial boundaries. Some blacks in Frankfort expressed the opinion that the two men were guilty and deserved the noose—legally or otherwise, they did not specify. According to one newspaper account, "A number of colored people went into a store...and said if they had some white people to lead them, they would hang the culprits themselves in order to relieve their race of the stigma, which, they said, usually attaches to the commission of a crime by a colored man."

In the face of the growing threat, the jailer quietly spirited Turner and Patterson out of Frankfort and held them in a secret location—or so he said. When word got out, the members of the would-be mob looked at each other for a few moments, shrugged, and went home to bed. With the morning light came the revelation that the jailer had planted a false rumor and the prisoners had been in Frankfort all along. By the time the truth was known, the denizens of Frankfort had cooled down and Turner and Patterson faced no threats of being lynched—at least for the time being. We might congratulate the jailer for his cleverness, but afterwards he did an odd and foolish thing: he allowed an endless stream of curious people into his establishment to stare at, comment upon, and threaten the caged prisoners. Any one of these unnecessary and unauthorized visitors might have caused serious trouble.

After Louisville was deemed sufficiently calm, the prisoners were returned to that city's jail. Their homecoming on April 27 was commemorated at nightfall by a crowd of 200 men, many the worse for drink, who gathered ominously near the jail. The members went their separate ways when the police showed up. The officers later opined that it was the most orderly and easily cowed throng they had ever seen.

A somewhat more spirited crowd rushed the jail on April 28. The members made incendiary speeches and went so far as to brandish a section of a telegraph pole with which to force open the jail door, but the crowd lost its daring when the Louisville Light Infantry and 125 policemen showed that the law meant business. The two chief ringleaders were quickly arrested and taken to jail. The crowd made a couple of halfhearted charges against the prison, for the sake of appearances, I presume. Then they gave up, but not before the police made over 200 arrests. People milled about until dawn, but finally left after having done no harm whatsoever. It made little difference to Turner and Patterson, who spent the night shaking with terror in their cells and praying with a minister.

On the night of April 30, an estimated 15,000 people roamed the streets of Louisville, many of them rowdies looking for trouble. They made a third and final attempt to storm the jail and seize the prisoners. At the jail, they met not only 150 policemen, but also the Louisville Light Infantry, 500 extra guards, and a Gatling gun. Thirty-eight arrests and numberless beatings later, the mob gave up for good.

The papers had been giving daily reports on Jennie Bowman's fluctuating condition. Members of the A. Y. Johnson family remained at her bedside and gratified her every need; women came by with presents of food and flowers. It was reported on April 25 that she had a stronger pulse and a normal temperature. On April 26, it was announced that the inflammation had left her wounds, that she could open both eyes, and that she had asked for milk and toast. However, her condition took a down turn on April 27, when she became delirious; on April 29, it was reported that she was raving so violently that she had to be restrained even though her left side was still paralyzed. Then she sank into a coma. On the night the mob faced a Gatling gun at the jail, the cause of all the excitement lay thrashing in her bed in tremendous agony, battling imaginary enemies and occasionally emitting bloodcurdling screams.

Some Louisvillians were convinced that Patterson was innocent; that Turner, for whatever reason, had implicated a guiltless man as an accomplice. They pointed to discrepancies between his story and the story told by the semi-delirious Jennie Bowman. She said that she let Turner into the house, while Turner claimed he had already broken into the house before she came home. How Turner got into the house was a minor matter. According to the press, Bowman had at first described one burglar, not two, and that intruder was Albert Turner. Yet, Mrs. William Johnson—who had been among the first people called to the house after the crime was reported—swore later under oath that the newspapers had been wrong and that Jennie had always said that there were two attackers. The position and height of the bloodstains on the stairwell walls seem conclusive proof that two men had been in the house. On April 30, Jennie rallied and was able to answer questions clearly in detail and she unequivocally stated that she saw two burglars in the house that morning: "I would know both of them if I could look at them for a minute." When she described her attackers, the details fit the appearances of Turner and Patterson.

There was no doubt about Turner's role in the crime; his conscience troubled him so much that he was quick to tell anyone who would listen that he was guilty. To one reporter he said: "I done that deed, and I am ready to die for it; that's all I can do…. [Y]ou don't know what suffering I have gone through since that deed was done. Before they arrested me my good angel kept me from sleeping…. I have died in [my] mind at least a hundred times." He often expressed the opinion that he richly deserved a quick, legal hanging by the sheriff, though he feared the brutality of a mob. William Patterson, by contrast, maintained his innocence with considerable surliness. His already wobbly alibi received a further drubbing when George Hall, whose occupation was selling books door to door, identified Patterson as a man he had seen hurrying out of A. Y. Johnson's yard on the morning of the attack. Hall, who for some reason also went by the name A. L. Shannon, visited the jail on April 27 and, recognizing Patterson by his clothes, picked him out of a lineup "without a moment's hesitation." Patterson lost his nerve and seemed on the verge of confessing, but changed his mind. He stuck to his alibi, but when told that his explanation had been investigated and discredited, he quickly invented a new tale, the details of which appear to have escaped the press.

The second story must also have been demolished upon investigation because he soon told a third one just as rich in detail as the first, again naming acquaintances and streets and remembering times of day with startling clarity. He claimed that early on the morning of April 21, he had been killing time at the train depot at Tenth and Maple. Shortly after 8:30 a.m., he strolled up Eleventh Street, where a man named Ike Ballou asked if he would help haul grain to the Crystal Springs distillery on First Street. Patterson declined and instead walked to Twelfth and Madison. Around 10:30 he rode in a coal cart with one Willie Woods. They accidentally delivered the coal to the wrong address, finally delivering it correctly to the home of Scott Parker. After a few more misadventures, he visited a woman named Eliza Haley at 12:30 p.m. The alibi continued in this vein for considerable length, loaded with mundane details that gave it the ring of truth.

Detectives found that Patterson's story checked out. Many persons remembered seeing him riding in the coal wagon; Willie Woods's receipt for the coal delivered to Scott Parker was indeed dated April 21. The occupants of the house where the two had erroneously delivered the coal remembered that they had started unloading their freight around 11 a.m. Other witnesses swore they had seen Patterson that day in locations where he claimed to have been.

Yet, the alibi had a flaw. The earliest news accounts erroneously state that the attack on Jennie Bowman had occurred between 10:30 a.m. and 11 a.m. Mrs. Abbie Johnson confirmed that it actually had occurred much earlier, around 9:45 a.m. Patterson was only able to prove his whereabouts at 8:30, when he turned down Ike Ballou's offer of work, and after 10:30, when he climbed into Woods's cart. Patterson claimed he had spent the missing two hours walking from Eleventh and Maple to Twelfth and Madison—a distance of only two or three blocks. "There was ample time to commit the outrage and give Patterson an opportunity to go to Twelfth and Maple, where he met Willie Woods," said Chief Whallen. If Patterson's story truly explained his whereabouts, asked the chief, why did he wait so long to tell it while his life was being threatened by lynch mobs?

On the first of May, Jailer Bailey found that some of Turner's visitors had been trying to persuade him to take back his accusations against Patterson. Acting on Judge W. L. Jackson's orders, Bailey decreed that until further notice, no one but the proper authorities would be allowed to visit the prisoners—an order the jailer himself would soon defile, trample, and eviscerate much to the disgust of the national press. Since Turner and Patterson had no company for the nonce, they whiled away the days by arguing with each other from their adjoining cells—Patterson insisting that he was innocent and Turner replying with ripostes such as, "If it wasn't you, then it was your twin brother."

Jennie Bowman had made so much progress that almost two weeks after her beating, the *Courier-Journal* announced in a headline: "Miss Bowman's Recovery Certain." Her friends and relatives were joyous, as were the Johnson family, the Louisville community at large, people in other states who had read in their newspapers about her brave struggle, and Albert Turner and William Patterson—because as long as Jennie survived, they would be charged with lesser crimes than murder. However, all hopes were cruelly dashed. Just when Jennie's miraculous recuperation seemed a certainty, she sank into a maelstrom of physical agony and mental delirium in her bed at A. Y. Johnson's house. There she died at 9:15 p.m. on May 9, more than two weeks after she had the misfortune to surprise the burglars. In her last moments, she was surrounded by grieving members of two families: her own and A. Y. Johnson's.

"[T]hroughout the ages the spot where she sleeps should be marked by tributes to heroism and virtue," eulogized the *Courier-Journal*. Even before Jennie died, Bishop C. C. Penick had suggested that should she not recover, a memorial be erected to the girl's memory. The idea was endorsed by both the community and its leading newspaper, so the Jennie Bowman Benefit Fund became the Jennie Bowman Memorial Fund. The *Courier-Journal* urged all citizens to send contributions—"We trust the response will be generous and prompt"—for the money collected to date was not enough for a suitable tombstone, which was to serve double duty as a grave marker for a brave young woman, but also as "a monument... to tell how—poor and lowly though she was—she excelled the best of us, in the nobility of her life and the travail of her death." Yet, the public, who cared so much for Jennie while she was alive, was slow to contribute to her monument. Over the next few months, the *Courier-Journal* would alternately wheedle, browbeat, and shame Louisvillians into sending money.

Coroner Miller conducted a post mortem examination on Bowman's body, not at the morgue, but at the home of A. Y. Johnson— as though the mansion at 1522 Brook Street had not already seen its fill of horrors. After Dr. Miller sawed off the top of her skull, he could see that a large blood clot had formed, resulting in inflammation of the brain. Despite Jennie's many appalling injuries, this was the official cause of death.

On May 10, Jennie Bowman was buried in Cave Hill Cemetery in a plot purchased by A. Y. Johnson. Weeping relatives and friends accompanied her to the grave, including a grief-stricken German youth whom she was soon to have married. Some days before, a former employer had reminisced that Jennie had been so phobic about burglars that she had refused to sleep with the windows open even in the hottest weather. She had had a premonition that someday her life would end in violence.

————

A *Courier-Journal* editorial remarked, "In a sense, it may be said that [Bowman] dies that Justice may live. There can now be no escape for her assailants from the full penalty of their crimes"—something Turner and Patterson well knew. When the coroner's inquest came on May 12, the jury got to examine such morbid memorabilia as Patterson's gory clothes, the broken water goblet, and the bloody pokers. They heard testimony from several witnesses, including Mr. Johnson, police officials, and John Wesley Adams, a janitor at City Hall, who testified that on April 28, Patterson had confessed to him and added, "I hope the girl will forgive me." After ten minutes' deliberation, the jury concluded that Jennie Bowman had been murdered by Albert Turner and William Patterson and that they would have to stand trial.

The court appointed Major Lawson to be Turner's lawyer. It is complained that defendants in capital cases often do not receive proper and competent representation, but that certainly was not true in Patterson's case because he had three prominent lawyers. Matt O'Doherty, a rising star in the Republican party, was to make the statement of the case for the defense to the jury and cross-examine the prosecution's witnesses; N. R. Harper, the first black attorney in Kentucky, was to perform the direct examination of the defense witnesses; Thomas Martin was to cross-examine the State's rebuttal witnesses.

Turner was tried first. His lawyer could not cloud the issue since the defendant was not insane and could not claim self-defense. Major Lawson could only plead for the jury's mercy on the grounds that his client had confessed. The officials of the Louisville court system feared that the defendant would be lynched if they delayed, so he was tried by the grand jury the very next day, May 13; after only an hour and five minutes, the jury had indicted Turner, heard the witnesses and arguments, and sentenced him to be hanged on July 1. In fairness to the court, it should be noted that the verdict was a no-brainer. Turner had entered a guilty plea. He did not even attempt to offer an alibi. Objects stolen from the Johnson house were found in his apartment. He bore wounds identical to those Jennie Bowman claimed she had inflicted upon her attacker. He had admitted his guilt, and had said that he deserved capital punishment. The jury agreed and after the sentence was pronounced, Turner was taken back to prison.

While they were at it, the grand jury also indicted William Patterson, whose trial began on May 18. Unlike Turner, Patterson pled not guilty. His defense hung on a slender thread: his alibi—the third one, upon which he had finally settled. If the jury believed his alibi when he went to the witness stand, he would be spared. If they did not, he certainly would share Albert Turner's fate.

Such was the level of interest in Patterson's trial that when an epileptic collapsed to the floor in a fit, hardly anyone in the packed courtroom noticed. The first witness was Coroner Miller, who testified as to his findings at Jennie Bowman's autopsy. Next came a draftsman from the City Engineer's office, who swore to the accuracy of the maps placed on exhibit showing the Johnson residence. The third witness was Dr. I. S. Hoskins, Jennie's primary physician from the day she received her injuries to the day of her death. He described the experiment in which two policemen carried a substitute for Jennie upstairs and proved that the locations of the bloodstains could have come about only if she had been carried by two men. Defense lawyer O'Doherty's vigorous cross-examination served only to make Dr. Hoskins more certain and emphatic in his belief. Next, Police Chief Whallen told of Turner's identification of Patterson in the lineup at the Frankfort jail and of finding the blood on Patterson's clothes. Under cross-examination, he denied promising Turner protection from the lynch mob if he confessed. The following witness, a chemist, offered his opinion that the blood found on Patterson's clothes was from a human. Under cross-examination, the chemist asserted that the stains were recent.

The most sensational witnesses came at the end of the trial's first day. Albert Turner was called to the witness stand and told the same story he had confessed to the police. Next, the book agent pointed out Patterson as the man he had seen leaving the Johnsons' yard, but rather than identifying Patterson positively said only that he was "pretty sure." Lizzie Caldwell testified that it was not her blood on Patterson's clothes, as Patterson had told the police. A *Courier-Journal* reporter and a Franklin County magistrate recounted how Turner had picked out Patterson immediately from a lineup, corroborating Whallen's testimony.

On day two of Patterson's trial, Mrs. Abbie Johnson and her sister Mrs. R. W. Johnson testified to the all-important chronology of the mundane events that had occurred on the morning of April 21, before Jennie Bowman had been found battered. Under cross-examination, Abbie Johnson swore that she had never heard Jennie say that only one man had attacked her. A. Y. Johnson testified that it would take only a few seconds for anyone who ran around his house to become completely invisible from the street and that he had seen footprints leading around his house after the attack. Important testimony came from professional nurse Fannie Westby, described by the *Courier-Journal* as "self-possessed and a most admirable witness." She related that on April 28, when Jennie's mind was clear, Jennie said she had been beaten by a large black man downstairs and by a small black man in a short coat upstairs. The next witness, Charles Hickey, was the policeman who had arrested Patterson. Hickey testified that as he took the prisoner to jail on a charge of allegedly stealing shoes—remember, these were pre-Miranda days—Patterson had remarked to a passerby that he actually was being arrested for "that murder on Brook Street," although he was not charged with that crime until he reached the stationhouse. The passerby, George Moore, corroborated Hickey's testimony under oath. Another witness, Mose Tucker, told of an interesting and damning thing his longtime friend Patterson had said in his presence on the afternoon of April 21. Patterson appeared to know about Bowman's beating at a time when relatively few people in Louisville had heard the news. Tucker had seen Patterson nervously searching for a late afternoon edition of the *Louisville Post*. By way of conversation, Patterson asked Tucker if he had heard about a woman who was "murdered on Brook Street."

"Who murdered her?" asked Tucker. "Her husband?"

"No. Burglars," replied Patterson.

The reader may wonder at Patterson's choice of words in both instances; he referred to the crime as a "murder" even though Jennie Bowman would not die for several days. The inference is that he was in fact one of her assailants and when he abandoned the Johnson house he assumed he had killed her.

Officer Hickey also told the court of finding blood on Patterson's underclothes. Spirited cross-examination failed to shake him on any point. Another officer testified that Patterson had attempted to hide his hat; when the hat was discovered, he refused to give it to the jailer; that when he finally agreed to do so, the police saw him surreptitiously tear out the lining and hide it before he handed the hat over; and when the lining was retrieved and examined, it was found to bear a bloody thumbprint. John Wesley Adams, the City Hall janitor, testified that Patterson had confessed the crime to him on April 28 as mobs surrounded the jail. Under cross-examination, Adams remarked wryly: "I don't claim the distinction of being the only person to whom Patterson confessed his guilt. I don't see any distinction in it. I have frequently said that if Turner and Patterson were guilty, they ought to be punished, but I have not been in any mob or endeavored to excite one." A couple of policemen described the scene when Turner picked Patterson out of the lineup at Frankfort jail, a doctor testified about the blood spots found on Patterson's clothes, and then the Commonwealth rested its case.

The defense began with a speech by N. R. Harper, in which he assured the jury that "in common with his white fellow citizens, he was shocked at the brutal murder of Jennie Bowman, and was behind no one in the intensity of his belief that the cowardly assassins should have meted out to them the severest punishment of the law"—by using the plural, was he acknowledging that there had been two attackers?—but he insisted that William Patterson's alibi would be proven in court. On the witness stand, Patterson once again displayed a phenomenal memory as he retold the detailed story of his peregrinations on the morning of April 21: how he had gone to the train depot, how he had helped Willie Woods deliver coal to the wrong address, and so on.

Patterson's chief strategy was to flatly contradict most of the testimony against him: he had never had such a conversation with that liar, Mose Tucker; Lizzie Caldwell also was a liar because he had been intimate with her; Officer Hickey had told him at the time of his arrest that he was wanted for the assault on Jennie Bowman, not for stealing shoes; Chief Whallen had used violent language against him when they rode the train on the way to the Frankfort prison in hopes of scaring a confession out of him; janitor Adams lied when he said Patterson had confessed, for he had only asked Adams to fetch a preacher; he had hidden his hat and torn out its lining only because he had a particular dislike for the officer who asked for it; despite the many people who had recognized his clothing, Patterson maintained that the bloody coat was not even his, but belonged to a fellow prisoner called "Mock Turtle" for reasons that have eluded the net of history. The warden had given the pre-bloodstained coat to Patterson, undoubtedly as part of a diabolical conspiracy to frame the unwitting prisoner. Under cross-examination, Patterson refused to state whether the hat and underwear also were the original property of "Mock Turtle," and undermined his own claim by admitting that when the book agent picked him out of the lineup, he wore the same clothes he had worn when the police arrested him—implying that the clothes really were his. Later, it was revealed that Mr. Turtle did not even own a coat at the time of his incarceration.

According to Patterson, the biggest liar of all was Albert Turner, who was blaming an innocent man, probably to save himself from a mob. If that had been Turner's plan, it was remarkably unsuccessful, since he and Patterson had been threatened with lynching on at least three occasions. Turner did not positively identify him at the lineup in Frankfort, Patterson maintained, but merely had said that he "looked like" his erstwhile accomplice. Patterson added that Turner knew nothing of the bloody underclothes until Chief Whallen told him (but even if that were true, how did Whallen know about them?).

After Patterson was dismissed, a number of people took the stand who attested to meeting him that morning in the places he described. But as noted earlier, there was a troubling two-hour gap in the defense's timeline. No one could definitively verify Patterson's whereabouts between 8:30 and 10:30 a.m.; and, according to Mrs. A. Y. Johnson, the attack on Jennie Bowman must have taken place around 9:45 a.m. Many defense witnesses gave testimony too vague to be helpful. A. J. Lewis claimed to have met Patterson at Eleventh and Maple Streets and asked him for help hauling tanbark "between nine and ten o'clock." Isaac Ballou also saw Patterson at Eleventh and Maple and had asked him to help haul grain to the Crystal Springs Distillery "between nine and ten o'clock—nearer ten than nine....I had no watch with me and had not looked at any clock." (Previously, Patterson claimed this encounter had taken place closer to 8:30 a.m.) Willie Woods swore that he met Patterson at Twelfth and Madison and had given him a ride in the coal wagon. Woods could not remember the exact time, but thought it was between ten and eleven a.m. Two women in Scott Parker's household who received the load of coal from Woods and Patterson were quite sure the time of delivery was 10:35 a.m., for they had an accurate "eight-day" clock. Although the testimony was not as precise as one might wish, the defense did appear to successfully establish the possibility that Patterson might have been seen away from the Johnson manor at the time the burglars broke in.

The third and final day of the Patterson trial, May 20, featured the prosecution's rebuttal. Remarkably, Commonwealth's Attorney Aaron Kohn used post office records to establish that all the defense witnesses were honestly mistaken as to the time they had met William

Patterson on the morning of April 21. Several witnesses (including Patterson himself) agreed that a mailman had delivered Scott Parker's mail just before Patterson and Woods unloaded Parker's coal. The delivery records proved that the mail carrier had made his rounds an hour later than everyone had thought. In other words, all the people who thought they had seen Patterson between 10:00 and 11:00 a.m. actually were seeing him between 11:00 and noon. Since the assault on Jennie Bowman occurred a little after 9:45 a.m.—the prosecution took care to establish that the Johnson family clock was accurate— Patterson's well-crafted alibi did not help him.

(Perhaps the reader is wondering how so many people could have been wrong about the time. Correctly telling the time of day was a far more difficult task in 1887 than it is today. Not everyone could afford a watch; people who did own clocks and watches had to wind them daily or they would be inaccurate. Also, since there were no established time zones yet, most communities set their clocks by "solar time"—that is, they guessed what time it was by basing their estimates on the sun's position in the sky. Thus, it was possible for every clock on an average neighborhood street to provide widely varying times. As one might expect, conflicting time-of-day accounts drove many a homicide investigator to the solace of drink in those days.)

A State witness named J. Douglass swore that he had been present when the book agent identified Patterson in the jail lineup. Douglass stated: "Nothing whatever was done to assist the book agent in the identification, which seemed to be a very positive one. Indeed, the Chief seemed to guard particularly against anything which could suggest the identity of the man suspected." (The bookseller's testimony might not have been the most reliable since he admitted under oath that he "sometimes ate morphine.") Chemists testified that bloodstains on Patterson's garments were of recent origin, rendering it doubtful that "Mock Turtle" or prison staff had given him the bloody clothes. A witness who had been with Chief Whallen when the latter interrogated Patterson swore that the Chief had used no rough or opprobrious language. Whallen swore the same and added that he had not known about Patterson's bloody underclothes until Albert Turner told him about them.

Two defense attorneys, Martin and O'Doherty, took turns making a final plea to the jury. When they finished, Commonwealth's Attorney Kohn gave a closing speech that the *Courier-Journal* published in its entirety, so majestic did the editors find it. Or maybe they were gratified that Kohn spent much time roasting a rival paper, the *Louisville Commercial*, for its biased reporting and one of its reporters in particular for "trying to throw filth and slime upon every man who has dared to do his duty" in the Bowman case by vilifying representatives of the law.

A side note, then we will return to Mr. Kohn's speech. Albert Turner was undoubtedly guilty. He bore telltale facial wounds; he freely confessed, not once but on several occasions; Johnson family items were found in his possession. Patterson's guilt was less certain. Jennie Bowman was often delirious, so it is difficult to decide how much weight to give her words. When feverish, she described her attacker with a singular pronoun—"he"—but her varying descriptions indicated two different men, one tall with a long coat and the other smaller in a short brown cottonade coat. It may (or may not) be significant that Turner wore a long coat while Patterson wore a short brown cottonade coat and that Turner was taller than Patterson. The Johnsons' neighbor, Mrs. William Johnson, testified that when lucid, Jennie always stated that she had been beaten by two men. Believers in Patterson's innocence had some uncomfortable questions to answer. If he were blameless, how were Albert Turner and the book agent able to immediately pick him out of police lineups at the Frankfort jail? How had Turner known that Patterson was wearing bloody underclothes? Assuming that Lizzie Caldwell's testimony was true, why did Patterson lie about how the blood got on his clothes? Why did Patterson feel the need to cook up three alibis? He did confess to janitor John Wesley Adams, if Adams told the truth. (A fellow prisoner named Robert Crow told reporters that Patterson had admitted his guilt to him, but no one seems to have taken Crow's story very seriously.)

Circumstances seemed to point to Patterson's guilt, but many still believed his alibi. Therefore, the most crucial part of prosecutor Kohn's final speech came when he attempted to explain the chronological difficulties and demolish Patterson's alibi once and for all. By using the testimony of three witnesses, including the very precise Mrs. William Johnson, Kohn was able to establish conclusively that the beating occurred between 9:40 and 9:50 a.m. It has been noted that Patterson was able to remember in extraordinary detail every trivial aspect about his stroll through the streets of Louisville on the morning of April 21—he even remembered the number of the train he saw at the depot and the address of the house where he had delivered coal. Patterson had claimed in his testimony that the fear of being hanged had sharpened his recollection of the events of that morning, but the prosecutor found a sinister purpose behind his uncanny memory. Kohn theorized that Patterson had spent time before the crime and afterward memorizing such details with the intention of establishing a convincing alibi. The reader will recall that two laborers had offered Patterson opportunities to work that morning and he refused both of them. He told one that his back was weak. Yet, minutes later, he readily agreed to the strenuous job of delivering coal with Willie Woods. Perhaps he accepted Woods's suggestion because it offered him a chance to ride ostentatiously in a coal wagon and thus make sure a lot of people saw him in a certain place at a certain time.

Kohn had shown that nearly all the defense witnesses had been mistaken as to the time when they saw Patterson on the street; discounting their testimony, that left a window of time between 9:10 and 10:15 a.m. during which Patterson easily could have committed the atrocity on Brook Street and gone to Eleventh Street, where Ike Ballou first saw him. The only witnesses who had access to an accurate clock were the women at the house of Scott Parker, where Patterson and Woods delivered coal. They claimed that Patterson had visited their house at 10:35. Kohn pointed out that there was slightly over an hour unaccounted for in Patterson's alibi; had he committed his crime close to 9:45 a.m., as the police believed, he would have had a half hour to make it to Eleventh Street by 10:15. It was determined that Patterson could have walked leisurely from the Johnson house to Twelfth Street, a distance of a mile and a half, in only twenty minutes—ten to twelve if he had hurried. That left twenty minutes for him to meet Lewis and Ballou, ride on Woods's cart, and deliver the coal.

When Kohn finished his oration, Judge W. L. Jackson provided an evenhanded charge to the jury. Among other things, he cautioned the jury to ignore Patterson's previous convictions for other crimes. He also told the jury that neither a confession from Patterson, "if there be such," nor Albert Turner's testimony warranted a conviction unless corroborated by other evidence, and added: "[I]f, upon the whole case, the jury entertain a reasonable doubt of the accused, or of any material fact necessary to his guilt having been proven, they should find him not guilty."

The jury returned after twelve minutes with a guilty verdict and a recommendation of the death penalty. Patterson was taken back to his cell, where he complained that he did not receive a fair trial. It is true that the evidence against him was largely circumstantial, but the public erred then (and errs now) in the belief that circumstantial evidence is by definition weak or inadequate. On the contrary, often it is more trustworthy than the eyewitness testimony so beloved by dramatists and filmmakers. Witnesses can be made to look like fools through cross-examination. Witnesses can be mistaken or forgetful. Witnesses can lie under oath. Witnesses can be bought or otherwise unduly influenced. Witnesses can contradict each other.

Lawyers often make the specious claim that circumstantial evidence is like a chain; break one link, they say, and the whole thing falls apart. However, the celebrated attorney Vincent Bugliosi has argued forcefully that a rope is a better analogy: "[E]ach fact is a strand of that rope. And as the prosecution piles one fact upon another we add strands and we add strength to that rope..... [I]f one strand does break, the rope is not broken. The strength of the rope is barely diminished. Why? Because there are so many other strands of almost steel-like strength that the rope is still more than strong enough..." While no one circumstance against Patterson is convincing in and of itself, put the many suspicious circumstances together and his apologists had to jump through hoops to explain them all away. In the early days of the investigation, there had been considerable feeling in Louisville that Turner was attempting to frame Patterson, as expressed by the *Courier-Journal*'s "In and About" columnist as early as April 26—that is, until the full weight of the circumstances against Patterson became evident; then, such talk was largely confined to conspiracy theorists and Patterson's attorneys.

On May 30, Patterson again stood before Judge Jackson. In the past, Jackson had sentenced him to the penitentiary for lesser offenses and had warned him that the scaffold would be his destiny if he did not reform his ways. "You are a man of more than ordinary intellect," remarked the judge, "and have some education. It was in your power to have become a useful citizen." So saying, Jackson officially passed the death sentence: Patterson would hang alongside Albert Turner on July 1. "You are sentencing an innocent man," said the prisoner.

The two prisoners were polar opposites in their personalities: Turner continued to admit his guilt and calmly awaited his fate while Patterson constantly protested his innocence. As is too often the case with convicted murderers, the phlegmatic Turner and the loud, excitable Patterson became celebrities. Thousands of people with nothing better to do attempted to visit them at the Louisville prison; more often than not, Jailer Bailey permitted them to do so, as had the man in charge of the Frankfort prison. Kentucky prison officials do not come across very well in the Jennie Bowman saga. Some of the visitors expressed sympathy for Turner and Patterson and left money and gifts, while others came to insult and menace. Patterson was so angered by the words of a couple of young "visitors" that he threw a cup of water in their faces.

Turner was not above begging for monetary contributions from visitors. He had his photograph taken and eventually sold over 200 copies. He spent his income on luxuries such as jelly-cake and cigars, but he also intended to save enough to pay his final debt: his burial expenses. Turner regaled a reporter who visited him with stories of his romantic conquests (he had nine illegitimate children) and the promise that the authorities would "make no monkey" of him on the scaffold. The scandalized journalist remarked: "A talk with this brute is one of the most depressing things that a sensitive person could subject himself to. Turner seems to contradict every optimist theory of moral philosophy and to be a living defiance of every hope of Christianity and every tenet in an orthodox creed concerning the creation of man." Yet, Turner could not have been as amoral as the reporter thought, since he felt tremendous remorse for the murder of Jennie Bowman.

Perhaps the reporter was really bothered by Turner's happy and joking nature around fellow prisoners and the fact that he anticipated his death. On one occasion, he was heard playing a presumably jolly song called "Johnny, Get Your Hair Cut" on a harmonica. At night he would pray for hours. Still, he refused to exonerate Patterson, stating: "I would save him if I could, but I don't go to Heaven with a lie on my lips." About a week before the hanging, jail officials found mysterious white powder in his cell and, fearing that he was contemplating suicide via strychnine or the popular rodent poison Rough On Rats, they took away all his privileges. Turner became livid and threw spectacular and fearful tantrums, because he had come to enjoy the attention he received in prison, including flowers from admirers. (Regarding the floral tributes, the *Courier-Journal* remarked with disgust: "Remembering the awful nature of the crime for which Turner is to die, it is difficult to understand how a woman should wish to decorate his cell with flowers. Who has sent a wreath to Jennie Bowman's grave?") The powder turned out to be only whitewash and he was permitted visitors under close scrutiny. When he was again allowed callers, his old calmness returned.

As Turner happily awaited his doomsday, the public exhibited two completely opposite, though equally unattractive, facets of human nature. While hundreds of bloodthirsty and morbidly curiously people, white and black, unsuccessfully tried to get official tickets to see Turner's hanging, hundreds of mawkish types attempted to visit him in jail so they could compete to see who could shed the most tears over him. Turner became the beneficiary of the maudlin sentiment that too many people lavish on a condemned man, no matter what he may have done. In addition to the aforementioned bouquets, Turner received letters and money. It is doubtful that most of his well-wishers would have given him so much as a nickel under ordinary circumstances. On Turner's last weekend, Jailer Bailey broke his own visitation rules and allowed over 2,500 persons to troop by the cell and gape at the condemned man. His visitors included relatives and friends, as is right and proper, but also complete strangers, including well-to-do businessmen and ladies donning the latest fashions. It was estimated that over half of the gawkers were women representing every social class, race, and age.

Turner jocularly threatened to haunt his relatives if they failed to have a "big funeral" for him. He wanted to be buried in no mundane pine box, but rather had his heart set on a seventy-five dollar imitation rosewood model with satin trim, silver handles, a brass nameplate on the lid, and a glass window so mourners could peer in and contemplate his lifeless face. In order to acquire this wonderful coffin he posted a large placard reading, "LADIES AND GENTLEMEN: Please donate something to help bury me, July 1, 1887." A great many persons did as requested and after a few expressed reluctance, Turner refused to show his face to anyone who did not drop money in his cigar box. (In the meanwhile, the *Courier-Journal* had been haranguing readers to donate to the fund intended to buy a monument for Turner's victim.) The prisoner had a splendid time, laughing and joking with visitors and having a sweet jailhouse romance with an eighteen-year-old former girlfriend from Chicago who happened to be confined in another part of the prison for the "malicious cutting" of another human being. Another weeping ex-mistress of Turner's bought a couple of his photographs. In all, Turner made nearly $300 by exhibiting himself like a sideshow attraction in an era when the average worker's yearly wages were less than $500. More than a few commentators complained that because he was permitted to profit from his imprisonment, become a celebrity, and die as a folk hero rather than as an example, it negated the seriousness of his crime and trivialized the gravity of his punishment.

Turner spent his last day charging a steady stream of well-wishers and the merely curious for the privilege of seeing him. He also prayed and consulted with two ministers, Rev. George Scott of the Zion Baptist Church and Rev. C. C. Bates. Some of the prisoner's tranquility vanished when his lifespan became a matter of hours. His formerly robust appetite dwindled; he had trouble sleeping. Nevertheless, he retained a veneer of cheerfulness and the reverends baptized him in a tin bathtub. The swanky coffin he had purchased was brought to his cell, where he inspected it with delight.

On the morning of July 1, the execution of Albert Turner was held privately in the jail yard, but it was easily visible from the upper floors of City Hall, houses on the south side of Market Street, and a local firehouse. Naturally, these prime viewing spots were filled with haste by the throngs who wanted to watch a man die. One spectator held a pair of opera glasses; the technology of photography was sufficiently advanced in 1887 to permit amateur photographers to take pictures of the proceedings. Louisville was so fascinated by the hanging that the publishers of the *Courier-Journal* did something that appears to have been unprecedented in the paper's history: they put out an early morning edition in addition to the usual afternoon edition. Thus, readers got the details of the execution on the morning it occurred rather than having to wait.

As the sun rose, Turner dressed in the clothes Police Chief Whallen had purchased for him shortly after he was arrested. Prison officials entered the cell and manacled Turner. As they escorted him to the prison yard, he managed to sell two final photographs of himself to a couple of cooks. Turner approached the gallows "as cool as an iceberg," mounted the steps without a second's hesitation, and stood on the trap as the hangman placed the noose around his neck. With only minutes to live, Turner confessed to an assault and robbery for which another man had been sent to prison. Then he startled everyone by making a brief speech in which he insisted that William Patterson was innocent after all. At precisely 6:30 a.m. the trap was sprung and Turner died almost instantly of a broken neck. There was a clamor to retrieve the rope and cut it up for souvenirs—an ugly and inevitable facet of hangings in those days. Despite Turner's hankering for a "big funeral," the officers at the church of his choice, Rev. Scott's Zion Baptist, unanimously voted not to allow their church to be the scene of the pompous spectacle Turner had intended to purchase with the money gained from his prison peepshow.

At the last possible moment, Turner had recanted his charges against Patterson. In addition, Rev. Scott produced a letter written by Turner on June 22 in which he claimed he had framed Patterson. The minister said that he had promised Turner he would keep the contents of the letter secret until after the hanging. That would seem to end matters, but the night before his execution, Turner wrote a second sealed letter that he insisted should not be opened until after his death. It read:

DYING STATEMENT OF ALBERT TURNER. Jail, June 30.— I, Albert Turner, have never give...any person any statement in regards to anything different from what I have said in the courts on the witness stand as to the guilt of Patterson, and what I said on the stand was the truth and the whole truth, so help me God.

The letter was signed by the prisoner and four witnesses. Which of Turner's statements was the truth? The overwhelming weight of evidence pointed to Patterson's guilt, so the general consensus was that Turner had "died with a lie on his lips." Turner had claimed in the letter of June 22 and on the gallows to have railroaded Patterson, but on neither occasion did he explain why. In the letter to Rev. Scott he also claimed to have committed the crime by himself, something that the forensic evidence indicated was impossible. If Patterson were innocent, why hadn't Turner admitted it long before and spared him the ordeal of the trial? And why did he ask Rev. Scott to keep the letter confidential until after his death? No answers were forthcoming and since Turner was no longer around to explain his reversal, few people took stock in his last confession.

The reader will have noticed that Patterson did not hang alongside Turner as had been originally planned. At the time of Turner's execution, Patterson's attorneys were appealing his case, which went before the Court of Appeals in September. Commonwealth's Attorney Kohn traveled to Frankfort to make a case against allowing Patterson an appeal. On October 6, the Court upheld the decision of the lower court. Albert Turner's last-minute contradictions concerning Patterson's role in the crime could not be taken seriously; there simply was no compelling new exonerating evidence and even if there were, the higher court could not consider anything that had not been brought out at the trial. Patterson expected to be pardoned and when he got the news to the contrary, he was so astonished he could not speak for several minutes. Nevertheless, one of Patterson's three attorneys stood by him. Matt O'Doherty was determined to see his client get a second trial and filed a petition for a rehearing by the Court of Appeals.

The officials at the Louisville jail, still smarting from the harsh criticism they received for allowing Albert Turner to exhibit himself to the public, refused to allow William Patterson any visitors except family, his legal advisors, the occasional reporter and any preachers who dared drop in. Patterson was often rude to members of the clergy. Like Turner, he enjoyed being an object of respect and awe in jail and he cultivated a reputation for bullying other prisoners, who called him Mr. Patterson and saluted him when he went to exercise. He always got to read the newspaper first and the other jailbirds felt compelled to ask his permission before singing. His bravado had diminished only briefly and his spirits were kept high by his absolute conviction that he would never be hanged.

His adamant belief was shaken considerably when attorney O'Doherty's second petition for a new trial was overruled by the Court of Appeals on November 23. When Patterson heard that the appeal had been turned down he nearly fainted and upon recovering, he cried: "I am innocent, I am innocent! Turner done it, and he said so." But the indefatigable O'Doherty swore that he would save Patterson if he had to spend thousands of dollars to accomplish this noble work. Nothing now could spare Patterson but executive clemency—i.e., a pardon or a commutation of the sentence to life in prison. It all depended on whether Governor Simon Bolivar Buckner could be pressured into being a "merciful ass," as Mark Twain put it in *Tom Sawyer* when well-meaning, but naïve, citizens wanted to have multiple murderer Injun Joe pardoned. O'Doherty expressed a wish to start some petitions—the sooner, the better since Governor Buckner had set the date of execution as January 27, 1888.

The optimistic O'Doherty granted a too-candid interview in which he boldly predicted that Governor Buckner would not merely commute Patterson's sentence, but would set him free with a full and abject pardon. For one thing, there was Turner's statement on the gallows. The attorney argued, with more sentiment than sense: "If the statement of a dying man, who has no interest at stake save to clear his soul of perjury before he goes to face his Maker is lightly treated, it will establish a most dangerous precedent." (Perhaps Turner had convinced himself that it would be pleasing in the sight of God to save the life of a fellow human with a lie.) In addition, O'Doherty dropped hints about some new evidence that would set matters right as soon as he informed the governor. When pressed, he stated that he had found two hitherto undiscovered witnesses, whose names he would not release as yet. Despite O'Doherty's insistence on maintaining his witnesses' anonymity, he revealed that one was a former Senator, which would seem to greatly narrow down the possibilities for those intent on determining his true identity. He allegedly told O'Doherty that when he had visited Turner in prison, the latter confessed that he had no idea whether Patterson was the right man. Why hadn't the ex-Senator come forward with this evidence? Because, O'Doherty explained, "he did not want to be mixed up in the case, and thought Patterson deserved punishment on general principles." It would be interesting to ask the attorney why he thought the ex-Senator was such a find, since this admission hardly redounded to the man's credit.

O'Doherty's other secret weapon was "a very prominent businessman" whose testimony would prove that the assault on Jennie Bowman was discovered more than an hour after the prosecution claimed. "I asked him why in the world he had not come forward sooner, and he said that he had expected to be called as a witness in the case and was surprised at not having been." Maybe the unnamed businessman thought the defense attorneys had psychic powers and would find him even if he did not step forward. O'Doherty added that the businessman's timeline would be confirmed by Dr. Hoskins, who lived across the street from the A. Y. Johnson family. However, the attorney was perchance overconfident, because the next day Dr. Hoskins officially announced: "I made no explicit statement in regard to the time. I was called in to see Jennie Bowman at about half-past ten o'clock. Such was my statement on the witness stand. So it is obvious that [my] testimony rather militates against than helps Mr. O'Doherty's claim that the assault on Jennie Bowman was discovered a few minutes after eleven." Despite O'Doherty's zeal, he must have decided that the ex-Senator and the prominent businessman were not believable, because he appears never to have mentioned them again.

When Christmastime came, Patterson started reading his Bible and lending a more interested ear to the exhortations of visiting ministers, though he still hoped that he would be freed by the petition now circulating in full force. A week before the date of the scheduled execution, Matt O'Doherty had a conference with the governor, during which he earnestly explained why his client ought not to be hanged. Aaron Kohn argued the opposing viewpoint equally forcefully. Among O'Doherty's new arguments was that the police had put the blood on Patterson's clothes in order to frame his client, but this imaginative forerunner of Johnny Cochran sidestepped the delicate matter of how the coppers applied blood to Patterson's underpants and then convinced him to wear them. He also brought in an affidavit signed by respected Louisville detective Delos Bligh, who swore that he had been present when Albert Turner was first brought to the police station for interrogation and that, at the time, Turner said that he had no accomplice. However, Turner's statement could have only signified that at first he lied to protect somebody. Not to be outdone by O'Doherty in the eleventh-hour testimony business, Kohn took a statement from David White, "an old and respectable colored man... [who] bears an excellent character for truth and veracity," and who had been acquainted with William Patterson for many years. White swore that on the morning of April 21, he had seen Patterson only 150 yards from A. Y. Johnson's house. Kohn did not explain where White had been when the prosecution needed him during the trial.

Governor Buckner granted a thirty-day reprieve, during which he would review the evidence and reach a final decision. He must have found the problem a difficult one, because on February 15, he extended the reprieve by another ninety days, setting May 25 as the date for the hanging. During that month and a half, a remarkable development transpired. On April 18, 1888, almost a year after the assault on Jennie Bowman, the press reported that Dr. Evans, a Presbyterian minister from out of town, had seen William Patterson running out of an Oak Street alley and in the direction of Eleventh and Twelfth Streets between 9:30 and 10:00 on the fatal morning. Reverend Dr. Evans had not reported it because he had scruples against the death penalty. The news got out only because he had reported the sighting to a fellow minister. Defense attorney O'Doherty wrote to the papers: "I presume that [Rev. Dr. Evans] is everything that his sacred profession demands he should be—a gentleman and a Christian. I feel, therefore, no hesitancy whatever in saying that the use of his name in the report referred to was unauthorized by him, and that he will not be found to substantiate a single statement concerning Patterson therein made." On both counts O'Doherty was correct, sort of: Evans's name was dragged into the case against his will and the minister never substantiated his claim—not necessarily because it wasn't true, but because he did not want to get involved. He abruptly made himself scarce and never could be found, even though the governor requested an interview with him. Partly because of the difficulty in finding the timorous minister, Buckner granted Patterson another respite until June 22.

At long last, the governor made his decision. He had gone to Louisville to personally inspect the evidence and found Kohn's arguments more persuasive than O'Doherty's. On June 14, he declared that he would not interfere with the judgment of the Circuit Court. Patterson must be hanged. Both O'Doherty and the prisoner expressed the utmost astonishment. "It's murder to hang me!" cried the latter. He went on to blame his problems on everyone but himself and complained about a dark conspiracy between the police and the prosecution: "I hope that my ghost will follow them all. They're spilling the blood of an innocent man, and I hope my fate will be that of every one, from the governor down." On the same day Patterson learned that his hanging was a certainty, he received news that his seven-month-old child had died. Prison officials took up a collection to pay for the infant's funeral and Patterson remarked, "Well, I hope to meet it before long." O'Doherty, much deflated, admitted defeat. There was nothing more he could do to help his client.

Patterson spent the next eight days waiting for the hangman's footsteps. He no longer sent ministers away with hurled insults and epithets for their pains. The day before his death, he happily announced that he had at last found God and felt he had been forgiven for all his sins. Some local preachers gave him a rushed baptism. He spent his last day praying and reciting religious and sentimental poetry of his own invention, some of which was reprinted in the *Courier-Journal*.

Long before dawn on June 22, crowds assembled on the rooftops and in the windows of every building which provided a vantage point for witnessing the hanging. Around 6:00 a.m., Patterson walked the same route to the jail yard that Albert Turner had taken nearly a year before. Like Turner, he walked with a steady gait and a calm demeanor. Yet, while Turner had reaffirmed his guilt while standing on the gallows, Patterson protested his innocence for the final time, saying he knew nothing more of Jennie Bowman than he knew of Queen Victoria or Marie Antoinette. There was another, more horrible, difference between the two executions. While Turner's hanging had gone successfully, Patterson was not so lucky. He was considerably lighter than Turner and the rope had not been properly adjusted; instead of receiving a broken neck and an instant death, Patterson slowly strangled to death. Over four minutes after the trap was sprung, people standing nearby heard him whisper, "Oh Lord, take me, take me." He was dead after a little more than ten minutes of swinging. Ghastly as his death was, however, unforgiving souls noted that it did not compare to the two weeks of torture endured by his victim.

The hanging of Patterson did little to resolve the racial tensions that had gripped Louisville since the day Albert Turner was arrested. The older black residents of the city tended to believe in Patterson's guilt, while the young tended to believe he had been wrongfully prosecuted. Many blacks held a mass meeting on the night of June 23 to express their conviction that Patterson had been the victim of a racist conspiracy, overlooking the fact that several black witnesses testified convincingly against Patterson—including Albert Turner, John Wesley Adams, Mose Tucker, George Moore, and Lizzie Caldwell. For some reason, Patterson's funeral services were held at the Ninth Street Colored Baptist Church on July 8, two weeks after his execution. The services were marked by several gossamer-thin comparisons between William Patterson and the Lord. Said Reverend Mitchell: "The meaning of our discourse will be that the innocent are put to death….Jesus Christ was put to death, but He was innocent of all the crimes laid to His charge." Governor Buckner came across as being not unlike Pontius Pilate—but the Governor of the universe had pardoned Patterson, even if Buckner had not, said Mitchell. The sermon included much more in this vein.

The bad feelings engendered by the hanging affected politics as well as religion: at the end of the month, many Louisville black men organized to vote against the sheriff who had hanged Patterson. Some citizens were troubled for years by the fact that Patterson never confessed, but that can be explained. Attorney O'Doherty had filled Patterson's head with false hopes and he expected a reprieve until almost the end of his life. A confession would have spoiled his chances forever of getting that commutation.

Nearly four months after Patterson's death, the monument for Jennie Bowman was finally paid for. A dedication ceremony was held in Cave Hill Cemetery on October 6, 1888. It was made of "teardrop" granite delivered from Maine and the inscription read: "Public Recognition of the Heroism of Jennie Bowman, Faithful to Her Trust Even unto Death."

William Patterson may have expressed a wish to haunt all of those who, in his view, were responsible for his downfall, but the other two principals in this story allegedly did return to this sad world as ghosts. After Turner's execution, an eerie rumor spread that he had been revived with electricity after death and that his reanimated corpse was awaiting a chance to sneak out of the city. That tale soon gave way to reports that his ghost haunted Tillie Goodall's cottage near Walnut Street. Knowing a good thing when she saw one, Mrs. Goodall held regular séances that were attended by up to a hundred paying believers. Customers were treated to the sight of the late Mr. Turner's head, which always appeared in a cottage window, bathed in lights of changing colors. Attendees swore that they could feel the impression of a rope indentation around the ghost's neck. Turner's ghost reported that right after his hanging he had gone straight to Hell as a punishment for lying on the scaffold. Once there, he got a job as a fireman aboard a steamboat that carried recently deceased souls to the infernal regions. After a few months, however, God showed mercy and allowed Turner's ghost to ascend to Heaven. Apparently, he was often given permission to leave Paradise and visit Walnut Street, Louisville. Mrs. Goodall made sure skeptics were not allowed to attend the séances, a suggestive fact that speaks for itself. It has been many decades since anyone has reported seeing the gainfully employed ghost of Albert Turner.

Jennie Bowman's phantom is no laughing matter. As though the murdered maid's fate were not hard enough, there are those who believe her restless spirit still haunts her old neighborhood. According to author David Dominé in his book *Ghosts of Old Louisville*, residents on Brook Street have seen the ghost of a small young woman wandering the sidewalks. She is dressed as a maid from the Victorian era, complete with lace apron and bonnet. Dominé writes that "she seems to float along the sidewalks at night, usually with her face turned away from the viewers, and they almost always hear a long, piercing scream before she vanishes into thin air." On occasion, witnesses have seen her cover her face with her hands—perhaps she is reluctant to show herself because of the brutal, disfiguring beating she received? A. Y. Johnson's house on Brook Street in which she was murdered has long since ceased to exist, which some believe accounts for the fact that she is seen on the sidewalk.

Modern Brook Streeters have reported seeing her not only on the street, but also in their houses; maybe her befuddled spirit is searching for Johnson's nonexistent house. Interestingly, considering that Jennie first encountered Albert Turner at her master's fireplace, residents who claim her ghost has invaded their homes report that incidents often center around their fireplaces. Most disturbingly, keeping in mind that Jennie was struck with fireplace pokers, the residents of one Brook Street house claim that at least twice they have found their pokers mysteriously arranged in the shape of a cross.

Never Tease
an Angry Sheriff

Kentucky's oldest town, Harrodsburg, was founded in 1774 by James Harrod. One of his direct descendants was Dr. Frank L. Harrod, who graduated from the Louisville Medical College in 1890. He moved back home to Mercer County to practice medicine. Things were looking good for Dr. Harrod—then he made an enemy of Sheriff John I. VanArsdale. (The contemporary press and court records give the lawman's name in several creative variations including Vanarsdal, Vanarsdel, Vanarsdell, VanArsdel, and Vanarsdall, but I have chosen to use the spelling that appears on his death certificate.)

Harrod and VanArsdale met in 1890 and became friends; the doctor and his wife boarded with the sheriff's family for a while. In September 1893, they had a falling out. VanArsdale later claimed that Dr. Harrod was angry because the sheriff would not loan him money.

When Sheriff VanArsdale ran for re-election in November 1894 he was soundly beaten by his Republican opponent, F. P. James. VanArsdale did not take his defeat philosophically. He blamed it on a series of anonymous letters that had circulated before the election which accused VanArsdale of beating his wife and terrorizing his family. The sheriff was convinced that Harrod was responsible, something the doctor never exactly denied. Harrod only said that everything in the unsigned circulars was true and that he "would say to [VanArsdale's] face all he had ever said about him."

On January 4, 1895, VanArsdale had only a few days left until his term as sheriff expired. He walked down Office Street, brooding. Only a few minutes before this stroll, his friends had teased him for having lost his job to a Republican. Unfortunately for all concerned, the sheriff's department was located next to Dr. Harrod's establishment. VanArsdale saw the man he blamed for his troubles opening the door to his office.

A few moments later, several witnesses, including a patient named Dan Hines waiting inside Dr. Harrod's office, heard someone on the sidewalk swear a loud oath. This was followed by three shots. Witnesses ran to the scene to find the forty-three-year-old doctor lying helpless on the icy pavement. The sheriff went to his own office, where he was arrested by Chief of Police K. C. Smith as he reloaded his pistol at his desk. Dr. Harrod, who had been shot below the shoulder blade and in the back and abdomen, died in his own office minutes later without regaining consciousness.

It was announced that VanArsdale would be prosecuted by Hon. C. J. Bronston of Lexington and two other attorneys. Part of their fees was paid with contributions from the poor people of Mercer County, to whom Dr. Harrod had been a great friend. VanArsdale retained Col. Phil Thompson and seven other defense attorneys, whose services he needed rather desperately since he claimed he had killed Dr. Harrod in self-defense even though Harrod was unarmed and had been shot once in the front and twice from behind. Perhaps the small army of defense attorneys could have argued that the murder was committed in a fit of anger; however, at the preliminary hearing on January 11, witnesses swore that on the night before the murder they had seen VanArsdale standing with a shotgun on a corner that Dr. Harrod regularly passed to get to his office. This suggested that the shooting had been premeditated.

The soon-to-be-ex-sheriff told his side of the story in court on January 12. He said that he had been walking up the street when Dr. Harrod "ran his hand behind him," a gesture that made it seem he was reaching for a weapon, and shouted an attention-getting oath. Thinking he was being attacked, VanArsdale shot the doctor three times. He denied having shot the man as he lay on the ground, contradicting a number of prosecution witnesses who swore they had seen him do exactly that. VanArsdale stated that Dr. Harrod had often threatened him; for example, the doctor had been in the habit of impudently brushing by VanArsdale on the sidewalk as the latter attempted to converse with friends.

VanArsdale also testified that he had never harmed his family, but three rebuttal witnesses swore otherwise. A neighbor named Mrs. T. S. Marimon said she had seen the sheriff "whipping his child and using her very roughly." A former boarder, Mrs. T. H. Carter, had seen Mrs. VanArsdale upset and crying; after Mrs. Carter asked what was wrong, Mrs. VanArsdale claimed that her husband had poured a bowl of water on her. (Sheriff VanArsdale stated under oath that he had only sprinkled her with water in jest.) Dr. Harrod's widow, Mary, testified that when VanArsdale's teenage daughter, Lottie, had been expelled from school, the sheriff had pinned her to the ground with both knees and beaten her with a barrel hoop. (On the other hand, seventeen-year-old Lottie testified that she had not received corporal punishment from her father since she was ten—and then he had only spanked her with a switch.) Despite the contradictions in the testimony, Judge James Neal decided to deny bail for VanArsdale and declared that he would have to stand trial. Reporters noted that those who attended the court session were barely able to restrain their applause. VanArsdale was led to jail by his hated Republican replacement.

In short order, VanArsdale was indicted and no-nonsense Judge Saufley set the trial to begin on Valentine's Day. Public interest was at such a high pitch that spectators brought lunches to the courtroom so as not to miss a second's worth of testimony. By the trial's end, persons outside the courtroom were so desperate to hear the proceedings that they pressed against the windows until they shattered and many a disappointed Mercer Countian went home with cut and bloody hands. High-powered lawyers represented both sides; the most prominent was one of the eight defense attorneys, William O. Bradley, who would become Kentucky's first Republican governor later in the year. Also arguing for the defense was VanArsdale's brother James. Both the prosecution and the defense announced that new evidence beneficial to their side had been discovered since the examining trial; a rousing courtroom battle seemed to be brewing.

The first witness for the Commonwealth was David Chatham, Mercer County jailer, who stated that he had spoken with VanArsdale on Chiles Street just before noon on January 4. Moments after their conversation, he heard a shot on Office Street (which intersected with Chiles). Turning, he saw VanArsdale shoot Dr. Harrod twice and then walk into his sheriff's office. On cross-examination the defense got Chatham to admit that before the shooting, VanArsdale had seemed to be "in a good humor," as though that proved anything. Only one witness could be found who had seen VanArsdale fire the first shot: thirteen-year-old Carrie VanArsdale. (I have been unable to find out if she was a relative of the accused; possibly not, since VanArsdale was one of the most common names in Mercer County.) Perhaps the defense could have tried to negate her testimony, but it would have had very little effect as a half-dozen people saw the sheriff fire the second and third shots: Chatham, Ben Gabhart, Alice Benton, William Carrick, Clayton Phillips, and Buzz Bell—and besides, the victim was unarmed, as indicated by the testimony of numerous witnesses. Two other witnesses, Alvin Taylor and Charles Corn, did not see the shooting, but ventured outside just in time to see the doctor lying on the ground and VanArsdale standing over him with pistol in hand.

Calvin Johnson testified that he had seen VanArsdale standing on a street corner with a shotgun two nights before the murder. W. T. Curry had seen the same unnerving sight the night before the murder. There was considerable testimony involving a broken doorknob found near the wounded doctor, significant because the knob to his office door was missing. The implication seemed to be that the doctor was in the act of opening his door when the first bullet entered his back, causing him to spasmodically tear the knob from the door. In fact, Carrie VanArsdale swore under oath that that was exactly what had happened. It is surprising that the defense did not claim that Dr. Harrod had removed the knob from the door with the intention of using it as a weapon, forcing the terrified sheriff to shoot in self-defense.

Perhaps Dr. Harrod did write the scurrilous circulars that led to VanArsdale's electoral defeat, but the prosecution proved that VanArsdale had often made offensive remarks about the physician in the presence of others. In the summer of 1893, James Terhune heard him sneer that Harrod "only doctored prostitutes and niggers." (On rebuttal VanArsdale denied having made the remarks.) Reuben Williamson had heard him use a four-jointed epithet when referring to Harrod and saw him draw his pistol for emphasis.

After the prosecution rested, defense attorney Col. E. H. Gaither appealed to the jury by referring to the defendant's good character and his Mercer County ancestry. The latter tactic was widely regarded as a mark of desperation. The Colonel added that VanArsdale "had filled the office of sheriff so well that he had received the praises not only of the highest tribunals, but of the lowest citizens for his protection to them"—and yet, it appears they did not think highly enough of him to reelect him. The real cause of the trouble between the two men, said Gaither, was that Dr. Harrod was heavily in debt to VanArsdale. The defense promised to prove that Harrod had been bent on destroying the reputation of the VanArsdale family and that Harrod had vowed to murder the sheriff if he ever got a chance; therefore, VanArsdale was fully justified in shooting the doctor out of fear for his life.

In order to prove the animosity Harrod had for VanArsdale, the defense suggested that the doctor kept a hatchet in his office for the alleged purpose of performing unorthodox and unnecessary surgery on the sheriff's head if the opportunity arose. VanArsdale's attorneys claimed that the shotgun he had been carrying out on the street the night before the murder was actually a present for a boy named Matt Curry, and VanArsdale had only been taking it to his office for safekeeping. (A problem with this version of events: he was seen in public with the gun two nights in a row.)

VanArsdale took the stand and stated that Tom Wheeler, Dave Teator, Dr. Merideth, and Abe Armstrong all told him that they had overheard Dr. Harrod threatening his life. Interestingly, Harrod's words of violence always seem to have gotten to the sheriff by secondhand, for VanArsdale did not testify that Harrod had ever threatened him up close and personal. However, he did often see the doctor glare at him and stick his hands in his pockets and he thought Harrod had once set off a firecracker at his doorstep. He claimed to consider these gestures menacing and terrifying. VanArsdale declared that he had not been looking for trouble on the morning of January 4; he had been heading for his office in a jovial mood when the doctor had confronted him and called him a bad name while simultaneously reaching behind his back as though grabbing for a gun. The sheriff argued that under those circumstances, he was justified in believing his life was in danger and in firing a shot in self-defense. (Problem: even if this were so, why did he fire twice more after his opponent was rendered helpless?)

Several defense witnesses took the stand to affirm that they had heard Dr. Harrod speak abusively of the sheriff. Their testimony as a whole was not compelling. Lee Coleman had heard the doctor use a common, but crude, phrase that cast aspersions on both the sheriff and his maternal unit in the bargain. Dick Vandiver saw the doctor pass the sheriff on the street with—horrors!—his hand in his coat pocket. John Davis testified that Harrod had told him that if he ever crossed paths with the sheriff he would kill the "d—d scoundrel," but this conversation had taken place several months before the shooting, so apparently the doctor was in no big hurry. About three weeks before the shooting, W. D. Green, Henry Sallee, and Clayton Phillips saw the doctor throw up his arm and strike the sheriff's elbow as they passed on the street. Green admitted that he "noticed nothing particular in [Dr. Harrod's] manner," so the incident could be interpreted as nothing more than an accidental jostling. VanArsdale's current boarder, M. W. Curry, said that when he was in James Tomlinson's grocery store he had overheard Harrod express a wish to batter the sheriff with a hatchet handle. Mrs. James Divine corroborated the statement. The defense considered this evidence that the doctor intended to violate his Hippocratic Oath to "never do harm to anyone." However, on the same occasion, Curry also heard Harrod say that a glance from the sheriff could turn sorghum into vinegar, which raises the distinct possibility that the doctor was making idle threats and/or joking.

The next day's proceedings yielded more of the same. David Teater had heard Dr. Harrod say in his office that VanArsdale abused his family and rightly should be in Hades. Marion Cloyd said he had heard Harrod state that he would kill VanArsdale if he ever crossed his path. Ex-magistrate Thomas Wheeler had heard Harrod say that VanArsdale was not fit to hold office and that "all he wanted was a chance to get at him." Wheeler also heard Harrod express the desire to borrow a pistol, "as he might need it." It did not seem to occur to the defense that this comment could be interpreted to mean that the doctor felt the need to protect himself against the angry sheriff. E. W. Jackman testified that he had seen the doctor carrying a pistol several times; of course, on the one occasion that mattered, the day of his murder, Harrod had been unarmed. In classic blame-the-victim style, the defense attempted to put on the stand a Boyle Countian with the unlikely name Nimrod Buster, who intended to bring up some scandalous act on Dr. Harrod's part. Judge Saufley ruled that none of this testimony would be presented as it was irrelevant. One major problem the defense faced was that none of this testimony proved much more than that there was bad blood between the doctor and the sheriff. After all, if Dr. Harrod had been so keen to pick a fight with the sheriff or even kill him, why was there no evidence that he had threatened VanArsdale to his face? Their offices adjoined, so if Harrod had been serious about killing VanArsdale, he had had plenty of opportunities to do so.

On February 21, Judge Saufley gave instructions to the jury. If the members believed from the evidence that VanArsdale had killed Harrod with premeditation, he should be found guilty of murder and given the death penalty or life imprisonment. If they believed the killing had been done in the heat of the moment and without malice aforethought, they should find VanArsdale guilty of manslaughter and sentence him to no fewer than two years and no more than twenty-one years in prison. If the jury believed VanArsdale had fired because he perceived that his life was in immediate danger, they should acquit him. After the judge spoke, attorneys for both sides made their final arguments.

The case went to the jury on February 23. To recap: before a number of witnesses, VanArsdale had shot an unarmed man three times: twice in the back and once when he was on the ground; according to some witnesses, Harrod's back had been turned when the sheriff commenced firing; the defense had shown that Harrod had said plenty of violent things behind VanArsdale's back, but conspicuously failed to prove that the doctor had ever tried to carry out his threats. The broken doorknob at the crime scene indicated that the doctor had been engaged in nothing more sinister than opening the door to his office when the sheriff "shot him down like a dog on the highway"—or sidewalk, to modify a line from Alfred Noyes's poem "The Highwayman." Despite all of this, the jury returned after a few minutes with a verdict: acquittal on grounds of self-defense.

(It seems that Mercer County had a problem at the time with juries soft in heart and head. A contemporary of VanArsdale's, Ed Bunnell, celebrated his seventeenth birthday on September 30, 1894, by rearranging the atoms that comprised his uncle Neal Freeman with a shotgun. He received a paltry two years in the penitentiary. Similarly, in May 1895, George Norvel was sentenced to two years in jail for murdering a professor named Colson without provocation, but at the same time, a farmer named John Parson was sentenced to one year for stealing a bushel of corn from his neighbor. Thus the Mercer Circuit Court established that a human life was worth exactly twice as much as a bushel of corn.)

The press's reviews of the verdict soon came in. From a local paper, the *Harrodsburg Sayings*: "As a self-respecting journal with the best interests of our community at heart, we must go on record before the world in instant condemnation of the crime and the decision of the twelve men." From the *Paducah News*: "It is easier for a camel to go through the eye of a needle than for a murderer to be punished in Mercer County, and more's the pity, there are other counties in Kentucky of which the same thing can be said." The *Danville Advocate*: "At Harrodsburg the verdict was received with consternation and disgust, and there was some ugly talk indulged in by good citizens who believed that Mercer's sense of justice had been outraged." The *Henry County Local*: "The verdict is another proof that it is fast becoming impossible to get an impartial jury in the state. It is reported that some of the jurors were perjurers....The man who will swear to a lie in order to get a chance to acquit a friend deserves the penalty of the law in the most rigid form." The *Richmond Climax*: "With this acquittal...is it any wonder that mob law at times seems expedient?" The *Jessamine Journal*: "It is no wonder that the press throughout the country calls Kentucky 'the dark and bloody ground.' On what charge Mr. VanArsdale received his acquittal was never fully known except to the court and all respecters of law and fair play in the state must now hide their faces in shame....As long as the aristocrats of Kentucky are permitted to kill whom they please and the law turns them loose, in the name of God how is a good citizen to be protected?" The *Williamstown Courier*: "Thus another stain is added to the many that blacken the history of this good old Commonwealth."

Eventually, the uproar subsided and normality returned to Harrodsburg. The 1910 Mercer County census reveals that VanArsdale became a hotel keeper. He eventually sold real estate. Dying at age eighty-six in August 1943, he took with him the secret of whether he had shot his enemy in self-defense or in a spirit of vengeance nearly a half-century before.

Sketches in ―――――
Kentucky Murder

I.

Tripped by His Big Toe

T he *History of Union County, Ky.* (1886) covers all the material that one expects to see in a county history, such as biographies of prominent settlers and significant dates and details on local agriculture. It also includes the details of a contemporary crime so heinous that the author felt compelled to include it along with more savory matters. The anonymous historian's account begins with admirable directness of style: "Intense excitement was caused… on Monday, August 17, 1885, by the discovery of one of the most revolting crimes ever committed in Western Kentucky in which a beautiful young lady of this county was murdered by her uncle."

The beautiful young lady was eighteen-year-old Lyda Burnett, the granddaughter of Dr. Myers, one of Union County's pioneers. One account states: "Though a poor girl, her character was as spotless as the finest lady's in the land, and she was remarkably popular among the young people of the neighborhood." She lived in the charmingly-named town of Persimmonville along with her grandmother, Mrs. Myers, and her uncle and aunt, Mr. and Mrs. Robert Fowler.

Mr. Fowler was an ugly, hulking six-footer who weighed nearly 250 pounds. He had once romantically pursued Lyda Burnett, but when she discouraged his attentions, he married the girl's aunt in 1884, although he was twenty-three years old and she was nearly fifty. It was generally understood that he had married the aunt out of spite. Lyda's uncle Bob, in other words, was her ex-boyfriend. The fact that they all lived in the same household would have been a source of endless comedy had they been characters in a French farce, but in the real world their living arrangements were guaranteed to cause trouble. That trouble came in April 1885, when Lyda announced her plans to marry James Hall by the end of August. Uncle Robert furiously declared that the nuptials never would occur, but no one paid any attention.

On Sunday, August 16, Mrs. Myers received company: her daughter, Mrs. George Whitworth of Boxville, and Mrs. Whitworth's two children. At the end of the day, Lyda Burnett rode with the Whitworths as far as the village outskirts in order to see them off safely. Several hours later, her horse ambled home without its rider. Nobody was alarmed at first, since Lyda often visited relatives and sent her horse home without her, but she had not returned when morning came. Mr. Whitworth was located and said that Lyda had not spent the night at his house. Clearly, something sinister had happened to her after she parted company with the Whitworths and started home.

A search party found Lyda's remains in the forest only a half-mile from her home. She was lying under a tree with her right hand clutching her throat and her left hand grasping her right wrist. The slayer had carefully wrapped her skirt around her feet, but had snapped her belt with brutal force. She had been nearly decapitated by two deep slashes to the throat; a newspaper account cryptically refers to this deed as "the mercifulest thing the murderer could do," which suggests that before her death Lyda Burnett had been abused in some atrocious manner. She was to have been married the following Tuesday.

Law enforcement officers have seldom had an easier job. Lyda's attacker had gone barefoot and his footprints were found all over the scene. Their distinctive features included a deformed, bony big toe and a second toe larger than the big toe. Searchers easily followed the tracks through woods, weedy fields, and across dusty roads; at one point, investigators found a bloody pool where the killer had stopped to wash his hands in a stream. The tracks formed a line across a cornfield; the space between tracks at this point indicated that the panicked murderer had been running. A bloody handprint on a fence rail showed exactly where Lyda's killer had crossed. The tracks ended at the girl's own home, which certainly helped narrow the list of suspects. Searchers looked in Fowler's smokehouse and found bloody gray trousers and a recently washed white hat that nevertheless bore traces of blood. They also found a bloody shirt hidden under Fowler's mattress and a bloody two-bladed pocket knife concealed on his person; an inspection of his hands revealed dried blood under his fingernails. One of his feet proved to be malformed in exactly the same manner as the footprints found at the crime scene. Investigators took Fowler to the site of the murder and made him put his foot in one of the tracks. It fit perfectly. Later, in court, he would claim that he had made the tracks while hunting hogs a few days before the murder, but he failed to explain adequately why he had felt the urge to run across a cornfield and bound over a fence with bloody hands while hunting hogs. Even the motive was not hard to guess, since everyone recalled that Uncle Robert had opposed Lyda's impending marriage.

Fowler was placed in jail and threatened with lynching in the usual style of those days, but the sheriff sent him to Henderson. When he was tried in Morganfield in September, there was no exculpatory evidence whatsoever. The prosecution made certain the jury knew about the bloody knife, the shirt, and the distinctive footprints. George Whitworth testified that the bloodstained pants and hat found on Fowler's property were the same ones the suspect had worn the day Lyda Burnett disappeared. Fowler's only hope was to convince the jury he was insane, a proposition they did not buy. He was found guilty and sentenced to adorn the gallows on November 27.

To make a long story short, the case was appealed and the verdict sustained, but on the morning of the hanging Fowler received a temporary stay of execution from the governor. The prisoner had to be taken to Henderson to avoid renewed threats of lynching. The verdict was sustained a second time and Fowler climbed that lonesome stairway on the morning of April 23, 1886, the center of the attention of at least 5,000 souls. In his final speech, he said that five men had sworn lies against him, but at the same time he admitted his guilt—something he had confessed privately to his attorney and to the jailer. He had met his ex-girlfriend in the woods and had "accosted her familiarly," and was angered into violence when she rejected his familiarity by striking him in the face with a riding switch. He added that he deserved his punishment.

Most legal hangings went without a flaw. This was not one of them. When the gallows trapdoor opened, the rope broke, flinging Fowler five and a half feet to the ground but effectively snapping his neck. Just to be on the safe side, the authorities picked him up and hanged him again from the crossbeam.

II.

The Acid Assassin

November 2, 1897, was Election Day in Vanceburg, Lewis County. At nightfall, most people were concerned with election returns and did not notice a man wearing a fake beard carrying a couple of bottles. He walked furtively down the dark city streets to the residence of Captain Thomas S. Hoobler, a contractor who specialized in building bridges for the Louisville and Nashville railroad. The man knocked on the door; the Captain's fifteen-year-old son, George, answered. The man with the bottles asked where he might find the Captain. At this moment, Hoobler came to the door. The visitor responded by breaking a beer bottle over the Captain's head. While Hoobler was stunned, his assailant threw the contents of the other bottle in his face: muriatic acid, now better known as hydrochloric acid. The corrosive fluid burned out Hoobler's eyes and seared his face horribly. The assassin poured much of the acid down his victim's throat.

Hoobler's married daughter, Mrs. Evans, ran to her father's rescue. The acid thrower threatened to kill her if she interfered. At this inopportune moment, his fraudulent facial hair fell off and the man hurried away, but not before Mrs. Evans got a good look at him.

Hoobler died in agony the next day at noon. A quickly assembled coroner's inquest suspected a man who had borne a grudge against the Captain. Suspicions grew greater when this particular man, Henry D. Halbert, abruptly left town. Halbert was a civil engineer and expert chemist who also happened to be a former business partner of Hoobler's. The two had had a falling out after Halbert was caught up in a breach of promise suit and Hoobler sided with the woman in the case. Despite rumors that he had fled to Cincinnati, Halbert was soon found in Brownsville, W.V. He swore that he was innocent and said he would voluntarily return to Vanceburg when the excitement died down. He wrote in a letter to a lawyer: "I had no idea of leaving that night until I heard it expressed on all hands that they believed I did it. The public knew that I had a grievance against Hoobler, and on that their suspicions were based. The public forgets that Capt. Hoobler had many other enemies, men who had openly avowed their intentions to kill him."

Despite his protestations, Halbert had no intention of clearing his name in Vanceburg. On November 17, a man who was heavily armed as though expecting trouble, and who answered to the description of Halbert, jumped from a train as it arrived in Huntington, W.V. The man received fatal injuries when he landed on his head. The mysteries of whether this man actually was Halbert, whether Halbert had been Hoobler's assassin, and whether Halbert had cheated the gallows by committing suicide remain unanswered.

III.

Murder at the Revival

The Votaw brothers had a bad reputation. In 1894, Luther Votaw killed two brothers named Masterson in a fight. His brother, Richard, was said to have been a ringleader in raids against local tollgates and, despite being cross-eyed, also was considered Mercer County's champion pistol shot. Richard's father later claimed that he had not been in his right mind since suffering from an attack of the grippe.

On the night of July 2, 1898, a group of sanctificationists held a three-week tent revival meeting at Cornishville, Mercer County. For reasons now unknown, Dick Votaw, described as "a drunken bully of Washington County"—and this was one of the nicer things said about him—held a grudge against certain members of the church, specifically Thomas Hale, B. Lawson, and Dr. Carrier. After drinking and gambling all day, he threatened to break up the revival's final meeting and kill the three gentlemen named above. The next night, he rode to the revival armed with two revolvers and a considerable amount of ammunition. He got everyone's attention by swearing and raving. Preacher Turner Bottom of Perryville asked if someone would please calm Votaw down. The elderly Thomas Hale approached the intoxicated loudmouth and asked him, in a polite and friendly way, to please refrain from using such foul language. Votaw shot Hale in the chin with a .44 caliber Colt pistol, killing him instantly.

As the crowd of about 700 scattered, Votaw fired indiscriminately, killing a young man named Merritt Adkinson. He shot at his enemy, Dr. Carrier; to the physician's good fortune, the bullet passed through his coat and missed him entirely. However, the bullet struck Julia Poulter, resulting in a fatal wound. Another bullet passed through the body of fifteen-year-old Nora Campbell, daughter of a local preacher. Votaw screamed nonsensically at the crowd: "This is a free country and I am a free man!" Then he mounted his horse and rode away as fast as he could, in order that he might remain a free man. Although a posse followed Votaw almost immediately, he proved difficult to locate. Large groups of citizens helped in the search; some were armed with ropes rather than rifles.

Votaw was cornered in Boyle County. Sheriff George Coulter demanded that he surrender. The outlaw responded by reaching for his revolver. Sheriff Coulter offered a similar, and quicker, rejoinder with a double-barreled shotgun. A news correspondent noted that Coulter had spared Mercer County "the disgrace of an illegal hanging" and also "saved the State a vast expense by his accurate aim." Votaw's body was taken to Mercer County, where hundreds of people came to see it at James Stagg's undertaking establishment.

In the fall of 1902, Richard's brother, Thomas, was also overwhelmed by the urge to disrupt religious services. He tried to kill a man named Butler Daniels in a crowded Cornishville church. Daniels escaped by crawling through a window. Thomas Votaw evaded capture until April 1903, when he was charged with assault and battery, carrying a concealed weapon, disturbing religious worship, and willful and malicious shooting without wounding.

IV.

The Fatal Barnyard Fowl Impersonation

On Mildred Road in Jackson County there is a church—Blooming Grove Missionary Baptist Church. Across the road from this house of worship there is a modest cemetery. And in that cemetery there is a pockmarked gravestone, badly worn by weather and time, with a barely visible, erratically spelled inscription: "John Vaughn. Born Aprl th 10 '77. Murdered by George Johnston an others Oct. 31 '99." If local legend is correct, the monument stands as haunting proof that Kentuckians take their politics seriously.

At the turn of the last century, Jackson County was overwhelmingly, almost unanimously, Republican. John Vaughn was one of the county's few Democrats. Because the rough terrain sometimes meant delays in tallying votes, elections were often held in mountain counties a few days before the official Election Day. John Vaughn's date of death, October 31, happened to be Election Day in Jackson County that year. No doubt the reader knows instinctively the direction in which this story is heading.

Elections could be scary events in those bygone days. Vote fraud, whether paid for or coerced, was widespread. Men came to the voting booths liquored up, armed, and yearning for trouble. For years, Kentucky newspapers reported election violence days after the ballots were cast. In fact, there had been a politically-inspired fight complete with gunfire at McKee, county seat of Jackson, a couple of months before the events in this story unfolded.

One other particular the reader should know: we are accustomed to the Democratic party's symbol of a donkey and the Republican party's symbol of an elephant, but in the late nineteenth century the two were symbolized by the rooster and the raccoon, respectively.

On October 31, 1899, the men in some eastern Kentucky counties were voting for governor. John Vaughn went into the booth at Welchburg, a town on the Jackson-Clay County border, and cast his vote for the Democratic candidate, Mr. Goebel. Local legend holds that when emerging he was unable to resist an ill-advised display of political wit. He looked at the crowd of surly (and possibly drunken) Republicans and crowed a defiant "Cock-a-doodle-doo!"

It was almost the last thing he ever did. As the tombstone notes, one man present was George Johnston, a member of a family with whom the Vaughns had been feuding for years. Vaughn's father had been killed in a fight with the Johnstons several years before at Dughill, Clay County. Johnston flew at Vaughn with a revolver; Vaughn, like the man in the old joke, had come to a gunfight armed with a knife. He managed to give Johnston an exploratory stab, but Johnston "and others" shot him to rags on the spot. Thus, Jackson County lost one of its few Democrats, but the soon-to-be-murdered-himself Goebel was doubtless grateful for Vaughn's vote. I was unable to discover whether Johnston and his cronies were punished for the murder.

It appears the accusatory inscription on Mr. Vaughn's tombstone did not please some locals or perhaps they felt like doling out some post-mortem punishment; whatever the reason, his gravestone once bore the marks of having been used for target practice. It is now so old and worn that it is difficult to tell natural blemishes from manmade ones. John Vaughn's wife, Mariah, followed him to the Hereafter—where politics are unknown—a few years later on November 26, 1905. If his shade feels any emotions, perhaps it takes pride in the fact that he is probably the only man in history to have been killed for impersonating a rooster.

V.

A Corpse in the Closet

Henry S. Church lived in his grocery shop at 1215 West Market Street, Louisville. Three policemen near his store heard what sounded like firecrackers being set off inside the building on the night of June 22, 1901. They found Church sitting in a chair, mortally wounded from a suicide attempt. Or, rather, three attempts: in order to make certain he accomplished his mission of self-destruction, Church had shot himself in the chest with a revolver, slit his wrist with a razor, and drunk laudanum.

After calling for an ambulance, the police searched Church's apartment for a note. Instead, they found a sinkful of unwashed dishes, signs of a struggle, and a torn dress at the foot of a bed. "I thought he was single," remarked a lieutenant. Then they noticed a hearty stink emanating from a closet. When they opened the door, they beheld a middle-aged, wide-eyed, bloody-haired female corpse clad only in a nightgown and in an advanced state of decomposition. (All of these discoveries, by the way, were made by the light of a single lamp, which must have added immeasurably to the nightmarish atmosphere.) The coroner found that she had been strangled with a gingham apron, which was still wrapped around her neck—and also that she had been dead two long, hot summer days.

This last bit of news upset the stomachs of Church's more delicate neighbors, who recalled with a shudder that he had been running his store and conversing with customers as usual, although after a certain point he hung a "closed" sign on his establishment's door and stayed inside. All the time, he had borne the secret of the increasingly pungent corpse in his closet.

Church died at the hospital on the morning of June 23. Investigators found that the dead woman was Emily Stuart of Frankfort, whom

Church falsely had claimed was his wife. The question of motive was a mystery. Since Stuart was a co-owner of the store, some thought that Church had murdered her in an attempt to take over the business. On the other hand, the fact that she was wearing a nightgown when she died implied that Stuart and Church were more than just business partners. Police also discovered that Mr. Church, the friendly neighborhood grocer, was a morphine addict.

Church was buried in Frankfort next to his real wife. On June 29, a week after his death, he was the subject of one final mystery. Merchants came to his store to buy unsold stock. As workers cleared the building of its merchandise, someone uncovered a trapdoor beneath the counter. "It was large enough to admit a body and the sawdust which was lying upon the ground was fresh, so that it was certain that the contrivance was not old," wrote a reporter. "Several of the boards had been nailed together, so that the door could be lowered or raised at will." Had Church intended to hide Emily Stuart's body under the floorboards?

VI.

Murder Near the Springhouse

Zoda Vick—the sixteen-year-old daughter of prosperous farmer Charles Vick of Homer, Logan County—undertook the task of retrieving milk from a springhouse on the afternoon of August 20, 1902. It was the last chore she would perform in this world. When she failed to return, a search was made for her. She was found slumped in the corner of a rail fence located near the spring, covered well with leaves. Her head had been battered almost beyond recognition by a bloody rock that still covered her face. "The object was to hide an attempt to assault the girl," said the press. "She had evidently died hard, as signs showed she had made a great fight for her honor" fifty yards from the springhouse.

One man had been willing to assault and kill Zoda Vick, but

hundreds of others were willing to avenge her. Soon, more than 500 angry men streamed into the woods with bloodhounds borrowed from authorities in Russellville and Bowling Green. (Vick's body was left at the scene of the crime for several hours so the dogs could nose out some evidence.) There was open talk of lynching and the possibility of burning the perpetrator at the stake was not excluded. A contemporary describes the scene:

> *Immediately people congregated in groups on the square. On their faces was written determination to run down the murderer of the young girl, who was the idol of her parents and popular among all who knew her. Groups of ten to fifteen could be seen to leave the town until more than a hundred persons had gone, some in buggies, some on horseback and some on foot to offer their services to help capture the murderer.*

Nor were they blindly searching for just any old scapegoat; the identity of the most likely suspect was passed around by word of mouth and the 500 avengers were scouring the county in search of that one man, who happened to be a former employee at the Vick farm.

For that one man, times were pretty warm. An "indignation meeting" was held at the courthouse, ensuring that hotheads would whip each other's anger into righteous fury.

All Russellville businesses were closed because virtually every able-bodied man in town was on the hunt. By the day after the crime, the county and state had chipped in on a $1,000 reward, resulting in an even greater number of persons on the manhunt. The house of Suspect Number One was searched and a bloody pair of ripped trousers was found, a discovery that did nothing to improve his standing in the community. The man's wife and children were away on an extended visit and the man himself was nowhere to be found. It was inferred that he had waited until his family was out of sight, then sought to have his way with Zoda Vick by fair means or foul.

The authorities were confident that the man would soon be caught and that he would then be royally mistreated by mobs. Steps were taken to spare the man's life. The members of Company M of the State Guards, a Russellville military company, got armed and ready to escort any captured men to jail and Governor Beckham promised to call out more state militia should circumstances require it.

All these precautions proved unnecessary. Just before noon on August 22 a farmer named J. M. Bilyon entered the barn of William McCarty, located four miles from the scene of the murder, and found the overripe body of the wanted man, Hugh Marshall, hanging from a tier.

Marshall was about thirty-eight, tall and handsome, and had always been considered an outstanding citizen. He had somehow managed to elude posses for several hours before reaching the solace of McCarty's barn. The killer, realizing his situation was hopeless, had lynched himself. The men of Logan County were aggrieved by the news, "as they had a more terrible punishment in store for the murderer," said the *Louisville Courier-Journal*, which did not specify what nameless horrors the mob had had in mind. They requested that the corpse be turned over to them after the coroner's inquest so they could subject it to public cremation, but the sheriff refused. Marshall's family took immediate possession of the body and buried it with haste a mile from the barn where he had killed himself and less than a mile from where Zoda Vick paid with her life when Marshall's passion overruled his reason.

There was no doubt that Hugh Marshall had murdered Vick. Metal heelplates on his shoe perfectly matched shoe prints found near her body.

VII.

At Least He Had a Good Motive

Frank Underwood's family and friends wondered about his

whereabouts. The nineteen-year-old had gone out on the morning of February 10, 1903, in order to chop some crossties but still had not returned to his Enterprise, Carter County, home by the late afternoon. As the hours dragged by, their concern turned into unease, then dread, and at last fear. Would-be rescuers entered the woods searching for Frank. They found him late that night beside his unfinished crossties. Someone had ambushed him from behind with a shotgun, much to the detriment of Underwood's shoulder and the entire back of his head. He had been blasted with such force that in his last moment he had spasmodically thrown his ax several feet away.

There was some good news: Underwood's assassin had left behind tell-tale fragments of paper wadding and shoe tracks. Soon, the police had in custody a local teenager named George Henderson, an acquaintance of Underwood's, who had been seen emerging from the woods near the place where the victim had been chopping wood. The communities of Enterprise and Olive Hill were puzzled; Henderson was only seventeen years old and had never been known to have a grudge against Underwood. He confessed the day after his arrest.

At his trial in March, the prisoner claimed self-defense on the grounds that Underwood had threatened him with his ax. But the nature of the wounds indicated that Underwood had had his back turned to Henderson when the latter fired. The jury at Grayson didn't buy Henderson's story and, on June 19, the youth was sentenced to eleven years in the penitentiary.

Ah yes, the motive. It seems that Underwood had owed Henderson $1.50, and Underwood didn't want to pay it back.

"Bad Tom" Smith
Entertains 5,000 Spectators

The family feuds of eastern Kentucky are the stuff of legend. These frequently pointless fights involved dozens of members of warring families and sometimes lasted for generations. Several are still well-known events in state history: the French-Eversole feud in Perry County; the Hill-Evans feud in Lawrenceburg; the Baker-White feud in Clay County, which lasted nearly seventy years; the Turner-Howard feud in Harlan County; the Martin-Tolliver feud in Rowan County. And of course, everyone has heard about the fracas between the Hatfield and McCoy families which nearly caused a war between Kentucky and West Virginia.

A small incident with large repercussions took place in "Bloody Breathitt" County in 1887, when John Hurst shot and killed a young man named Alfred Rader after an argument over a division fence, despite Robert Frost's later poetic assurance that "good fences make good neighbors." Hurst was sentenced to eighteen years in the penitentiary; although he had murdered an unarmed man in cold blood, he was paroled in autumn 1892 after serving only about four years—a fact that may help explain the prevalence in Kentucky of the lynch mobs reviled by the nation's press in those days when our ancestors supposedly were so resolute about "law and order." After his release, Hurst became a grocer in Lexington.

The victim's elder brother, Dr. John E. Rader, swore vengeance when he learned that Hurst had been paroled. The doctor's desire to assassinate the assassin became so all-consuming that he neglected his practice, leaving his wife and three children in dire poverty. (Incidentally, Rader's long-suffering wife was destined to face tragedy until her dying day. Shortly after her husband was murdered—as shall be seen—she married Levi Johnston, County Judge of Jackson County. At the end of August 1898, the judge snapped after a quarrel and shot her and then himself with a Winchester rifle at their home near McKee.)

John Hurst, having heard that Rader was gunning for him, lived in a constant state of dread. One night he even dreamed that Dr. Rader had invaded his home and filled his hide with buckshot. The very next day, Hurst would have the unique experience of seeing his nightmare come true.

At sundown on May 12, 1893, the vengeful doctor entered Hurst's establishment and shot the murderer-turned-grocer five times with a pistol before Hurst could get up out of his chair. Hurst was luckier than his victim because he survived; in October Dr. Rader was sentenced to two years (!) in prison. In autumn 1894, Dr. Rader also received an early parole. Hurst, who no doubt previously had appreciated the legal system's absurd leniency, did not take the news of this particular parole very well. He fled the state in terror before Dr. Rader could return and finish the job.

Hurst had been transformed from a criminal into a grocer, but Rader underwent a contrary metamorphosis: he went from a respectable physician to a hardened outlaw. Denied the chance to fulfill his dream of blowing out Hurst's brains, the embittered thirty-eight-year-old former doctor was unable or unwilling to make his living an honest way. He drifted home to Breathitt County.

On Quicksand Creek, four miles from Jackson, stood a house occupied by a forty-eight-year-old farmer of murky reputation, Catherine McQuinn. She shared the house with her live-in paramour, thirty-year-old Tom Smith, originally a native of Perry County, where lived his wife and two children. Despite his reputation for being a man best avoided, Smith has been described by a reporter as soft-spoken and melancholy: "[T]he sad expression of his eyes would indicate anything but the mountain desperado." The same journalist unchivalrously described Mrs. McQuinn as "a large woman, with a face almost masculine in its coarseness…. [H]er nose is large and her mouth is of enormous size, with thick sensual lips. When in repose her face is actually repulsive, but when she begins to talk it lights up, and her large eyes fairly sparkle with intelligence."

On the night of February 5, 1895, Mrs. McQuinn persuaded Dr. Rader on some pretext to spend the night at her house. The dwelling was small, so McQuinn, her boyfriend Tom Smith, and Rader all occupied the same room. At some point during the night, Dr. Rader was shot to death as he slept in the bed. When the authorities inspected his body, they found two bullets in his heart. Mrs. McQuinn surprised everyone by confessing to the murder, though she declined at first to provide a motive. The police arrested her and took her to jail. At the same time, they organized a manhunt for Smith—who for some inexplicable reason had made himself scarce. He was nowhere to be found at the house when the police arrived, but was soon located and arrested.

Despite having an unlovely appearance, Catherine McQuinn managed to leave behind her a trail of broken hearts and cooling corpses. She is described in early press reports as being "a widow," but her husband was very much alive. He was an inmate at the Eastern Kentucky Asylum for the Insane in Lexington, having been driven mad by an illicit affair between his wife and a clerk at the Day Brothers' store in Jackson. The clerk was so guilt-ridden that he committed suicide. Mrs. McQuinn, the fair charmer, had barely escaped a jail term several years before for braining a woman with a garden hoe. Despite this evidence of violence in her past, the police believed her to be not the murderer of Dr. Rader, but merely a conspirator. The bullets lodged in Rader's body were large, indicating a high-caliber weapon unlikely to be used by a woman. In addition, McQuinn's boyfriend had the worst imaginable reputation in the community for being an arsonist, horse thief, murderer, and overall nuisance. He was well known by his nickname, "Bad Tom," and had long been a key player in the French-Eversole family feud. The police suspected at first that Smith had murdered Rader after finding him in a compromising position with McQuinn. But there were no signs of a struggle. Rader obviously had been murdered in his sleep, hinting that the true scenario was a cowardly assassination rather than outraged jealousy.

The reader may be idly wondering, as did the court, how it came to pass that John Rader, Catherine McQuinn, and Tom Smith were sharing the same bedroom and partaking of a gallon jug of whisky on the night of the murder. Early in January, Smith told Dr. Rader that he suffered from epilepsy; he claimed that whenever he went to sleep, he would have violent spasms. Smith persuaded Rader to spend the night of February 5 at his girlfriend's house so he could witness the nighttime seizures—but then, to hear McQuinn tell it, the doctor took advantage of Bad Tom's drunkenness and tried to rape her. Few believed either Smith or McQuinn. Contemporary accounts suggest that Smith lied about having epileptic seizures as a pretext to get Dr. Rader in McQuinn's house, where he could be slain and robbed at leisure. It strains credulity to believe that Bad Tom could have carried out his lengthy career of outlawry while suffering from such a severe untreated disorder.

The examining trial for Smith and McQuinn was held before County Judge N. B. Day on February 9. Mrs. McQuinn embroidered her story under oath, claiming that Dr. Rader had attempted to rape her while her boyfriend lay on the bed in an alcoholic haze. She said that she had shot Rader in self-defense as he sprawled on the floor. However, her story did not square with forensic evidence: when the police arrived, they found Rader's body in bed, not on the floor, and even McQuinn did not dare suggest that she shot the man and then helped him into bed. In addition, the floor was bloodless while the bed was soaked in the late doctor's gore. Rader's bed clothing was brought into the courtroom. They bore bloodstains and powder burns, proving he had been fully dressed when shot. The icing on the cake, as it were, came when Rader's corpse was borne into the courtroom for the judge and doctors to examine. In one bullet wound they found a fiber from the blanket, proving conclusively that Rader had been in bed when he was shot. Judge Day officially declared that McQuinn's story reeked of fish; she and Bad Tom were ordered to stand trial. They were sent back to jail with bail fixed at the then-princely sum of $3,000 each.

Before his arrest for murdering Rader, Smith had been in trouble with the law many times. He sided with Fulton French's family in their war against Joe Eversole's clan and by 1895 he had been indicted for seven separate shootings. Many, if not all, of them were feud-related as the victims tended to be friends or relatives of the Eversoles. The dismal roll call began with Joe Hurt, whom he shot in 1887. In April 1888, Smith and some accomplices killed Nicholas Combs and Joe Eversole; he was later heard to laugh that when he shot Combs in the head, the youth's eyeballs detached and came rolling out. Smith was tried for those two murders, but after he made a few prudent threats, no one dared appear as a witness against him and he was set free. Later the same year, he hid in the brush and shot Shade Combs as he played in his yard with his children. In 1889, an especially busy year, Smith killed Ambrose Amburgey and Robin Cornett in cold blood; that autumn, he shot Jacob McKnight and Ed Campbell in a general fight between the French and Eversole factions on the streets of Hazard. To be fair about it, there is some confusion as to whether he or someone else killed Campbell, but as Smith boasted about it, let's give him the benefit of the doubt.

Six of Smith's pre-Rader homicides occurred in Perry County. The exception was the murder of Amburgey, which took place in Knott County. Except for the murders of McKnight and Campbell, who at least had a fighting chance since they were slain during a gun battle, all of the killings were cowardly ambushes. When there was talk of indicting Smith for his many crimes, he attempted to solve his legal problems by setting fire to the Perry County courthouse, thus destroying incriminating records. The grand jury indicted him for burning down the courthouse, but then let the matter drop. After the arson, the sense of terror that gripped the county was vividly described by a reporter in April 1895:

> Men who had expressed themselves as being opposed to
> his methods left the county, their wives and children remaining
> and trying to take care of what little property they had. That
> year, no crops were raised by those who feared the vengeance
> of Smith and his friends. The County Judge had to go disguised

as a woman when at home and was shot at several times in his own field, finally being permanently driven from the county, fleeing to save his life.

Others who found it wiser to run away than face Bad Tom's wrath included Ira Davidson, a Perry County Circuit Clerk who happened to be Joe Eversole's brother-in-law, and superintendent of schools Abner Eversole.

The seven murders Bad Tom Smith committed before he killed Dr. Rader well illustrate the perils society faces when serious crimes are left unpunished. Smith was indicted for slaying Robin Cornett, but the case was put on hold indefinitely as though the officials were afraid to try him. He finally forfeited his bond and walked the streets ready and willing to perform more mischief. Five of the other homicide cases went to trial but ended in acquittal because jurors feared for their lives. Jacob McKnight's murder was the only one for which Smith was tried and found guilty, but only after the governor sent the state militia to Hazard to ensure that the judge was not killed and then later changed the venue to Pineville. Yet, after all of this trouble to see that justice was done, the Court of Appeals reversed the guilty verdict. The newly freed Bad Tom skipped off to Breathitt County and Dr. Rader was measured for a winding sheet soon afterward.

Local officials, long smarting from the bad publicity given to eastern Kentucky by its never-ending pageant of feuds, fights, and murders, saw the eighth arrest of Bad Tom as a means of restoring some luster to the region's reputation. He was tried only six weeks after his final murder. At his trial, Bad Tom gallantly shifted all the blame on Catherine McQuinn, claiming in the face of all the evidence that she had killed Rader in self-defense. Nevertheless, after three minutes' deliberation on March 13, the jury found him guilty and sentenced him to death. Virtually every historical account of Dr. Rader's murder takes pains to mention that Smith was the first and only man ever to be legally hanged in Breathitt County, so I will not break the tradition.

Mrs. McQuinn's trial began the next day. She pled not guilty and took the opportunity to retaliate against her former beau. Formerly, she had refused to testify against him; now, she claimed she had only been acting on the advice of her attorneys. She said that her lover had shot Rader out of jealousy since the doctor "was importuning her to submit to his will," which certainly is a very dainty way to put it. She claimed that Smith threatened to kill her if she did not take the blame for shooting Rader and that Bad Tom was a member of a secret society "sworn to avenge injuries to each other." She even named some locally prominent men as fellow society members, including B. F. French, Jesse Fields, and Joseph Adkins. Mrs. McQuinn claimed that her boyfriend warned her that if he were hanged or sent to prison, his buddies would show up looking for revenge.

When the recently convicted Bad Tom took the stand, he reiterated that he had gone to bed drunk but had awakened in time to see Mrs. McQuinn shoot Dr. Rader in self-defense. Those not easily impressed by the story believed that he and Mrs. McQuinn had plotted the murder together, that she had invented the story about the secret society in order to conceal her own role in the shooting, and that the chief motive was robbery rather than defending her alleged honor since the doctor had been shot while lying down, fully dressed in bedclothes, and under the blanket. In the end, the jury consisted of cynics rather than believers and on March 17, Mrs. McQuinn was found guilty of first-degree murder and sentenced to life in prison. She got off relatively easily for no discernible reason other than that she was a woman. Academics and activists who make a career out of squawking about the awful treatment women received back in those evil times never consider that many a richly deserving female prisoner escaped the death penalty, or received no punishment whatsoever, simply because of her gender. Just ask the shade of Lizzie Borden.

On March 19, Judge Redwine declared that Tom Smith would become Breathitt County's first legally hanged man on the last day of May. Smith received the news with such indifference that the judge felt moved to remark that the condemned man would have been much better off had he found a better outlet for his nerve. Mrs. McQuinn went to her life sentence with a stoicism that was no less remarkable than Smith's.

Possibly the only person in Perry County who was unhappy with Bad Tom's death sentence was his brother Bill. When he heard that most of the evidence convicting his brother had been unearthed by Detective George Drake, Bill passed along a threat to the effect that Drake had only a week to live. Rather than skipping town, Detective Drake went out looking for Smith and found him in the Day Brothers' store. Striding up to the would-be avenger, Drake said: "I understand you give me but a week to live. I will make the best use of that time by killing all the bushwhackers I can, and as you are the worst one I know of out of jail, I will begin on you." Then he drew his pistol and aimed it at Smith's head. Bill Smith quickly realized that he was not quite the big, bad villain he fancied himself to be. He fell to his knees and pleaded for his life until Detective Drake left in disgust.

Bad Tom's attorneys appealed his sentence in vain. He had gotten lucky once before, when the Court of Appeals unaccountably reversed the guilty verdict for the murder of Jacob McKnight, leaving him free to resume his infamous career. He would not be so fortunate a second time. On June 20, the Court of Appeals overruled his attorneys' motion for a retrial and on June 21, Governor Brown set the date of execution for June 28—exactly a week away.

While his appeal was being processed, Bad Tom gave a number of interviews to newspaper reporters. He usually comes across as optimistic and looking forward to good times in Heaven, but the most striking feature in his interviews is his refusal to take responsibility for his own actions. Despite the fact that six of his eight murders were committed via ambush, he repeatedly made the claim that he had killed only two men, both in self-defense. He pointed out that he had been acquitted several times, neglecting to mention that he got off so easily because everyone in the community was afraid to stand up to him. From Smith's perspective, everybody had been picking on him: "When I first came here [to jail], I felt mighty hard against the men who prosecuted me, but that's all gone….I have no hard feelings against any man. No, not even the ones that put me here."

The primary person who "put him there," of course, was himself.

Some thought that Smith's eagerness to paint himself as a dirt-poor, persecuted farmer stemmed from the knowledge that a pardon would be forever out of the question if he confessed. When his appeal was turned down and he realized that he would not outwit the law this final time, Smith weakened. The only question was whether he would "die with a lie on his lips" or confess before the hangman got his work in.

As many a man has done in the same peculiar, unenviable situation, Bad Tom took up religion with a vengeance. He claimed to have seen the light and requested that he receive baptism before it was too late. It was expected that Breathitt's county seat would be visited by the largest throng in its history because people from other counties were already vowing to witness the hanging of such a notorious desperado. The owners of Jackson's mills, stores, and factories planned to close their establishments on June 28, considering it a sort of dark holiday. Saloon owners agreed to sell no whisky that day in order to help keep the crowd peaceable. The city fathers swore in an extra police force and citizens formed a militia to thwart troublemakers. To accommodate the thousands of anticipated sightseers, the Lexington and Eastern Railroad provided a special chartered train called "The Bad Tom Smith Flyer," bearing nine coaches—round trip fare only $1.50! The company placed an exquisitely tasteless circus-style advertisement in the *Lexington Evening Leader*: "EXCURSION TO JACKSON. A Chance For All to See Bad Tom Smith Leave This Earth." After promising patrons that the train would arrive in Jackson at 11 a.m., the ad continued: "As the hanging of 'Bad Tom' Smith does not occur until 12 o'clock, persons going upon the special will have ample time to secure good seats at the big event."

As the excitement over the impending hanging demonstrates, honest mountaineers were tired of being intimidated by the likes of Bad Tom Smith and they were tired of their region being considered a joke in the national press. The hanging was intended to send a message to feudists and outlaws. In addition, there was a financial motive to see justice done: eastern Kentucky had lagged far behind the rest of the state in terms of economic development because its reputation for lawlessness was so bad that investors were afraid to start businesses there. As a correspondent for the *Louisville Courier-Journal* explained:

> *It is the opinion of the best people here [in Jackson] that the hanging of Smith will be worth many thousands of dollars to this town and county. It will show to the world that there are enough law abiding citizens in this county who have the courage to enforce the law against men who hold human life so cheaply, and they believe that capitalists will not be afraid to invest their money in the valuable coal and timber lands of this section....A brighter day seems to be dawning for these people, and within a decade the mountain feud will be a thing of the past, as it will die a natural death under the influence of civilization and the rapid progress of Christianity and education in eastern Kentucky.*

On June 25, three days before the scheduled execution, the newly formed militia formed a picket line around Jackson and guarded every entrance into the city in case Bad Tom's friends decided to attempt a rescue mission. By June 27, Jackson was overflowing with spectators who had come from as many as a dozen counties. The prisoner could hear the sound of the scaffold being constructed only a hundred feet from his cell, yet he was noticeably calmer than the jailhouse officials. He spent the day singing hymns and praying and he promised that he would make a full confession on the gallows. This news was pleasing to Catherine McQuinn, by then beginning her life term in the Frankfort penitentiary. She believed that Bad Tom surely would confess that she had no role in Dr. Rader's murder. Why, that pardon from the governor was as good as hers! She was wrong. I have found no evidence that she served out her entire life sentence, but certainly she spent plenty of time in jail regretting her taste in boyfriends.

Early on the morning of June 28, Sheriff Buck Combs fulfilled the prisoner's last wish by allowing him to be baptized in the Kentucky River about 400 yards from the jail—under heavy guard, of course, after which he was taken back to his cell to await his hanging. The size of the crowd awaiting the sight did not fail to live up to expectations. Some people walked for many a mile across inhospitable mountain terrain to see the execution; some rode horses or mules; others took buggies or wagons. People arrived singly, in duos, in trios; entire families came. Some people even brought their dogs. A sizable percentage of the crowd consisted of women and children. No doubt the kids were present in order to learn a harsh lesson in the dangers of being bad. It was estimated that about 5,000 people were on hand to see Bad Tom expiate his sins—a sizable crowd that would have gratified the Prince of Wales, though a two-headed calf might have done even better.

The prison officials could not have chosen a more picturesque spot for the hanging. The gallows was encircled by high hills, so when Smith mounted the steps at 1:00, fashionably late by one hour, he was surrounded on all sides by spectators who must have felt as though they were watching a show in an amphitheatre. The sheriff had promised him all the time he wanted to address the crowd and Bad Tom took advantage of his generosity by inflicting upon his audience a forty-five minute confession. He admitted that he had committed six of the eight murders attributed to his industrious hands, and some who heard him recount his crimes thought he did so with callousness and lack of regret. He did not number Ed Campbell and Ambrose Amburgey among his victims.

Smith told the vast multitudes that he did indeed shoot Dr. Rader, the crime for which he was actually being hanged, but added that Catherine McQuinn had put him up to it and assured him that she would take the blame. The inference was that she hoped she could avoid paying for the crime if she claimed Rader had made unwanted sexual advances. Smith also said that McQuinn had taken money from the dead doctor's pocket. Contrary to McQuinn's hopes and expectations, Smith's gallows confession only reaffirmed her role in Rader's murder. While he was at it, Smith also confessed to his prominent role in the French-Eversole feud and implicated his friends Jesse Fields and Joseph Adkins in the infamous murder of Judge Josiah Combs. (At the time, Fields and Adkins were being held in the jail at Barbourville, Knox County, on the charge. They expressed their belief to a reporter that Smith had not actually named them in his confession—the acme of wishful thinking, since his declaration of guilt was heard by 5,000 witnesses!)

Years later it would be recalled that in addition to making that interminable spoken confession, Smith sang a toe-tapper of a ballad which he had composed himself about his life of crime. The rather depressing lyrics went:

> *I don't want you to grieve after me,*
> *I don't want you to grieve after me;*
> *Oh, when I am dead and buried*
> *In the cold and silent tomb,*
> *I don't want you to grieve after me.*

"Bad whisky and bad women have brought me where I am," Bad Tom told the crowd, at last taking some responsibility for the choices he had made in life. "Take warning from my fate and live better lives than I have lived. I die with no hard feelings toward anybody. There ain't a soul in the world that I hate. I love everybody." So saying, he knelt on the trapdoor and prayed for ten minutes "in a hysterical way," according to one eyewitness. After this, he was allowed, for reasons unexplained, to walk around in circles on the scaffold like a caged tiger for several minutes more. Perhaps it was to help him get his nerve up. After one more brief prayer, the sheriff manacled Bad Tom's legs and arms, placed the black hood over his head, and adjusted the rope. Just as the sheriff cut the rope that pulled the lever, witnesses heard Smith cry out, "Save me, O God, save me!"

The drop instantaneously broke his neck. The *Courier-Journal* ran an editorial protesting that such executions should be held in the seclusion of the prison yard, not in public. Undoubtedly, the editors were correct, but the crowd was full of men of Bad Tom's ilk who needed a graphic warning.

At nightfall, the authorities turned the remains over to Smith's kin. They placed the corpse in a mule-drawn wagon and made a long, slow, fifty-mile trek over the mountains in the heat of summer—a scene reminiscent of Faulkner's *As I Lay Dying*—to the family cemetery at Carr's Fork, Knott County. The rest of the community felt ill-disguised joy that Bad Tom was gone, never again to trouble anyone. The owners of the mills and stores and factories reopened on the morning after his hanging with a newfound sense of optimism and hopes for prosperity. "The Lexington and Eastern railroad is proving to be the means of advancing the civilization in the mountains," wrote a journalist. "And now that the French-Eversole feud has been wiped out there is no longer any barrier to improvement, and the next few years will show great advancements in this section of the state." In other words, while in modern times capital punishment often is disparaged as being "barbaric" and "uncivilized," the hanging of Bad Tom Smith was considered a sure sign that civilization had come to eastern Kentucky. The people who lived in the region acknowledged that a change had occurred in their attitude toward crime and the necessity of punishing evildoers. A few days before Smith was hanged, an editorial in the *Jackson Hustler* stated:

> Word comes to us from every direction of the revolution in sentiment of the people of this section of the mountains in regard to punishing criminals. A man told us this week that he had been to eight counties since the Fields-Atkins trial at Barbourville, and that the intense feeling against lawlessness was universal.... In the counties where lawlessness has been worst this feeling is greatest. The revolt from the state of terror and death will sweep a number of men into the state prison and some into their graves. Woe to the desperadoes of these counties now. Their race is run. The grand juries are doing their work and the petit juries their duty.

Feudists Fields and Atkins got off luckier than their friend Smith did; they merely received a sentence of life imprisonment and even then the punishment didn't stick. (Fields was tried again and acquitted in July 1899; Adkins was paroled in December of the same year. It would have been better to keep Fields, at least, in jail. He was shot to death on April 26, 1900 and at the time of his death three murder charges were pending against him. Rumor held that he made many interesting confessions on his deathbed.)

Six weeks after Bad Tom pioneered a new use for hemp in Breathitt County, a special correspondent for the *Courier-Journal* reported that matters had improved dramatically in Smith's home county. The headlines told the story: "It Is Safe to Go to Work Now in Perry County Fields. The County Has Reformed. Law-Defying Gangs Have Fallen to Pieces." The writer stated that he had seen much bloodshed in the county over the past decade and compared living in Perry County to constantly being on a battlefield, but "since the execution of 'Bad Tom' Smith and the conviction of Fields and Atkins, it is like another country. Everybody feels secure."

It would be absurd to claim that all violence in the mountain counties ceased after Smith's hanging—most certainly, it did not. However, the execution had the salutary effect of showing criminals that the law finally meant business and the hanging put a permanent end to Bad Tom's one-man campaign to devastate families and terrorize communities. I wonder what anti-capital punishment busybodies, such as Sister Helen Prejean, would think about the possibility that hanging Tom Smith might have saved dozens of lives—not only those of his future victims, but also the potential victims of those outlaws who were sent to jail in the wake of reform or who were scared into changing their ways when the law made an example out of their idol.

Perhaps the most striking symbol of the changes that were blowing in the mountain wind came just after Smith's funeral. As related in John Ed Pearce's 1994 book on Kentucky feuds, *Days of Darkness*, Bad Tom's widow agreed to allow another widow, Susan Eversole of Perry County, to adopt the executed man's children. This was an especially remarkable act of generosity when we remember that Bad Tom had spent his adult life exterminating the Eversoles, the enemies of his friends, the French family. One of his victims had been Susan Eversole's husband, Joe, and another had been her father.

What Came of
Stealing Some Quilts

One might not expect to see many Jews in southeastern Kentucky in the late nineteenth century, yet there were at least two: Gustav and Julia Loeb, married itinerant peddlers who made their home near Pineville, Bell County. Since 1890, the Loebs had made the rounds in Harlan County and had become well known to the citizens. They spent the night of June 21, 1895 at the home of one Charles Hensley, manufacturer of illegal homemade whisky. June 22 would be their last day on earth.

On that morning, W. R. Riddle was hauling a load of mail about ten miles from Harlan Courthouse, a town whose name would later be shortened to just plain Harlan. As he descended Black Mountain, he heard gunfire issuing from nearby Martin's Fork; witnesses later claimed that they heard between twenty-five and thirty shots. Riddle had not gone far when he met a small boy running in a state of terror. The boy paused only long enough to tell him that a man and a woman had been shot. Riddle hurried back to Harlan Courthouse to inform the sheriff and the coroner.

In the meanwhile, the family of the marvelously named Longstreet Cloud also had heard the shots only a few hundred yards from their house. The curious family saw an oncoming driverless horse pulling a spring wagon. As the wagon passed, they could see bullet-riddled boxes and the obviously dead Mr. Loeb lying on the floor with his head and shoulders dangling over the edge of the wagon's rear gate. The Clouds knew that Mr. Loeb had been traveling with his wife, so they went to investigate the area from which they had heard shots. There they found Mrs. Loeb lying dead in the road.

When the sheriff and coroner arrived, they examined the bodies, having managed somehow to stop the runaway wagon with its dead occupant. Sixty-year-old Mr. Loeb had been shot three times, including once in the chest and once in the back of the head. Mrs. Loeb had been shot in the chest and the foot and had received a facial wound that nearly removed her jaw.

The three men who had committed the cowardly murders were quickly identified; it was their misfortune to have been seen by about a half-dozen witnesses chasing the Loebs' wagon. The assassins had crossed Stone Mountain and gone to Rose Hill, VA. At C. E. Baylor's store they made themselves conspicuous by brandishing Winchester rifles and purchasing lots of ammo as though preparing for a siege. Some witnesses overheard the men foolhardily discussing a couple of murders they had committed back in Harlan County. Two of the men were brothers from Hancock County, TN, William and Buford Overton, and the third was a native Harlan Countian named John Scott, an illiterate and easily led young moonshiner. When the trio left Baylor's store, they pretended to be heading for Tennessee. Instead, they doubled back and stupidly returned to Harlan County and almost literally to the scene of their crime, where they were cornered in a house. The sheriff enlisted the help of armed citizens. In the ensuing gunfight, John Scott escaped, Buford Overton was captured, and his older brother William fatally wounded. Scott was captured the next day by his cousin, a deputy sheriff who also happened to be named John Scott. The younger Scott was nervous and when in jail made many incriminating statements that would come back to haunt him and his companion Overton.

The Loebs must have been well-liked by the community because as soon as the desperadoes were captured, there was talk of lynching them. The intense hatred for the prisoners soon gave way to a calm willingness to allow the law to take its course. Instead of performing an illegal hanging, citizens undertook the nobler task of burying the Loebs near the spot on Martin's Fork where they were murdered.

The young murderers' motive was a topic of debate. What

conceivable reason could they possibly have had to kill the harmless old peddlers in cold blood—particularly Mrs. Loeb, who was blind in one eye and deaf? Robbery was advanced as a possible motive, but it seemed less likely when the coroner found about fifteen dollars each on the bodies of the Loebs.

It turned out that the murders were inspired by neither robbery nor anti-Semitism, but were a sort of contract killing. Mr. Loeb noticed on the fatal morning that some of his counterpanes (quilts) were missing and had reported it to the law. Overton later claimed under oath that the thief had been the daughter of Charles Hensley at whose home, the reader will recall, the Loebs had stayed the night before their murder. The peddlers had been on the verge of having Sally Hensley arrested. According to Overton, Hensley was worried that if the police came looking for Loebs' coverlets, they would also find his moonshine still. Therefore, he cooked up the brilliant, criminally sophisticated scheme of hiring the Overtons and Scott to ambush the Loebs in order to avoid prosecution. Hensley was immediately arrested and thrown in jail without bond.

The citizens of Harlan had grown weary of their county's reputation for violence and were determined to see Overton and Scott pay the ultimate penalty for their crimes. A contemporary writer stated: "Harlan County had just emerged from the smoke and fog of a great feud, and peace, quiet and contentment prevailed throughout the county until these Tennessee criminals invaded the county.... There is a determination among the good citizens of Harlan County to wipe this stain out by a strict enforcement of the law and a first-class hanging."

Buford Overton was tried for murder in August. The Commonwealth so thoroughly proved its case against him that all he could do was to confess and hope for leniency. Under oath, he swore that the shots had been fired by John Scott and his conveniently dead brother William:

[R]ealizing the great crime about to be perpetrated, [I] begged my brother...not to harm the peddlers; that we could return and tell Charles Hensley the Loebs had traveled too

fast, and we could not overtake them and they made their escape; that if we killed them we would be hung for it; that we had come publicly down the road in pursuit of the wagon, passing several dwelling-houses, and seen by divers persons, and for God's sake let us leave without doing them any harm. My brother, being greatly under the influence of whisky, pushed me aside and said "D— you, if you do not want to do it, stand out of my way."

Overton concluded his testimony with a rather too obvious attempt to tug at the collective heartstrings of the jurors: "I have neither father nor mother; they both died before I was one year old; I have neither brother nor sister; I am a friendless stranger in a strange land, never through life having had a home. I am wholly devoid of an English education. I can neither read nor write, and throughout my life I have been buffeted about and kicked from pillar to post, a friendless orphan boy. I have now told you the whole truth, and my case is in your hands to deal with as you may deem proper." Oddly, despite his claim that he had done everything he could to prevent the murders, he pled guilty.

Overton was found guilty and sentenced to be hanged on October 18. Though only nineteen years old, he was tough—he was covered with scars and bullet wounds and claimed that he and his brother had killed six men in Tennessee—yet, he nearly fainted when the sentence was read and had to be carried back to his cell. John Scott was tried in September and received a sentence of life in prison, a judgment that did not sit well with many who felt that Scott was equally as guilty as the Tennessean and deserved the death penalty.

Buford Overton's courtroom oration won him some friends and supporters; a reporter who had been present noted that when the doomed teenager finished speaking, "a wave of sympathy swept over the faces in the courtroom and tears trickled down the bronzed faces and grizzled beards of many sturdy old mountaineers, who but a short time before would have been willing to have aided in his execution without a trial." However, the twelve men who actually sat on the jury had been unmoved by sentimentality. Some Harlan Countians felt that mercy should be shown to Overton, whom they considered the pawn of more cunning criminals. There was talk of sending a petition to the governor in order to have the prisoner's sentence commuted to life in prison because of his youth, his illiteracy, his admission of the crime, and the fact that he could not testify against Charles Hensley if he were dead.

The philanthropists probably changed their minds about Overton's character when the allegedly innocent convict escaped from the county jail on the night of September 13 while his two guards were at dinner. A politician named W. J. Hendrick was scheduled to give a speech on October 18, the date set for Overton's hanging—I wonder whether he intended to speak before or after the main event—and a local joke held that Overton had left behind a note stating that "he did not mind the hanging so much, but he did not want to hear Hendrick speak." Overton took with him a loaded Winchester rifle that the guards had been foolish enough to leave behind in a hallway. He almost certainly had help: the iron bars of the cell door had been destroyed and the lock had been broken from the outside. Even more suspiciously, somehow Overton had managed to break the hinges of the jail's inner door, a feat that would have been nearly impossible for one man. Rumor held that Overton's friends in Tennessee and Virginia had secretly offered a $1,500 reward to anyone who could spring him out of jail.

Governor John Young Brown offered a $200 reward for Overton's capture, and jailer F. S. Hensley tendered an additional $100. The young criminal was traced as far as the Little Black Mountain, across the Clover Fork River, and down a hollow near the Martin's Fork Road. It was evident that he had been heading for Virginia, but at this point his trail stopped and he seemingly had vanished.

Almost exactly a year passed, during which people wondered if the Loebs ever would receive their full measure of justice. Then came the news, on September 1, 1896, that Overton had been re-captured in Chilhowie, VA. During the interim, he had learned to read the Bible and joined the Masons. He was even on the verge of getting married.

The law, clearly disgusted with him despite these self-improvements, speedily sentenced Overton to be hanged on October 12. His friends—and a misguidedly loyal lot they must have been—started another petition beseeching the new governor, William O. Bradley, to have his sentence commuted to life in prison. They promised the governor that if given thirty more days, they would provide new evidence proving Overton's innocence.

Overton expressed gravely misplaced confidence that he would not be hanged. As scheduled, on October 12 he stood on the gallows at Harlan Courthouse, looking across a sea of over 2,000 upturned faces. Not all the spectators were hostile; rumor held that some of Overton's friends would try to save him at the last moment. Sheriff Grant Smith doubled the number of guards just in case, but any would-be rescuers wisely decided not to interfere with the law. Overton admitted to the crowd that he had lied about his innocence: he had shot Mrs. Loeb himself and blamed his downfall on whisky. The rope broke his neck instantly.

The "new evidence" promised by Buford Overton's friends was never forthcoming. Conspirator John Scott eventually was paroled and married in 1909. He was shot to death on Wallins Creek on September 13, 1922 at age forty-four. The only man who got off lucky in the whole affair was the alleged instigator, Charles Hensley. Perhaps there was no solid proof against him, but it appears that he never was punished for his part in the murders. Did his daughter Sally ever consider the toll in human life that resulted from her simple act of stealing quilts?

The Fictitious and Real Ordeals of Robert Laughlin

At 4 a.m. on February 15, 1896, Mrs. H. M. McCracken of Bracken County was awakened by cries and poundings from outside. Opening her door, she saw her brother Robert Laughlin bleeding from a slight neck wound. He said that he had been attacked by two strangers in his home, which was located three miles from Augusta on Rock Springs Road. One had borne a torch while the other drew a knife across the sleeping Laughlin's throat. His sweet repose thus interrupted, farmer Laughlin grabbed his attacker by the coat collar. The man, who had a waist-length black beard, punched Laughlin; Laughlin managed to punch him back and the two wrestled on the floor. The second man presumably stood there illuminating the scene with his torch and egging on his companion. Laughlin noticed that the door was open and, after breaking free, he ran into the night. One of the villains chased him with a club for about fifty yards, then gave up. Weeping and shaken, Laughlin told the McCrackens that his wife Emma and her thirteen-year-old niece, May Jones, slept in a bed in the same room and for all he knew some harm had come to them as well.

After hearing this horrifying tale of home invasion and attempted murder, the McCrackens dressed and ran to the rescue, only to see the Laughlin home in flames. In the morning, investigators found a crime scene that seemed to emanate evil: the charred remains of the two victims were inside what was left of the house. The girl's body was found in the cellar beside a long-bladed knife. The horror of the events was compounded by the fact that the position of May Jones's corpse revealed that she had been trying to leave the house when a piece of roof fell on her and she burned to death.

Robert Laughlin initially was the object of much compassion, except among hardliners who thought him a coward to have abandoned his wife and niece in their moment of need. The period of community sympathy lasted only a few hours because people started noticing that Laughlin's story changed every time he told it. No one could discern the invaders' motive: nothing had been stolen because Laughlin owned nothing worth stealing. Laughlin admitted that he had no enemies and could think of no one who would wish such harm on himself, his wife, and niece. The first major blow to his credibility came when Marshal William Sayers and railroad detective Edward Fitzgerald, deeply suspicious of Laughlin, asked him to remove his clothes and found that his underwear was soaked in blood, far more than should have come from the trivial cut on his neck. Laughlin claimed to have run barefoot for a half mile on rough and rocky terrain to escape the club-wielding maniac pursuing him, but his feet were not bruised or otherwise injured. They asked Sheriff Henry Frank to arrest him, but he refused to do so. This was the first occasion on which a sheriff displayed a marked and peculiar partiality for the murderer Laughlin.

Searchers found the imprint of a man's boot, size nine, in Laughlin's yard, though of course there was no way to tell how long the print had been there. Some people suspected a couple of men who had been sighted in Augusta—one of whom somewhat resembled one of the attackers described by Laughlin. Two other men named Pease and Sellers were arrested aboard a shanty boat at Silver Grove and taken to the jail at Wellsburg.

The events of February 16 came quickly and with terrific force. When the police borrowed bloodhounds from William Britton of Williamsburg, OH, the dogs tracked the scent of only one man who had left the Laughlin house. That man was named neither Pease nor Sellers. The dogs ran straight from the burned house to the McCrackens' home and, once there, the hounds refused to go farther, saying in their doggish way that there were no other trails to follow.

The bloodhounds insisted on entering the house and sniffing the chair in which Laughlin had sat the night before while telling his relatives all about his fabricated tribulations.

Soon enough, there were few souls left who entertained the possibility of Laughlin's innocence with the principal exception of Sheriff Frank, who still refused to arrest his number one suspect until the coroner's jury reached a conclusion. Nevertheless, Marshal Sayers placed the thirty-seven-year-old Laughlin under guard, which amounted to his being arrested. Laughlin did not complain, as it was for his own good: rumor held that he had confessed, but had also put on a crazy act and many citizens were in a mood to get together and dispense their own summary brand of justice.

In the meanwhile, Emma Ann Laughlin and little May Jones were buried in a cemetery on a hill near the still-smoldering Laughlin house. The two were buried in the same coffin before a large and fuming crowd. The Methodist minister, Rev. Gideon Jolly, attempted to comfort the mourners at a church service with a text chosen from Daniel 12:13: "Go thou thy way till the end, for thou shalt rest and stand in the light till the end"—a Scriptural promise of God's ability to bring peace of mind despite suffering. Robert Laughlin was present at the funeral and it is to be hoped that he paid close attention to the minister's words because he was just starting a long ordeal of his own. Before the day was over, he would be charged with two counts of murder and taken to the jail at Maysville, Mason County. He was not there long. Rumors of an impending lynch mob so disturbed the authorities that on February 17 they sneaked their prisoner out of the jail and hid him in a secret location. Before he was taken away, a *Courier-Journal* correspondent was allowed to see him. The reporter noted that Laughlin "was nervous and acted or feigned to act like one demented."

The prisoner made a melodramatic confession to the journalist. Laughlin claimed that he and his wife of four years got along very well. When her niece May Jones came to spend the night, they slept in the same bed and Laughlin slept on a nearby lounge. He got up at

3 a.m. to stoke the fire and as he watched his wife sleeping, Laughlin claimed, a demon took possession of him. The next thing he knew he had beaten her to death with a poker. May woke up and tried to run away, but Laughlin caught her and threw her on the lounge. He then attempted to rape his barely pubescent niece, but they struggled and fell off the lounge. In a fury, Laughlin hit her twice with the poker—fatally, he thought, but he was mistaken. His pants somehow caught fire as he attempted to put them on. When he tore off his smoking trousers, he overturned a lamp and the entire house was ablaze. Thinking fast, he made up the story about the intruders (one with a ZZ Top beard), gave himself two very minor cuts on the throat with a dull knife and fled the burning house. Sobbing in his jail cell, Laughlin said that he could not explain his actions and knew that he was as good as hanged—legally or otherwise.

It should be noted that not everyone believed Laughlin's version of events and argued that it was more likely that his wife was awakened when she heard him trying to molest his niece and that he killed them both to prevent the story from getting out. Laughlin's subterranean public image sank even lower when it came out that his wife had been a few months pregnant—which, in itself, might have been his motive for killing her.

After a day in hiding, Laughlin was returned to Maysville and then the police sneaked him out a second time on February 18 disguised as a veiled woman—one of many strange little incidents in the case—and returned him later that day. Jailer Johnson had to deal with the possibility that a mob might break down his doors and abstract the prisoner. To prevent this, extra guards were stationed and the turnpikes leading into town were kept under surveillance. Johnson also had a water plug installed in the jail so that if any mobs came calling, he could spray them down with frigid water rushing through the hose. "This will be the cheapest and safest plan ever devised," enthused a contemporary news report. Such a strategy proved unnecessary, but this is the earliest example I can find of a high-pressure water hose being considered as a tool for crowd control. As the days went by, it became clear that people had lost their interest in mobbing, symbolized by the fact that Johnson returned a number of extra guns that had been stockpiled in the jail. The only trouble Johnson encountered came from one Sherman Nash, who demanded admittance to the jail so he could see Bracken County's most hated man. When the police arrested Nash, he joked, "You have arrested all the mob."

On March 11, the Bracken County grand jury returned four indictments against Robert Laughlin: two for murder, one for rape, and one for arson. In those days, rape was a capital offense, so Laughlin stood three excellent chances to swing at the end of a noose. Somehow, the penniless Laughlin managed to get a judge (George Doniphan) and an ex-Congressman (John B. Clarke) to be his attorneys; perhaps they agreed to work *pro bono* ("for the public good"), though in this case the "good deed" meant representing a confessed murderer and child-rapist who allowed one of his victims to burn to death. Everyone is entitled to a vigorous defense, but it is impossible not to wonder about the motives of these prominent men.

It is the usual practice of the defense lawyer to have his/her client's trial delayed as long as possible in hopes that public feeling will cool down and said client might escape with a lighter punishment or even an acquittal. Doniphan and Clarke won Laughlin a continuance until the court met at its next term in July. That was the last heard from the relieved Laughlin for a while, except when he indignantly denied being the murderer of an "idiot boy" named Charles Sands who had drowned, apparently by accident, a couple of years before.

Despite attorney Doniphan's attempts to have the trial postponed again until October, on July 9 Laughlin was brought back to Brooksville—a prospect that made him very nervous indeed. He feared being lynched and he expressed the opinion that he could not get a fair trial in Brooksville. Given the enormity of his crimes and the amount of proof against him, including a freely offered confession, and the fact that not a particle of evidence pointed to any other culprit, we can only assume that Laughlin was really complaining that a Brooksville jury could not be snookered into giving him an acquittal. As he well knew, Laughlin's problem was not that he would not receive justice, but that he would.

The trial began on July 10. It was one of the most exciting events in the history of Bracken County up to that point because there had not been a legal hanging in the county in forty years. On its first day, the trial was held in a local church because such a large crowd attended the proceedings. Should a similar circumstance arise today, the American Civil Liberties Union would likely declare it a violation of the doctrine of the separation of church and state and file a lawsuit, despite the possibility that their meddling might allow a killer to walk the streets as a free man. In this case, the defense fell back on a shopworn but all-too-often effective strategy. It was obvious from the first day that they intended to plead not guilty by reason of insanity.

Back in May, Laughlin had throttled a fellow prisoner, then said afterward that he had no recollection of the act—a safe claim to make because who could prove otherwise?—and hopefully suggested that this was proof that he must be crazy. In order to buttress this impression, Laughlin's attorneys brought in as witnesses four jailbirds who had shared a cell with the accused. They regaled the jury with tales of Laughlin's jailhouse eccentricities. In rebuttal, the Commonwealth put on the stand ten witnesses who had known Laughlin for as far back as twenty-five years, all of whom testified that his sanity never had been doubted.

The prosecution's first important witness was Marshal Sayers, who had suspected Laughlin almost from the beginning and who had insisted that the suspect display his underwear which proved to be soaked in blood. Laughlin had confessed before Sayers, as he did later before others; the defense objected to Sayers's recounting of the confession on the risible grounds that Laughlin had sung only because of "fear and excitement caused by the presence of the officers." Presumably, the defense would have had no objection if Laughlin had been in a calm state of mind when he confessed or if no officers had been present. Judge Harbison agreed to temporarily sustain the objection until he could investigate more fully.

The next day, the judge declared that Laughlin's confession would stand, much to his attorneys' dismay. Sayers, County Attorney Adair, and reporter William Lynch all took the witness stand and recounted confessions Laughlin had made to them which had differed only in minor details. According to one account, "When Mr. Adair reached that portion referring to Laughlin's relations with the little girl and her attempt to escape, a sensation scene resulted. The father of the child, sitting near Commonwealth's Attorney Sallee, overcome with horror at his child's tragic fate, began crying and wringing his hands and making desperate attempts to reach the prisoner, who sat on the opposite side of the room." Judge Harbison restored order to the courtroom with difficulty.

On July 16, the jury deliberated for slightly more than an hour and returned with a guilty verdict. They fixed the penalty at death to the surprise of absolutely no one, least of all Laughlin, who accepted the news with a stoicism that contrasted starkly with the reaction of his aged parents. The eighty-year-old mother threw her arms around her condemned son and wept, an action that won Laughlin a few microseconds of sympathy from court onlookers. The date of doom was set for September 18, but his attorneys appealed. In November, the Court of Appeals affirmed the judgment of the lower court. Laughlin's reaction to this news is of passing interest. He had taken up religion loudly and ostentatiously ever since he got into his scrape, but when told that he must die, he swore a dark and bloody oath and played cards in his cell at Covington, where he had been taken for safekeeping.

Governor William O. Bradley chose January 9 as the day of the execution. Maurice Hook had replaced Sheriff Frank as chief law officer of Bracken County, but—like his predecessor—he seemed reluctant to do his duty. Sheriff Hook flatly stated that he would not hang Laughlin because he was convinced that the prisoner was crazy, despite all the evidence. Sheriff Hook wanted to form a jury to examine Laughlin's sanity. When Governor Bradley got wind of this, he replied, with a frankness lacking in too many elected officials then and now, that the sheriff had a duty to enact the law whether or not he personally found it distasteful: "If he fails to perform this or any other duty he forfeits his office." Though Sheriff Hook had a legal right to convene an insanity commission—at least, according to some lawyers, but not others—he changed his mind and soon a disassembled scaffold was on the way to Brooksville. It was noted that the scaffold had previously been the means by which a dozen killers had paid for their crimes, including William Neal and Ellis Craft, two authors of the notorious Ashland Tragedy of 1881. Another man who met his Maker on the gallows was referred to by the press as "Mud Dauber" Smith. Regretfully, I have been unable to find any information about Smith's criminal career and how he came by his delightful nickname.

It should not be thought that Governor Bradley was vengeful or bloodthirsty. He refused to see any callers on January 7, spending the day reviewing the records on the Laughlin case. Some of the prisoner's friends had earnestly pleaded before the governor their belief that Laughlin was insane; Bradley was determined to assess the facts and make a final decision. After looking over the relevant documents, Governor Bradley took pen in hand and wrote: "I will not interfere with the verdict and the judgment in this case." Doom was sealed for the "crazy man" who somehow claimed to be aware of his own insanity.

The next day, Laughlin was returned to Brooksville. Authorities searched the jail for potential escape routes and means of suicide; fifty special deputies were sworn in to thwart potential mobs. Laughlin was "stolid and careless" and eager to discuss any subject except his double homicide. He was cheered somewhat by sentimental letters he received from two of his friends from the Covington jail: Scott Jackson and Alonzo Walling, the notorious murderers and beheaders of Pearl Bryan. No one was permitted to see him except his parents and a minister named James Cusack. William Laughlin, the prisoner's father, had an emotional breakdown when he stepped down from his buggy and saw the final stages of the gallows' construction. One of the father's melancholy chores on Laughlin's penultimate day was to purchase a cloth-covered casket in which to transport his son's remains to Mt. Zion Cemetery, Chatham.

We read so often about condemned men who sleep soundly the night before their executions that it is almost surprising that Laughlin spent his final night in a restless and nervous condition. He recovered himself by the morning of January 9, however, and after a hearty breakfast, he adopted a purposeful, unaided stride en route to the noose.

Although the execution was held behind a plank fence sixteen feet high, his demise was witnessed by what was described as the largest crowd that had ever assembled in Brooksville. As was usual in such grim circumstances, the surrounding maple trees were filled with roosting people who wanted a good view of the hanging. When someone in a tree shouted that Laughlin was on his way to the gallows, the crowd overpowered the fifty special deputies and, in less time than it takes to tell about it, the plank fence was gone. Everyone who cared to watch had an excellent view of the proceedings, but at least when they saw Laughlin, the rowdy crowd became quiet and reflective.

Sheriff Hook was noticeably more upset than the prisoner, who seemed carefree as he stood on the gallows with a rope around his neck. The sheriff read aloud Laughlin's will, in which he remembered his fellow murderers Scott Jackson and Alonzo Walling. After the shaking sheriff adjusted Laughlin's black cap, he sprang the trap. Laughlin's body shot downward and he died instantly of a broken neck. He had blamed his crimes on a demon and there were those who believed he had gone to keep company with his old acquaintance.

The crowd had gotten its show and the hanging was the talk of Bracken County for years. The family of May Jones did not attend.

In Which
Mr. Dever and Mrs. West Lose Their Social Standing

B ack when Grover Cleveland was president for the second time, a family lived in a small log farmhouse on Burdett's Creek, a small tributary of Cartwright Creek, about four miles from Lebanon, Marion County. The parental units were Thomas J. West and his wife, whose name was Hattie, Patty, or Julia, depending on which account is right. We shall leave it to the genealogists to solve that one.

Mr. West was not by any stretch of the imagination a good catch. Neighbors found him honest and harmless enough when sober, but if he had been imbibing—and he often had—he was transformed into a bully. He was known to abuse his family. In fact, it was proved in court under later unpromising circumstances that his wife had once miscarried after West kicked her in the side. Animals were not immune from his wrath. On one occasion, he shot a recalcitrant mule and on another, he split a horse's head with an ax when the beast refused to cross a ditch.

The real-life soap opera that is the Wests' saga illustrates how radically one's life can change in a month. Before November 1895, they were a well-respected farming couple, though the neighbors kept a judicious distance from Mr. West. Then it became public knowledge that Mrs. West had been paying too much attention to a stranger who had lived in the area for about a year. Perhaps any man seemed a dreamboat compared to the violent and mercurial Thomas West. The new man in Mrs. West's life (or rather, what remained of it) was William Dever, approximately fifty years old.

Both the Dever and West families were unusually ill-starred. Dever's wife and son both died soon after he moved to Marion

County from Knoxville, TN. The widower became acquainted with Mrs. West due to the fact that his fourteen-year-old daughter Alma frequently visited the West daughters. He must have hit it off pretty quickly with Mrs. West, who was described in one account as "far from good looking" and about forty, because within weeks of their initial meeting they were lovers. They didn't care who knew about it, either. It is impossible to say whether the folks around Lebanon were more incensed by the adultery or by the flaunting of it. Mr. Dever was cautioned several times to leave the county. He refused to do so and soon three people would pay for his stubbornness with their lives. The first was the wronged husband, Mr. West. In late November, he filed for divorce and on December 6 he confronted, in his characteristic manner, the man who had stolen his wife's affections—in this case, "confronted" means "tried to kill him by snapping a pistol at him twice." The gun misfired both times. Dever's gun had no such defect and, within moments, Mr. West lay dead with a bullet in his heart. Dever went to trial for murder and was quickly acquitted on grounds of self-defense.

Dever's older daughter Susie died of consumption on December 26. At the funeral held the next day, Mr. Dever was warned in no uncertain terms by the citizenry never to return to the West cabin. Dever replied that he wasn't afraid of any of West's friends and exacerbated matters the next day by moving into the double log house of the man he had killed in order to live in sin with the widow he had created. Perhaps worst of all in the eyes of the community, Dever's daughter Alma lived with the faithless couple. Mrs. West's own three grown daughters left the house in disgust and moved in with neighbors, never to see their mother alive again.

Mr. Dever and Mrs. West were permitted only a day to enjoy their love nest. They had been repeatedly warned to "knock it off," and when it became evident that they had no intention of doing so, a certain element decided to knock them off instead. Matters came to a crisis just after midnight on December 29. The inhabitants (and cohabitants) of the West house were awakened by pounding at the door and harsh voices demanding to speak to the putative man of the house. Young Alma Dever cautiously opened the door and was pulled out into the night by a roughneck who told her to run if she valued her life. Alma took the advice.

The assembly again commanded Mr. Dever to step outside. He said he would rather not. The crowd shot the house full of holes, not sparing the windows. When even this did not flush out their quarry, the mob decided it was time to stop being so nice about it. They set fire to the house. Several agonizing minutes later the door burst open and Mr. Dever ran outside with a pistol in each hand. He attempted to outpace the mob, but shots rang out and within seconds all his plans came to a permanent end. Ironically, Dever died wearing the same boots that Mr. West had worn when Dever shot him, for the widow had given the footwear to her new love.

The hours passed in their interminable way as the woods filled with smoke tainted by the odor of burned flesh. After the winter sun came up, a nearby neighbor named Thompson found Alma Dever in the woods. She had been so terrified by the night's events that it was a while before she could even tell Thompson what had happened. When he was apprised of the situation, Thompson gathered some neighbors and went to the West farm to investigate. They found Mr. Dever behind a haystack with four bullets in his person. His hair, eyebrows, and beard had been burned off since he had not left the house until the last possible moment.

Nothing was left of the house but the chimney, but it eloquently told of Mrs. West's last horrible moments. Her body was found "burned to a crisp" in the fireplace. Her torn fingertips revealed that she had made a desperate effort to climb up the chimney. All Thompson and the others could do was take her body out of the smoldering ruins and place it alongside that of the man for whose affection she had died.

Let it be said that most Marion Countians did not approve of the brutal morality play which had been enacted on Burdett's Creek. Nevertheless, the carnage had a powerful morbid fascination and shortly after word of the atrocity got out, hundreds of people went to see the remains of the house, undoubtedly destroying crime scene evidence in their eagerness. The corpses were not spared a thorough ogling, for crowds came to Creel's undertaking establishment to gape at the bullet-riddled, singed remains of the one and the blackened mortal husk of the other. An inquest was held the same day, but few useful facts came out. Alma Dever was still so rattled by her traumatic experience that she could barely speak.

Dever was buried in short order, but Mrs. West's charred body remained in the funeral home for an extra day. She was buried in Ryder's Cemetery on the last day of 1895. Her funeral procession consisted of only one buggy. Even the usually inevitable throngs of curiosity seekers failed to show up. Perhaps the lack of mourners was due to public outrage over the flagrant adultery that got her killed.

The day after the murders, the good citizens of Marion County of every race, religious creed, and political belief assembled at the courthouse in Lebanon despite a blizzard and drafted several resolutions expressing their horror and disgust and vowing to take all measures to identify, capture, and convict those responsible. Naturally, the press in far-flung states used the massacre as an excuse to yet again flog the barbarians who allegedly populated Kentucky. They compared the crime to recent atrocities in places like Armenia, Turkey, and Zululand; the *Kansas City Journal* was moved to lob a political brickbat: "Kentucky is now a Republican state, but it can't get over its Democratic ways all at once." However, the *Louisville Courier-Journal* saw hope in Marion County's reaction to the double murder: "This is an example that is worthy of imitation," editorialized the paper. "It is well that the voices of the law-abiding people should be heard in such cases, that malefactors should know in what estimate they are held by the reputable people by whom they are surrounded." In addition to expressing their outrage, citizens took up a collection to pay for a top-flight detective. Governor Bradley wired Judge R. A. Burton to tell him that a substantial $500 reward would be offered upon request.

The citizens' consciences were assuaged somewhat by certain

clues which indicated that the murderers had come from another county. (It appears that the Dever-West fling was the talk not only of Marion County, but of places far beyond.) Alma Dever told Justice Nooe at the inquest that only six men comprised the mob and that she had never seen any of them before.

Despite the hiring of a detective, the investigation of the Dever-West slaying was bungled from the start. The conventional wisdom among investigators is that the first thirty-six hours after a homicide are of critical importance; a week after the Dever-West murders, no significant clues had turned up. Burdett's Creek had been plagued for years by a band of midnight thieves who specialized in raiding meathouses and purloining livestock and farm supplies. Some thought they may have been responsible for the latest acts of mayhem, but it was an unwarranted logical leap to assume that men who would pilfer a sheep would be capable of assassination and burning down a house with a living woman in it. Nobody knew, or at least was willing to admit knowing, the identities of the men in the gang anyway.

Even the most horrifying murder case usually features some comic relief. Unfortunately for justice, the detective who came to Marion County was Capt. T. R. Phillips of Newport, Campbell County. Phillips made several claims to the press: he was working on the case by special order of Governor Bradley, he had made considerable progress at solving the crime, and the cowardly authorities of Marion County had been no help to him whatsoever. Worse, they had told him that no jury would convict anyone he arrested, and that he may as well leave the county immediately! Phillips noticeably did not mention any specific names, probably with good cause since the detective's statements were discredited as soon as he made them. Several local officials had offered him full support, including County Judge R. A. Burton, County Attorney Ben Spalding, and Sheriff R. E. Young. Detective Phillips had kept such a low profile while sleuthing that the Marion County Coroner, R. Davis, had not even known he was there.

Why did the detective make such unflattering comments to the press? County Clerk A. P. Carter noticed that every time Phillips visited his office, he invariably steered the conversation toward the reward. A citizen named John Barr flatly told Phillips that no reward would be given until the perpetrators were caught and convicted. Apparently, the detective was angry because he had been refused advance money. In addition, some people thought Phillips simply had been unable to find the killers and invented the Marion Countians' threat as a fig leaf to cover his failure.

Caught lying, Phillips backpedaled by making a contradictory claim: the killers had come from Washington County and it was Judge J. W. Thompson, an official from that county, who had told him that a fair trial and conviction would be impossible. Judge Thompson promptly issued a statement branding Detective Phillips a liar. By then, nobody cared what Phillips had to say anyway. His antics had cost the investigation precious time and resources.

In January 1896, the sheriff of Scottsburg, IN, reported that an ugly stranger calling himself Charles Fox had drifted through town, claiming to be en route to Michigan. Fox, if that really was his name, said that he had come from Marion County, KY, and dropped a few broad hints to all who would listen that he had been forced to leave against his will because he had "talked too freely" about the Dever-West murders. The press recorded no follow-up stories, so it is a safe bet that Fox was only an itinerant loudmouth and braggart.

It was reported in early February that a grand jury expected to indict someone for the infamous slayings. Many witnesses were from Washington and Boyle Counties, a circumstance indicating that the murderers likely were not Marion Countians. Two weeks and two hundred witnesses later, indictments were found against two men. There must not have been much evidence against one of them because he never went to trial and was never even named in press accounts. The other, whom the State felt it had a good chance of prosecuting, was Lee Boyle, "a dudish-looking young man of about twenty-four."

Detective George Hunter had found Boyle at Charleston, IL, with a suspicious unhealed bullet wound in his shoulder. People not inclined to believe in Boyle's innocence thought he might have received the wound as Dever tried to flee the burning cabin with pistols blazing. Hunter took his prisoner to Lebanon. The residents seemed menacing, so Hunter hurriedly took Boyle to a cell in Louisville, where the accused man maintained that he had nothing to say. There he stayed until the court convened in Marion County in April.

Hopes were high after Boyle's arrest. If he were guilty, perhaps he would confess and name his confederates. "There is no question but that the coil is gradually tightening on the perpetrators of the crime," wrote a hopeful newspaper correspondent, "but it may yet require several links to form a chain of evidence that cannot be broken." Things did not go so well, however, when Boyle actually went to trial on May 11.

A few witnesses were called on May 12, as opposed to the expected hundreds, the first of whom was young Alma Dever, the only survivor of the murderous raid. Other witnesses included Detective Hunter and Sheriff Young. However, the weakness of the case against Boyle was obvious when the State called the witness with the "most damaging testimony," Louis Steele of Charleston, IL, who swore under oath that Boyle had told him during a barroom conversation that he had been a member of the mob. The State appears to have provided no solid evidence that Boyle had engaged in anything more serious than drunken fabulating. "The remaining testimony was not important," said the *Courier-Journal* in an offhand remark that strips bare the poverty of the prosecution's case. Ordinarily in a case of this magnitude, the State might spend days, even weeks, laying the groundwork necessary for a guilty verdict; in the trial of *The Commonwealth v. Lee Boyle*, the prosecution rested its case after a single day's testimony.

On May 13, the defense presented its case, doing hardly a better job than did the prosecution. Rather than providing evidence of Boyle's innocence, defense attorney T. W. Simms spent most of his time harping on the sinful relations between Mr. Dever and Mrs.

West, as though they were the ones on trial. Like the prosecution, the defense limply concluded its case in less than a day. In the face of lackluster evidence from both sides, it came as no surprise when the jury members announced on May 14 that they had failed to reach an agreement, ten members being for conviction and two for acquittal. The jury was dismissed, Lee Boyle's bail was paid and he walked away a free man. Later he was tried a second time, but the prosecution's star witness, Alma Dever, was nowhere to be found. Without her testimony, the already shaky house of cards collapsed once and for all. The case was dismissed.

Despite a newspaper's optimistic statement a few days after the crime that "[i]t is believed the murderers will be captured, and within a short time," the killers of Mr. Dever and Mrs. West were neither caught nor even identified. The best efforts of Detective Hunter, the governor, and many Marion Countians all came to nothing and if we take our folklore at face value, the spirits of Dever and West wander their home turf, troubled at never receiving justice.

In addition to the major unsolved mystery concerning the identities of the men who killed the proudly adulterous couple, there is a minor mystery: whatever became of poor Alma Dever? Just after the murders she was described as being beautiful and intelligent; she had been "furnished with a good home." Yet, her behavior after the mobbing was so erratic that it was feared she had lost her mind. An article written the day after the murders noted: "It is not improbable that [Alma's] mind is permanently shattered."

Alma disappeared after Lee Boyle's first trial. It was reported that she had died in a Louisville hospital in December 1897. A Marion County man named J. H. Thompson insisted that Alma was dead and buried in the Lebanon city cemetery. He did not view the corpse himself, he said, but his children had seen her in the coffin. However, in September 1898, a woman from Springfield, Washington County, claimed to have had a recent conversation with the allegedly dead woman in Bardstown, Nelson County, during which Alma admitted that she had been living in a number of places under assumed names.

Did Alma Dever actually die in 1897? Or did she fake her own death? If so, how? Did she go into hiding for fear that members of the mob that killed her mother might track her down? Where did she eventually settle? We will probably never know the answers to these questions and Alma might have wanted it that way.

The Case of the Killer Coroner

The coroner is generally the corpse's best friend. Should a body turn up under suspicious circumstances, it is the coroner's duty to examine the evidence and, if the cause of death is unknown, to hold an inquest. Coroners are not expected to manufacture business for themselves by murdering people; such a breach of professional etiquette would likely be censured by the community and would cost the coroner some votes in the next election. And yet, a little over a hundred years ago, Louisville had a coroner who was also charged with murder.

This unique public official was Dr. Hugh McCullough, who had been re-elected Jefferson County's coroner in November 1897. He, his wife, Hattie, and his small son lived at Mellwood and Letterle Avenues. His neighbors across the street were Mr. William Owen, a veteran of the War Between the States, his wife Perrina and their dysfunctional family. Just as the protracted and bloody Hatfield-McCoy feud was allegedly triggered by the questioned ownership of a pig, the McCullough and the Owen families came to shed blood over a peafowl. The record is unforgivably silent as to whether it was a peacock or a peahen.

In better times, when the neighbors had gotten along, the McCulloughs had given the bird to the Owens as a gift. Trouble began on September 17, 1900, when Mr. and Mrs. Owen had a screaming match—or, as we might say today in our studiously watered-down language, "a domestic dispute." So loud were the Owens that Mrs. McCullough could hear every word of their spat from her home across the street. Instead of defusing the situation or minding her own business, however, Mrs. McCullough took the opportunity to ridicule

Mrs. Owen. She remarked to bystanders that if she were Mr. Owen, she would beat Mrs. Owen's face "into a jelly" and have her sent to an asylum. Unfortunately, the Owens' daughter Julia was standing in front of the McCullough home at the time and she overheard. She went home and reported it to her mother, requesting that she cease the argument, as people in the neighborhood were making fun of them.

The haughty Mrs. Owen transferred her anger from Mr. Owen to that busybody Mrs. McCullough. The two women had a scorching verbal exchange, after which Mrs. Owen retired to her kitchen. That should have been the end of it, but a few minutes later Julia Owen came home crying and saying that Mrs. McCullough had called her a "damned strumpet." Mrs. Owen ran outside and renewed her quarrel with Mrs. McCullough.

After a while, Dr. McCullough came home, visited Mr. and Mrs. Owen, and tried to smooth things over, remarking that he hoped the two women would stop fighting. Before Mr. Owen could say anything, Mrs. Owen sneered: "Yes, I will let it drop for the sake of you and your baby. It wouldn't do me any good to bring you into court, for you haven't got anything anyhow." (The reader will observe how much trouble could have been avoided if the persons involved had simply shut their yaps and been civil.) Dr. McCullough made no reply to the insult, but turned and walked home. The families brooded and nursed their anger. They had another inconclusive argument on the night of Saturday, September 22.

Then, on the morning of the twenty-fourth came the Peafowl Incident. The bird was tethered in the Owens' yard but somehow got loose. It paid a social call at the coroner's house. After a while, the peafowl went back to the Owen residence, where it roosted in a tree blissfully unaware of all the trouble it was about to cause.

From this point, incidents escalated at a furious pace; when it came time later to explain in court what had happened, each family tried to put itself in the best light while casting the members of the opposing family as deep-dyed villains, so the reader is advised to believe whichever version of events he/she likes best.

Mrs. McCullough sent two men to retrieve the peafowl. Mrs. Owen told them to get lost. The men came back empty-handed. Mrs. McCullough erupted in a tirade aimed at Mrs. Owen, who responded in kind. In a fury, Mrs. McCullough ran inside and returned with a revolver. As Mrs. Owen sang a treacly popular song from the period called "Ben Bolt" in order to drown out Mrs. McCullough's verbal abuse, the latter fired five shots at the Owen house. Whether the angry woman had intended to shoot at the house, at the peafowl, or at Mrs. Owen was never clarified; Mrs. Owen herself never could seem to make up her mind about it. Mrs. Owen later claimed—but not consistently—that Mrs. McCullough produced a second revolver and fired two more shots, both of which also missed.

Dr. McCullough returned home after getting a call from his wife. According to Mrs. Owen's take on the event, the furious Mrs. McCullough handed her husband a gun and said, "Take this pistol and kill her." The coroner approached Mrs. Owen with the gun and said, "Damn you, you will have to stop this trouble with my wife." Shortly thereafter, Mrs. Owen's son George, a twenty-one-year-old who worked at the Mellwood distillery, came to her defense. McCullough shot George once in the chest and also killed the family dog, an enormous Newfoundland named Nell, when it attacked him. McCullough fled home and a nearby physician, Dr. P. B. Morris, came to the scene and announced that the boy had died instantaneously. Of course, McCullough was not allowed to perform an autopsy on the corpse he had made and it fell to Magistrate Augustus to give it an examination. The body remained in the doorway for nearly five hours until officials came to take it away.

Immediately after the shooting, two policemen rang the coroner's doorbell. He greeted them by saying, "Well, boys, it looks like I'm in trouble." He was arrested and taken to the station without incident. The officers placed him in a cell at first, but soon he was allowed free access to the offices as he was not considered a flight risk. The coroner spent a troubled night in a surgeon's office at the jailhouse where he spoke frankly with a *Courier-Journal* reporter, to whom he claimed that he had been justified in shooting George Owen because the young man had rushed at him with a knife. "The whole [Owen] family have been terrorizing the neighborhood," he explained, "and George seemed to have a special hatred for me. They have always been obnoxious. The mother pried into the affairs of the neighbors and trouble often resulted. About two weeks ago they began their attacks on my wife and myself. They irritated us in every conceivable manner. It finally became unbearable and last week I reported them to the police." He added, more germanely, that he had heard rumors that George Owen had threatened to kill him. He stated that he had gone to the neighbors' house not with murder in mind but simply to remonstrate with Mrs. Owen. He claimed to have had trouble finding her in the dark though she sat on the front porch—but at the same time McCullough said, perhaps contradictorily, that he could see the knife in George Owen's hand as he advanced.

The proceedings of the examining trial in Police Court on September 26 offered a taste of the excitement to come. A patrolman named Maurice Dooling claimed to have gone looking for evidence in the Owen yard the morning after the murder. He stated that he had found an open bone-handled knife, purportedly belonging to the murdered youth, in the vines by the porch two feet from where George Owen was standing when he was shot. Prosecutor Nick Vaughn ridiculed this evidence. He revealed that while Officer Dooling looked for clues in the Owens' yard, Dooling had engaged in conversation with Mrs. Owen and her daughter Hattie as the two grieving women sat on their front porch. The patrolman had been unaware that another Owen daughter, Julia, was watching him from the side porch. Vaughn claimed that Julia had seen Dooling drop the knife in the vines when he thought no one was looking and Mrs. Owen said she could produce witnesses to prove that her son did not even own a knife.

Soon afterwards the coroner found himself sharing a jail cell with Caleb Powers, one of the men accused of conspiring in the assassination of Governor Goebel. This unpleasant state of affairs lasted only a day. McCullough's friends posted $10,000 bail money on his behalf and he was freed.

The examining trial continued on September 27. The mourning Mrs. Owen took the stand and told the peafowl story; asserted that Mrs. McCullough had handed the pistol to the coroner with explicit instructions to commit murder; and swore that her son had had no knife in his hands when Dr. McCullough fired. The defendant testified that the Owen family had been hostile and impudent to his family and that his wife had fired her gun not at Mrs. Owen, but in the air in order to get the attention of the police. Mr. McCullough swore, contrary to Mrs. Owen's statements, that the gun he carried in his pocket to the scene was his own: "I am an officer of the law and have a right to carry one. My wife gave me none." His testimony contradicted Mrs. Owen's in another major way:

> I walked across the street to Mrs. Owen's and when close to the porch, called Mrs. Owen. There was no answer. I repeated the call and then Mrs. Owen, who was on the front porch, said: "You — — —, get off my premises." I walked off and told her I would have her arrested. Then I heard her son's voice, saying: "Sic him! Sic the — — —!" I saw the dog and Owen advancing and, as God is my judge, he had a knife in his hand. I shot the man first and then the dog. The dog weighed about 170 pounds. I shot because I believed my life was in danger.
>
> (We are not privileged to know exactly what "— — —" stood for.)

When asked how he knew that George Owen had been threatening his life, McCullough replied that one Will Lee and a girl who lived with the McCulloughs, Katie Hogan, had told him so. The defense asked how he could have seen the knife since it was dark outside. McCullough answered that there was an electric light 300 feet away and it provided sufficient illumination.

The boarder Katie Hogan took the oath and corroborated McCullough's statements. She had heard Mrs. Owen browbeating the two men sent to search for the peafowl and had also heard her call Mrs. McCullough unspecified "insulting names." She had seen the coroner walk across the street to confront Mrs. Owen and swore that he had no gun in his hand. She added: "When he reached Mrs. Owen's house, I heard her call him a vile name and soon afterward her son stepped around a bush. I saw him draw his knife. He sicked the dog on Dr. McCullough and said: 'Now I have got you!' Then Dr. McCullough fired. I certainly saw the knife." Under cross-examination she reasserted that she had seen Owen draw the knife from his pocket. To give the jury an interesting puzzle, the defense produced Mrs. Owen, who again declared that her son had never carried a knife in his life.

The defense also brought forth Capt. John Oyler, the dead man's uncle, who testified that he was on the scene five minutes after the shooting and, having heard rumors that George had drawn a knife, had searched the body and the surrounding area for a weapon. He found none. The two policemen who had arrested McCullough testified that Owen had a knife, but admitted that they had been unable to find it. Three other people—Granville Hooper, Ed Hooper (a childhood friend of the deceased), and George Owen's sister Julia—all testified that George had not been in the habit of carrying a knife. Of course, it is possible that he had picked up the habit very recently, anticipating trouble with the friendly neighborhood coroner. The day ended with the defense making an eloquent appeal for the case to be dismissed on grounds of self-defense and the prosecution making an equally eloquent appeal that McCullough should stand trial for murder. The jury agreed with the Commonwealth and, a couple of weeks later, the defendant faced a grand jury.

McCullough was indicted on October 22. To make matters worse for the coroner, he was also investigated on charges of having extorted money from local undertakers; on October 24, his wife Hattie was indicted for maliciously shooting at, but not wounding, Mrs. Owen. Just when things couldn't look darker for McCullough, one of the prosecution's star witnesses, Officer Dooling, was indicted on a charge of being an accessory after the fact since eyewitness testimony indicated that he had planted the knife at the scene of the crime. Interestingly, despite all of the indictments and scandals, the county appears to have kept the coroner on call because in mid-November, just days before his trial began, he was reported to be investigating the death of Thomas Kelly, whose head had deflected a blunt object on Election Day.

The trial began on November 21 after the usual difficulty in selecting a jury. (A hint for those who wish to avoid jury duty in a murder trial: just say that you are in favor of the death penalty and the defense will excuse you as though you were made of plutonium.) Before a packed courtroom, the coroner again told the story of the fight from his point of view. The reader is already familiar with the essentials of his version. Captain Hagan for the prosecution promised the jury that he would prove that George Owen owned no knife and never carried one. On the other hand, Mr. Phelps for the defense said in his opening statement that the coroner had been threatened in the past by George Owen—who, far from being a gentle young man, had once attacked his own invalid father with a club and in fact at the time of his death was under a peace bond, a legal promise given by a defendant that he will be on his best behavior and will refrain from committing disturbances. The Commonwealth successfully had these aspersions against Owen's character stricken from the record—for now, anyway.

The first witness for the State was Mrs. Owen, who told of the escalating tensions between the families—of course taking care to blame the McCulloughs. The most dramatic moment came when she was shown an undershirt and was asked if she recognized it. She did; her son had worn it when he was shot. He had been buried in it and the State had taken the trouble to exhume the body and remove the garment, which presumably was in need of laundering.

Under cross-examination, the defense brought out a contradiction in Mrs. Owen's statements; at the examining trial, she had said that she thought Mrs. McCullough had shot at the peafowl and later changed the story to say that the coroner's wife had fired at her. Mr. Phelps also extracted the admission that the McCulloughs had been kind to her in the past and had even loaned her money. She was inconsistent as to whether Mrs. McCullough had fired five bullets using one gun or seven bullets using two guns and whether or not her dog had bitten the coroner's hand on that fatal night. The next witness was Uncle John Oyler, who again testified that he had searched in vain for a knife in the Owens' yard.

On the night George Owen confronted the coroner, he had been followed by five friends; three of them made appearances on the witness stand. This was John Hawes's version of events: he, George Owen, Owen's father, and four other friends were sitting on the steps at Kamer's saloon when the party saw McCullough driving by rapidly in his buggy. Sensing trouble was afoot, young Owen said he was going to go protect his mother. Hawes heard Mrs. Owen tell McCullough to leave her yard; then George Owen said something inaudible to McCullough; the coroner answered, "What in the hell have you got to do with it?" This was followed by the sound of a gunshot. When he saw the astonished bystanders, McCullough said (according to Hawes): "If you don't shut up, I'll kill a couple more." His testimony lost its impact when one of the prosecutors, Aaron Kohn, demonstrated in court that Hawes was hard of hearing. The jury also heard from another of Owen's friends who had been present, Curtis Fields, but his testimony corroborated Hawes's statements only in the most general way.

The third witness called to testify that day was Owen's friend Fred Krause and the prosecutors soon wished they had never heard of him. Krause, a prosecution witness, testified instead in favor of the defense. The Commonwealth tried to prove that George Owen did not "sic" his fearsome Newfoundland on McCullough, but Krause, whom the prosecution expected to support its case, confirmed that Owen had indeed done so. Moreover, the coroner had backed up several steps before firing at man and man's best friend. Taken by surprise, the lawyers for the State could only say that Krause was not "an honorable man." One wishes the three witnesses could have cleared up the mystery of whether or not Owen had had a knife in his hand, but none mentioned it in his testimony. They had heard the murder occur but had arrived on the scene too late to see it.

Coroner McCullough took the stand on his own behalf and made an impressive showing. "He was perfectly self-contained and told his story in a plain, direct way," remarked an observer. He explained that he went to the Owen residence that night only to seek peace, but had received abuse from Mrs. Owen who demanded that he leave her property. McCullough said that as he started to leave he found himself facing George, who called him by an unflattering term and ordered Nell the dog to attack. McCullough started to back away, but George and the dog came after him. When he saw the open knife in the youth's hand he knew he had to act. He drew his pistol and fired in self-defense: "I fired as the dog was springing on me. I believed, I knew my life was in danger when I fired. I had no pistol in my hand [when first arriving at the Owens' porch], and I did not say to Mrs. Owen, 'I want the trouble between you and my wife to stop, — — you.' My wife did not hand me a pistol." McCullough ended his testimony by describing two recent occasions on which he was told that Owen had been threatening to kill him.

The second day of the trial was largely concerned with the Commonwealth's attempts to impeach its turncoat witness, Fred Krause. The defense had its own problems: a vigorous cross-examination of Dr. McCullough failed to shake him in any way. For example, the defense challenged his powers of observation by asking what Owen had been wearing the night he was shot. McCullough replied that he did not observe Owen's mode of dress, being far more interested in the knife in Owen's hand. However, McCullough's boarder Miss Hogan did not fare so well on cross-examination and the defense was able to point out several contradictions between her testimony of the day before and her testimony at the much earlier examining trial. The defense also produced a doctor who had examined Owen's corpse and swore that it bore no powder burns, which seemed to confirm that the coroner had been in the act of backing off in fear when he fired. Had he fired from close range, as the prosecution argued, there should have been burns on the clothes and the body.

By the end of the day, it had become an issue of character: McCullough and Owen were each presented by their legal teams as paragons of earthly virtue. Many witnesses—including a Senator—swore to the coroner's good reputation, but George Owen had far fewer defenders. Several neighbors, some of whom had known him for years, testified that they considered him little more than a dangerous thug. (One noted that the evil Owen had been known to "play marbles on Sunday.") Strangely, the prosecution appears not to have mentioned the recent charges that the coroner had accepted kickbacks from undertakers despite the fact that one mortician, W. S. Melton, had insisted the charges were true and said that the coroner demanded half the profits when he turned over an unclaimed corpse. During the time of the examining trial, the prosecutors had even turned up canceled checks from two undertaking establishments to McCullough which the coroner had promised to explain but apparently never did.

The case was submitted to the jury on November 23. Depending on which side you chose to believe, it was either a cowardly, pointless murder or a justifiable shooting in self-defense. After thirty minutes, the jury's members announced that they believed the latter. A reporter wrote: "In ten minutes the courtroom was deserted and the record of this celebrated trial had been made up and filed away, never to be opened on earth."

A little more than a week later, Dr. McCullough was hard at work performing an autopsy on Mr. Jacob Roeder, determining that he had died of alcoholism rather than a brick upside the head, as originally supposed.

There is a strange aftermath to the Case of the Killer Coroner. William Owen brooded over his son's murder and his own alcoholism until he finally committed suicide by swallowing whisky with an added ingredient, three ounces of carbolic acid, on October 7, 1904. Or at least that's what everyone thought had happened. Mrs. Joseph Stabb had been at the Owen house the night of the death, and she gossiped that Mrs. Owen—who appears to have been the champion virago of the neighborhood—had told her in no uncertain terms that she had poisoned her husband intentionally: "Mrs. Stabb, I fixed that up for him and he got it—I am glad of it." When the guest asked her what she meant by that, Mrs. Owen replied: "I mean that I put carbolic acid in whisky for him and he got it; that's what I mean." It came out that Mrs. Owen had sent her teenage son Rem to the druggist to purchase a nickel's worth of carbolic acid on the night Mr. Owen died. Authorities discovered that William Owen had been regularly abused by his wife and other family members, that he had been insured, and that his widow was to receive a pension due to her husband's military service.

The police found Mrs. Stabb's story credible and arrested Mrs. Owen on October 17. While Mrs. Owen had protested at first that her husband had committed suicide, she now claimed that she had put poison in the whisky in order to kill bedbugs and clean the family's beds and floors; her husband had drunk the concoction unaware of its contents. She added that Mr. Owen had been intoxicated the entire day of his death and for several days preceding, but a woman who worked as a domestic next door swore that she had heard the Owens arguing on the evening of October 7 and had seen him perfectly sober twenty minutes before he died. Mrs. Owen claimed that all of the witnesses against her were grudge-bearing liars.

The case went before Judge McCann. He dismissed all charges after the servant next door repudiated her statement that she had heard the Owens arguing on the day of the poisoning. Also, once on the witness stand, Mrs. Stabb softened her story. Before, she had said that Mrs. Owen had defiantly admitted poisoning her husband; now, Mrs. Stabb would claim only that Mrs. Owen had cynically muttered that she had put carbolic acid in the whisky in order to kill bedbugs, but she would not care if her good-for-nothing husband drank it. By sheer happenstance, the obliging man did exactly that a few minutes later and expired horribly. Mrs. Owen walked out of the courtroom a free woman on October 20.

The Jefferson County coroner who presided over the case was Dr. Harris Kelly, so Louisville was spared the irony of seeing Hugh McCullough testify at the trial of the woman whose son he allegedly had murdered.

Four Murderers

This is the story of three murders that took place in Lexington, Fayette County, over a hundred years ago. One was the result of two criminals acting in tandem; the others were committed by individual slayers who let jealousy or greed get the better of them. At one point, the lives of the four murderers converged like streams flowing into a river. Then, though they went their separate ways, all four paid for their crimes with their lives in some fashion: three were executed, while one cheated the hangman. Their crimes offer a glimpse into the life and customs of turn-of-the-century Kentucky, provide a microcosm of how the legal system worked in those days, and present a study in how citizens react to crime and how criminals react to punishment.

The Sixth Amendment to the Constitution's Bill of Rights gives citizens the right to a speedy trial—"speedy" being the operative word. Victims and their families often agonize over a trial process that can unfold for years before a verdict is reached. Historical true crime stories reveal that even in the "good old days," it often took an unconscionably long time for justice to be served. Every now and then there are notable exceptions. For example, William McCarty, an unemployed former worker for the Louisville and Nashville railroad, found the wheels of justice grinding exceedingly quickly as well as exceedingly fine—and not at all to his advantage.

McCarty and his twenty-year-old wife, Lucy, were married in Cincinnati in January 1901, after which they moved to Lexington. McCarty was a jealous, abusive husband. Mrs. McCarty confided to friends and neighbors that she felt it was only a matter of time until he killed her. Only fourteen months after their nuptials, he beat her so badly that she often required medical treatment. In March 1902, he increased his brutality by attacking her with a revolver. He paid a fine and spent a few days in jail but was released when his wife begged the court for leniency. On April 17, he rewarded her kindness by pistol-whipping her and dragging her over a railroad track. Then he scurried off to Louisville. When he returned to Lexington on April 19, he discovered, to his fury, that his bride had sworn out a warrant for his arrest.

That evening, Mrs. McCarty went to visit her friend, Mrs. Lizzie Swigert, at 245 West Main Street. As the two women conversed on the porch, a drunken Mr. McCarty approached with a .38 caliber revolver in hand. He fired before Mrs. Swigert could raise an alarm. A bullet lodged in his wife's back, to the left of her spine. The terrified wife ran into the house, but her husband caught up and fired another shot into her back. She had just enough time to exclaim, "Oh God, somebody help me," before she died in the front room. Ironically, she had paid the premium on her life insurance policy just two hours before her murder.

McCarty was sober enough to think it wise to disappear. He ran to the house of Nannie Bruen, but she refused to let him inside. He hid under her porch, but police found him when he went on a most inopportune coughing jag. As they hauled him off to the slammer, he remarked, "I don't care if I do hang." He was drunk, sullen, and refused to speak to the police or the press. Justice moved so swiftly that on the very same night McCarty committed his crime, a coroner's jury convened, weighed the evidence and accused him of murder. He wept and expressed regret in jail the next day as he sobered up. Only three days later, he faced the grand jury, the examining trial having been waived.

Although his attorney strongly advised him not to talk, McCarty held a press conference on April 23, at which he made a full confession and revealed the motive for his violent actions: it was all his wife's fault. He tried to convince the reporters that she had been unfaithful, despite the neighbors' consensus that she had been a patient and loyal wife, which he had not deserved—after all, she had refused to press charges the first time he was arrested for abusing her, at the cost of her life. McCarty explained that on the night of the murder he had been overcome with jealousy when he saw his untrustworthy wife talking to another man. In essence, he loved her so much he just had to kill her! While he was at it, he complained that the local papers had not quoted him when the news of the murder first broke—how they could have, when he was drunk and refusing to comment at the time, did not seem to trouble him. McCarty held another press conference the next day, at which he griped that the press still was not treating him fairly, i.e., they seemed not to be taking his rationalizations for his crime with what he deemed sufficient seriousness. As so many criminals have done, McCarty attempted to use the press to gain sympathy and "tell his side of the story," while at the same time complaining that the papers misrepresented him if they said something he didn't like.

As the investigation continued, authorities found that they could not locate the victim's family. Mrs. McCarty allegedly came from Boyd County, but telegraphs to Ashland and Catlettsburg failed to turn up any relatives. Her body lay at the mortuary, unclaimed like a lost suitcase, since her husband's family refused to assist in her burial. Her remains had to be removed to a public vault pending instructions from her family. When they proved untraceable, citizens took up a private subscription and Mrs. McCarty was buried in Lexington Cemetery. Eventually, investigators discovered that she had married McCarty under an assumed identity. Her real name was Frankie Huber (or Hubbard) of Prestonsburg, Floyd County. The reason she chose to go by an alias does not appear in the record.

McCarty's drunken violence claimed another victim, of sorts: Mrs. Swigert, at whose house the shooting occurred, went hopelessly insane a week later. She became convinced that McCarty was going to kill her for testifying against him before the coroner's jury. At other times, she thought she was going to be hanged. She described the details of the killing over and over and, at the end of the month, was taken via ambulance to her new home at the Eastern Kentucky

Lunatic Asylum. It took four men to get her into the vehicle.

McCarty's trial began on June 24, a mere two months after the murder. Bert Miller, the only person other than the insane Mrs. Swigert who had witnessed the shooting, provided damning testimony. Miller was a friend of McCarty's and had spent the fatal afternoon with him. He confirmed the statements that Mrs. Swigert had made before the stress of seeing a murder made her lose her mind; he flatly contradicted McCarty's claim that Lucy had been talking to another man on the Swigerts' porch. He added that McCarty had never complained about his wife being unfaithful. On the second day of the trial, the jury convened for an hour and found the twenty-seven-year-old McCarty guilty. The members fixed his penalty at death by hanging. The date was set at September 5, 1902.

After thinking it over for a while, the man who had said, "I don't care if I do hang," decided he did care after all—very much so—and his attorneys fought the impending execution tooth and nail. The case went to the Court of Appeals in August and McCarty spent a nervous seven months awaiting its decision.

A. B. Chinn was one of the oldest and best-loved merchants in Lexington at the turn of the last century. He was a Confederate veteran, the son of former mayor Dr. Joseph Chinn, and had spent many decades of his sixty-eight years as the senior member of the dry goods firm of Chinn and Todd. His career and his life both came to a tragic end on the night of Friday, October 10, 1902.

Shortly after 3 a.m., two thieves wearing bandanas over their faces slipped through a window in the room occupied by Chinn's elderly mother-in-law. Chinn's wife awoke her husband to tell him that she thought intruders were afoot. Just as he expressed his belief that she was only hearing the wind, the two burglars entered the bedroom and lit a match. In the dim light, the Chinns could see that the men were armed with revolvers. The burglars demanded money, to which Chinn responded that there was none on the premises but they were welcome to look for themselves. The burglars declined this polite invitation with a threat. At this critical moment, Asa, the merchant's twenty-four-year-old son, burst into the room and took on the invaders. In the exchange of shots that followed, Asa was wounded three times: one bullet hit his left arm, another grazed his nose, and a third broke his jawbone. His father took a bullet to the chest at point-blank range; it passed through his body and lodged in a wardrobe. A. B. Chinn managed to get out of bed and chase the burglars for a moment before he died in the hallway.

While lying on the floor, Asa managed to shoot one of his fleeing attackers with a .38 caliber pistol. Soon, the police rounded up two strangely-acting youthful hobos: Claude O'Brien and another who gave his name as Charles Thomas. They were found hiding in a boxcar of a train destined for Cincinnati. It had been raining the night of the murder and both boys had sopping wet coats, proving they had not been in the boxcar for long. Thomas was limping from a very recent wound. He claimed that he had just injured his right knee while trying to climb into the boxcar, but a doctor's examination revealed a freshly lodged bullet—of a .38 caliber and fired from an upward angle—just above the knee.

Thomas had some explaining to do. He abruptly changed his story and confided that he had been shot on Thursday, October 9, the day before Chinn's murder, by "a negro near Williamstown" for reasons unexplained. The cops didn't believe him, especially when his companion O'Brien gave a contradictory account. Further research uncovered more facts about the "boy tramps," as the press dubbed them: O'Brien came from Memphis; "Thomas" was from Nashville and his real name was Earl Whitney. Both boys recently had been inmates in a Nashville reform school. Whitney in particular had a long arrest record in Nashville, where he had been picked up on charges including burglary, vagrancy, and carrying a pistol. O'Brien and Whitney were, to make an understatement, "persons of interest" in the case.

They spent the next day in a jail cell, becoming increasingly nervous and restless as more suspicious circumstances against them came to light. A revolver had been stolen from the residence of O. L. Slade an hour before the Chinn shooting; the burglars had left wet, shoeless footprints in Slade's house. The prints matched similar tracks on the windowsill at Chinn's house. Prison officials examined the socks of both tramps and found them muddy and covered with a quantity of burs called Spanish needles, indicating that the thieves had been walking outside without shod feet. It so happened that the Chinn backyard was full of Spanish needles. Worse, the jailor declared that O'Brien and Whitney had actually dropped by the jail several hours before the murder in order to see a prisoner named Will Martin, who was O'Brien's brother. The jailer remembered that Whitney had not been limping that morning, as might be expected had he been recently shot in Williamstown as he claimed. (Note to aspiring murderers: It is not a good idea to visit law enforcement officials a few hours before you kill somebody.) O'Brien's story was demolished when the police discovered that the boy tramps had been under arrest on suspicion of burglary in Louisville on Thursday, October 9. A Louisville detective made a trip to Lexington to see the prisoners and recognized Whitney immediately since he was wearing the same clothes he had worn at the Louisville jail a few days before. In other words, O'Brien and Whitney were exposed as having a somewhat adversarial relationship with facts: they had been nowhere near Williamstown on the day they claimed and Whitney's story about how he had received his bullet wound was a bald lie.

At last, Whitney could stand the pressure no more. He folded like a lawn chair on October 15, stating that O'Brien had done the shooting and revealing that they hid their guns under a tool shed near the boxcar where they had been arrested. The immediate result of this outburst of honesty, other than a sense of spiritual relief for Whitney, was that a hostile mob—which even included women and children—came calling at the jail. The boy tramps had to be spirited away to Louisville, but not before Governor Beckham ordered two companies of the state militia to Lexington. Once there, the two obviously thankful youths struck the note of false bravado that rarely left them until the end of their days: they talked tough, cracked jokes, and told reporters that they would as readily have died at the hands of a mob as at any other time.

However, O'Brien was not as willing to accept his fate as he pretended. He turned on his partner in crime, claiming with the ingenuity of a defense lawyer that Whitney had shot Chinn, thus giving the State the burden of examining the hobos' contradictory stories and somehow proving which of the two did the actual shooting. Or perhaps, O'Brien declared somewhat less ingeniously, Asa Chinn had shot his own father by accident! Never mind the fact that Asa Chinn had done most of his shooting while lying wounded on the floor and A. B. Chinn had been shot in the chest at close range.

As the boys spent their time in Louisville trying to impress jailhouse visitors with their courage, Lexington legal matters were moving along at an admirable clip. A special grand jury met on October 22 and wasted no time returning six indictments against O'Brien and Whitney on charges of burglary, shooting, wounding, and murder. A month later the two returned to Lexington to face the music. They asked for, and received, separate trials when their cases were heard in early December. Earl Whitney, whom most onlookers considered the weaker and less defiant of the two, went on trial first. His limping walk as he entered the courtroom reminded spectators of the manner in which he received his gimpy leg. Two able attorneys, Charles Kerr and the superbly named Butler Southgate, represented Whitney.

Mrs. Chinn took the stand and recounted the home invasion and her husband's shooting. She was unable to positively identify Whitney as one of the burglars—not surprising since the invaders had worn masks and she had seen them only briefly by the light of a match. She was followed by Asa Chinn, who had slowly struggled his way to recovery. The Commonwealth's work took only a day or two and, on December 4, the defense put Whitney on the stand. His attorneys attempted to have his confession thrown out, but after Whitney admitted that he made the confession of his own free will and without promise of compensation, the judge allowed it as evidence. He insisted under oath that O'Brien had fired the fatal shot and that his own gun had jammed. Whitney's attorneys placed O'Brien on the stand, but he availed himself of his Constitutional right not to incriminate himself and steadfastly refused to answer every question they asked. The jury retired for slightly less than an hour and a half; after two ballots, the members unanimously decided Whitney was guilty and despite his extreme youth—he was only seventeen—they opted to treat him like the full-grown man he considered himself and gave him the death penalty. His studied machismo vanished and he "cried like a child," according to one witness. The crowd failed to appreciate the gravity of the verdict and cheered, much to Judge Watts Parker's disgust.

Claude O'Brien had good reason to be worried when he learned of his friend's fate. His own trial began on December 5. A strange moment occurred after a hard day spent selecting twelve jury members out of fifty-four veniremen. O'Brien's attorney, Captain John Feland, accidentally excused the members when he actually had intended to accept them. The process had to be started over again. O'Brien's defenders later claimed that Feland was drunk while in court, so perhaps this error originated from the bottle.

The Commonwealth called the same witnesses who had testified in the Whitney trial, but prosecutors also got some testimony from Whitney himself. He repeated what he had said before, emphasizing that O'Brien had killed Chinn. When O'Brien took the stand in his own defense, he contradicted Whitney by claiming that he had tried to escape the Chinn house when events took a violent turn and that Whitney had pulled the trigger. The jury did not believe him and he too was found guilty and sentenced to death.

O'Brien's lawyers immediately filed a petition to the Circuit Court asking for a new trial, charging that improper evidence had been admitted, proper evidence had been withheld, and the jury had not been correctly instructed. On December 13, attorneys for both youths pleaded for a motion for a new trial. Judge Parker asked O'Brien and Whitney if there were any reason the sentence should not be passed upon them. Calmly, even smilingly, they claimed to have had unfair trials; O'Brien repeated the claim that his attorney, Feland, had been intoxicated. The judge declared that he believed their trials had been fair and sentenced them to be hanged on February 13, 1903.

On the fine spring morning of Tuesday, March 10, 1903, passersby noticed a body in a reservoir near Lexington's Seventh Street power house. At first, it appeared that someone had fallen in and drowned, possibly while drunk. When the undertaker fished out the corpse of thirty-five-year-old Martha McQuinn Martin, he noticed that she had bloodshot eyes and dark marks around her throat. The coroner's autopsy determined that the woman had been dead four days. She had dislocated neck bones, finger-shaped bruises and fingernail marks around her neck, her heart was full of coagulated blood, and her lungs contained no water, proving that she had not drowned. Verdict: she had been strangled and dumped in the pond.

Within minutes, police found the prime suspect: James W. Bess, a villainous-looking married man who had been consorting with Mrs. Martin for a couple of years. He had been renting a cheap apartment over Reeder's Barbershop on East Main Street in order to carry out his affair with her. (I wonder if the mood was ever spoiled by a turn-of-the-century barbershop quartet crooning below.) Interest in Mr. Bess perked up when the police found that Mrs. Martin, a widow, recently had received an insurance payment of $225 when her house burned down—somehow Bess had had the foresight to remove her furniture to his apartment the night before her house caught fire—and Bess chose to keep $200 of the insurance money, despite Mrs. Martin's protests. Police interest in Mr. Bess increased exponentially when he was caught lying: he claimed he had not been with Mrs. Martin since Thursday, March 5, but witnesses had seen them riding in a buggy on Friday, March 6. An investigation showed that Bess had rented a buggy from a livery stable that night—not once, but twice. Caught in a tight spot, Bess first claimed he had not left town that night. His statement was proved untrue. He then confessed to renting the conveyance, but refused to say why. Finally, he stated that he had taken Mary Porter, not Mrs. Martin, for a ride in the buggy and said Mrs. Porter would come to the examining trial and prove his alibi. The police arrested Bess as a suspicious character, to the surprise of nobody.

Bess put on quite a show for reporters and other onlookers. He claimed that he had spent six months in an asylum. He "pulled and tore his hair in a fearful manner," according to one witness. "He said when he got excited he is desperate and dangerous." We may deduce what Bess was up to by a statement he made in his cell: "I am innocent of killing that woman. If I had killed her they could not convict me because I am crazy. I am not responsible." Yes, James Bess, who had functioned well enough in society to raise a large family and become a prominent and wealthy contractor, was laying ground for the good old tried-and-true insanity defense.

On March 12, the remains of poor Mrs. Martin were consigned to a lot in Lexington Cemetery. The more investigators searched, the worse things got for Bess. Despite his insistence on acting as his own lawyer, Mrs. Bess, perhaps sensing imminent disaster, hired attorney Samuel Tudor. She was willing to do more than that to protect her wayward mate: when police examined Bess's love nest over the barbershop, they found that Mrs. Bess had chopped several holes in the floor under the front window and even left the hatchet there. A detective asked Mrs. Bess about her peculiar ideas concerning apartment renovation, but would not divulge to reporters what she told him. Worse for Bess, hairpins, a hatpin, and a clump of hair were found in the buggy he had rented.

When the examining trial was held on March 17, the fabled Mrs. Mary Porter did not show up, contrary to Bess's promise. The grand jury promptly indicted Bess and he was arraigned in Circuit Court the next morning. When he went to trial on March 24, he pled not guilty due to insanity. To make sure everyone got the point, he wrote a letter to a friend (which somehow fell into the hands of the press) in which he referred to himself as "crazy." A Lexington reporter who covered the trial observed: "Only during lulls in the proceedings did [Bess] display any of the symptoms of the 'spells' to which he says he is subject.... At all other times, there was not a more interested person in the courtroom."

For extra insurance, just in case he could not convince the court he was insane, Bess claimed physical disability: he said that he could account for his whereabouts on the day Mrs. Martin disappeared except for one hour; anyway, he was too "crippled" to have murdered her in his seedy apartment and disposed of the body in just one hour.

The trial got started in fine style. Medical experts testified that Mrs. Martin had been strangled rather than drowned. The defense tried to convince the jury that she had committed suicide—which amounted to a theory that she had somehow manually strangled herself and cast her own body into the pond after death.

W. M. McGinnis, an employee of George Horine's livery stable, identified Bess as the man who had rented a buggy around 8:00 p.m. on Friday, March 6. Bess had driven off with a woman, but returned alone two hours later, saying he needed to rent the buggy for longer as he wanted to go to Sandersville. He seemed so nervous and impatient that McGinnis became suspicious. He noticed that Bess did not drive in the direction of Sandersville when he left with the buggy. The prosecution's theory was that Bess had murdered his mistress in his apartment over the barbershop, then rented the buggy in order to dump her corpse in the pond. Bess knew the body would be found, but hoped it would be thought a suicide.

Mary Porter, whom Bess had claimed would provide him with an airtight alibi, took the stand on March 30. Instead, her testimony was extremely harmful to him. She swore that they had gone for a buggy ride on Wednesday night, not Friday. Worse, she provided two letters in Bess's handwriting, both of which had been delivered by his son, in which Bess begged her to lie and say they had gone for a ride in the country on Friday and that he had spent the night at her house. In one letter, Bess provided a detailed list of charmingly mundane activities he wanted her to claim they had done on Friday and he ended with the words, "Learn this by heart." The letters could not have been more incriminating if they had been written in Martha Martin's blood—and they also demonstrated vividly that Bess was crafty rather than insane. When under oath, Bess could not satisfactorily explain why he wrote the letters. Out of desperation, the defense produced a woman named Maud Hardin who they claimed—surprise!—was the woman who had gone for the celebrated buggy ride with Bess.

The next day, the defense lawyers sheepishly announced they would not put Hardin on the stand after all. The reason for their change of heart was made plain when the prosecution took the opportunity to swear Hardin in as a witness and she denied having gone riding with Bess on the night in question. It may have seemed to the casual observer that things could not have gone any worse for Bess, but he was a talented man in that regard. When called to the stand, Bess claimed he had had an appointment with a woman named Sallie Walker on the night of the murder. He described her in some detail: she weighed about 125 pounds, had a round face, and black hair. He could prove it, too, because he had received a letter from her! Commonwealth's Attorney Allen then revealed that there was no such woman; the letter had been written by Detective Harry Stough's daughter under a pseudonym in order to trick Bess into providing a sample of his handwriting. Bess stuck to his story, though his expression must have been somewhat lacking in confidence.

The case went to the jury the next day. Bess and his attorneys had no illusions as to the probable verdict.

April 1 was a fateful fool's holiday for two of this chapter's subjects. The Kentucky Court of Appeals had announced its decision concerning wife-murderer William McCarty on March 26: the judges found no fault with the lower court's decision and refused to order a new trial. Therefore, on April 1, Governor Beckham announced that McCarty would hang. Meanwhile, in Lexington on the same day, the jury decided that James W. Bess was guilty of murdering Martha Martin and should expiate the crime with his neck. Bess laughed, claimed he was innocent, and said he would have no trouble sleeping. His attorneys filed a motion for a new trial.

Governor Beckham was reluctant to announce a date for William

McCarty's execution because a new development had arisen: McCarty was deathly ill with tuberculosis. (Perhaps the disease was the cause of the coughing fit that had led to McCarty's arrest as he hid under the porch.) The jailers brought in Dr. S. L. Helm to care for the patient. Undoubtedly, anti-death penalty zealots perceived irony in the situation, as they always do. Imagine, the State carefully nursing a man back to health with the object of putting him to death once he got well! If the zealots thought this, they did not stop to consider that there were perfectly logical reasons for tending to the condemned man: if left untreated, his contagious illness could have spread and afflicted innocent people, including prisoners not sentenced to die. One might ask which is the more humane action: easing McCarty's pain in preparation for a quick death on the gallows, or allowing him to suffer a slow, drawn-out death by consumption.

On April 3, James Bess was placed in a large steel cage in the Lexington jail. This event marks the moment when the histories of our murderers interconnected, because now they were all confined in the same place at the same time. Having four condemned men in jail at once was a new record for Fayette County. Bess made friends instantly with O'Brien and Whitney—at least, at first. For reasons never fully explained, O'Brien and Bess quickly developed a mutual loathing for each other which lasted until Death arrived on swift, silent wings. At one point, Bess threw a bottle at O'Brien's head. The bottle missed its target, hit a steel bar, and sent a shower of glass flying throughout the cell. Some time later, Bess made himself obnoxious by alternately crying, grinning like an idiot, and picking at his trousers. He claimed someone was trying to poison him. Once, he ripped a towel to pieces and said the shreds were paper currency. The skeptical prison doctor suggested these silly deeds were part of Bess's plan to feign insanity. Jailer Wallace, who would soon prove to be very kind to Claude O'Brien's mother, finally had enough of Bess's shenanigans and told him that if he didn't become sane very quickly, he would be strapped to a barrel and whipped. It was not an enlightened approach by our standards, but it was nonetheless effective: Bess's hallucinations instantly ceased and he became a model prisoner.

April 10 brought news suggesting that Bess had better learn to get along with his cellmates: Judge Parker of the Circuit Court refused to grant him a new trial and set June 12 as his execution date.

William McCarty's elderly mother, Josephine, died in Lexington on May 9 after a long illness, unaware that her son was to be executed on the 15th. (Physicians had kept the news from her, fearing the shock might prove fatal.) A petition was sent to Governor Beckham, asking that the sadistic wife-beating murderer's life be spared. The governor refused to consider it.

The *Louisville Courier-Journal* ran a story a week before McCarty's scheduled execution headlined "McCarty Preparing for Death"—and so he was, but not in the way everyone expected. On the night of May 14, McCarty went to bed and slept soundly for a man who was to be hanged in the morning—far too soundly. As dawn came, prison officials found McCarty impossible to stir. They realized he had somehow poisoned himself during the night. He had been scheduled to hang at 8 a.m. and he died of his overdose at 8:22, so he managed to extend his life by twenty-two minutes, all of which he spent asleep. An autopsy revealed the presence of morphine and cocaine. No one was certain how McCarty had managed to get the drugs, but suspicion fell on Alexander McKeever—a prison employee who had served as the death watch—who was a friend and former schoolmate of McCarty. McKeever denied all, but ignored a subpoena and failed to turn up at the official investigation. He left town on the double and was last seen on a horse car headed for Latonia, KY.

O'Brien and Whitney, having been sentenced to death by the Circuit Court, had better luck with two other courts: the Court of Appeals, which had agreed to consider their cases and make a decision in April 1903—resulting in a stay of execution for the boys—and the Court of Public Opinion. Petitions circulated on behalf of the killers. Many signers were convinced the two youths would somehow make amends for their deed if only their lives were spared, just as in recent times a certain element wanted to save serial killer John Wayne Gacy from the electric chair on the grounds that his ugly paintings of clowns demonstrated that he was capable of "giving something back to society."

Of course, people have different ideas of what constitutes "giving something back to society." A physician in New York, Dr. Justin DeLisle, took an interest in the O'Brien-Whitney murder case and suggested that the lads could help pay for their crime by allowing themselves to be used as human guinea pigs. His idea was that Drs. Bullock and Blue of Lexington should inoculate the prisoners with disease germs and study the results. Jailer Robert Wallace refused permission, possibly because O'Brien's widowed mother, Mrs. E. C. O'Brien of Memphis, sent a letter threatening to sue the county for damages if the experiments were performed. She added that the doctors in question ought to experiment on themselves.

Some people were not content to sign pieces of paper on behalf of the boy tramps. Jailer Wallace grew suspicious of a parcel of newspapers which had been sent to O'Brien. Upon inspecting them he found that someone had hidden within the papers eleven saws of varying sizes—an example of real life imitating the cartoons. O'Brien also receieved a lengthy letter, allegedly written by his mother, which planned out an escape for him and even offered advice on how to conduct himself once he managed to leave town. O'Brien denied knowing that the package had contained saws and his mother denied sending it. (It may have been sent by a certain local girl who had a crush on the prisoner.) Jailhouse officials remembered how William McCarty had pleaded with them to allow O'Brien to bunk in the same cell with him. It was widely suspected that one of the people "on the outside" who had arranged sending the saws was a friend of McCarty's and that McCarty and O'Brien had intended to break out together. Somehow it did not occur to them that all of their incoming and outgoing mail would be scrutinized.

While awaiting the all-important decision from the Court of Appeals, O'Brien came down with typhoid and had to be removed from the company of Whitney and Bess in the steel cage. He was taken to convalesce in the cell occupied by the recently self-dispatched William McCarty.

The promised decision by the Court of Appeals was announced on May 20, 1903, after nearly a month of pleadings from the attorneys of O'Brien and Whitney, who argued that the boys deserved a new trial because of errors made by the lower court. Nevertheless, the Appellate Court affirmed the rulings of the Fayette County Circuit Court. The attorneys had argued that the burglaries the boys had committed around town just before the murder were inadmissible as evidence, but the Court of Appeals sensibly ruled that information about the burglaries showed O'Brien and Whitney's motives for entering Chinn's house and also provided a means of identifying for the jury the pistols used in the commission of the crime. As for the alleged drunkenness of Claude O'Brien's lawyer, the higher court wondered why the attorneys failed to have the matter appear in the official record and did not complain to the lower court until making their motion for a new trial. Under Kentucky's Criminal Code, if such a seemingly critical error were mentioned for the first time only in a motion for a new trial, the Appellate Court was not obligated to consider it. Earl Whitney's attorneys tried in vain to argue that his freely given confession should not have been used as evidence. Worst of all—at least from the viewpoint of O'Brien and Whitney—the judges ruled unanimously that the atrocity of Chinn's murder warranted nothing less than the ultimate penalty.

The boys went back to jail. There was a new flurry of petitions, including one started in Memphis by the pathetic Mrs. O'Brien. The summer of 1903 saw the beleaguered mother making plans to visit Kentucky. She had two objectives: one was to present a petition to Governor Beckham and have her son's sentence commuted to life in prison; the other was to see her Claude for the final time in case her efforts failed. Friends had to raise money for her traveling expenses since she lived in poverty. Perhaps she would have been more affluent had Claude stayed at home, worked an honest job, and helped support her, rather than tramping about the country, burglarizing people, and assassinating the occasional elderly merchant.

Mrs. O'Brien arrived in Lexington on June 15. Jailer Wallace met her at the train and arranged for her to stay at a boardinghouse close to the jail so she would not have to take long walks to see her condemned son. However, his kindness had limits: he had learned a hard lesson from William McCarty, who had cheated justice with a little help from his friends, and made a rule that Mrs. O'Brien would not be allowed to kiss or touch her son. The jailer's steely resolve did not last long when he saw the affecting reunion between loyal mother and reprobate son. He permitted them to embrace—but only under the closest imaginable supervision. While in town, Mrs. O'Brien circulated a new petition among the locals for a commutation of her son's sentence. No doubt the Lexingtonians felt a pang for the bereaved mother, but the unpopularity of her son's actions may be gauged by the fact that after a day's work she managed to collect only eighteen signatures.

Mrs. O'Brien's hopes were shaken five days after her arrival when the Appellate Court overruled a petition calling for a rehearing of the Chinn murder case. Nevertheless, Governor Beckham agreed to meet her at his home in Frankfort and listen to her plea, though the papers noted that it was unlikely in the extreme that he would change his mind—only three days before Mrs. O'Brien met with Beckham, he had officially declared that the two boys would hang on July 24. When she met the governor, she made a heartrending speech urging him to reconsider. She admitted the crime was heinous, but it had been unpremeditated; her son deserved punishment, but "punishment tempered with mercy" in order that he might repent. Additionally, she claimed that her son had inherited insanity from his father—an argument which even his own lawyers had not dared make. This fact casts doubt on her assertion; when has a defense attorney ever failed to clutch at even the feeblest excuse to claim his murdering client is insane? Governor Beckham was sympathetic, but did not offer the mother any false hopes.

On July 7, Beckham did exactly what everyone but the most starry-eyed optimists expected: he declined to commute the boy tramps' sentences. Still, while there was life there was hope. O'Brien and Whitney continued to pin the killing of Chinn on each other just in case the governor changed his mind. Earl Whitney must have figured that if O'Brien's relatives could get a private audience with the governor, then why not his? About a week after Mrs. O'Brien's meeting with Beckham, the governor met Mrs. Abbey M. Hagan and Mrs. Ole Rothfeldt—Whitney's aunt and sister, respectively—who made a point of referring to the eighteen-year-old Whitney as a "boy" in the governor's presence. They said that he had a streak of hereditary insanity—which somehow nobody had noticed up until now—and claimed to have proof that the young man's mother had gone insane, been confined to an asylum, escaped, and had never been heard from since. (Of the four murderers who are the focus of this chapter, only McCarty failed to try the old insanity dodge.) Also, they stated that Whitney's father had died only five years before. This information was especially interesting, since Whitney had claimed on several occasions that both of his parents had been dead for many years and he had never mentioned any insanity in his family.

Whitney's relatives, like O'Brien's, had been busy circulating petitions; they managed to convince Governor McMillin of Tennessee to sign. Beckham gently told the ladies the same thing he had told O'Brien's mother: as far as he was concerned, the case was closed unless some striking new evidence surfaced before execution day. He added that if they filed the papers on time they could get the Fayette County sheriff to convene a jury and have an insanity hearing. Perhaps tellingly, they appear not to have done so despite their former vehement assertions concerning Whitney's abnormal mental condition.

The efforts made by the boys' relatives on their behalf were truly touching—but then they went too far. On July 8, prison officials searched O'Brien's cell and found six more saws; three were in his pillow and three were hidden at the bottom of a stationery box. It was not certain that the prisoners' relatives had sneaked them into the jail—their every movement had been watched by the lynx-eyed jailer, who was still on guard after William McCarty's suicide—but to be cautious, Mrs. O'Brien was not given a second's privacy when she said her final farewell to her son on July 9, an event notable for the lack of emotion on both sides. "I have resigned everything to God," said the forlorn mother. Before she left Lexington, Mrs. O'Brien took an opportunity to visit the widow of the man her son had murdered, to seek her forgiveness for the crime. When she arrived, she was told Mrs. Chinn was not at home.

Despite the petitions urging the governor to show Claude O'Brien the mercy that O'Brien had denied his victim, a drive was started in Memphis by more realistic persons to raise funds to have his body shipped back home for burial. Three days before the hanging, it was noted that the two criminals were not as devil-may-care as they formerly had been. They seemed nervous and spent much time finding solace in Scripture. Right up to the end, Governor Beckham was inundated with letters asking for clemency for the murderers, mostly on account of their youth. (The true crime aficionado is reminded of the Leopold-Loeb case of 1924, in which the renowned attorney Clarence Darrow urged the court to spare his two clients, who had committed the atrocious thrill-killing of a fourteen-year-old boy in Chicago, on account of their youth. No one was more surprised than the killers themselves when Darrow's sentimental drivel won the day. Leopold allegedly quipped that it would have saved taxpayers a lot of money if the judge had simply asked to see their birth certificates instead of holding a trial.)

Gradually, O'Brien and Whitney regained their composure—or at least pretended to. When Sheriff Wilkerson read the death warrant to them the day before the execution, they grinned and remarked: "Did you see how nervous that man was while he was reading that thing?" On July 24, as the morning birds filled the air with their sweet music, the murderous "boy tramps" were led from their cells. As they took their last walk, Claude O'Brien and fellow prisoner James Bess could not resist needling each other one final time. After Bess shouted out a goodbye, O'Brien remarked: "You will be next."

"I have some good evidence coming," retorted the ever-optimistic Bess.

The executions were carried out without incident. As was common in those days, the hanging was held in an enclosed jail yard, but hundreds of witnesses observed the festivities from trees and high buildings surrounding the yard. As also was the custom of the time, after the bodies were cut down they were enclosed in spiffy coffins and taken to nearby funeral homes, where any gawker off the street could come stare. In O'Brien's case, the morbidly curious were disappointed; his brother John left strict orders that no one but family was to see his remains. However, when Whitney's body arrived in Nashville it was put on display at his sister's house, which was soon "packed to suffocation" by a steady stream of 1,500 people who wanted a look-see.

The final word in the sordid O'Brien-Whitney affair came from O'Brien's pugnacious brother, John, who stayed in Lexington for a few days after the hanging. In a classic "blame the victim" moment, he gave an interview in which he fumed that the nearly mortally wounded Asa Chinn was responsible for his brother's fate: "[John O'Brien] said Chinn killed his father and caused the boys to be hanged because he would not ask for a commutation of their sentences. He said he wanted revenge on three people in Lexington, of whom Asa Chinn is one." In order to nip conspiracy theories in the bud, it should be noted that Asa Chinn shot at his father's attackers with a .38 caliber pistol; a bullet from a .38 was indeed found in the elder Chinn's body, but though the caliber was the same it had a different type of shell than the bullets in Asa's gun. John O'Brien also tried and failed to locate Governor Beckham. He had longed to give Beckham a thrashing for doing his duty.

Although Judge Parker had refused to grant James Bess a new trial, in December 1903 his attorneys convinced the Court of Appeals to reverse the lower court's verdict due to errors made in instructing the jury and for refusing to admit as evidence "certain statements of Mrs. Martin." Bess's new trial began on March 8, 1904. He was confident that he would be acquitted this time around, not least of all because two witnesses had died since the first trial.

He had learned nothing from his mistakes of the past. At the first trial, Bess had been humiliated when Mary Porter showed the letters he had written to her, urging her to lie in order to support his alibi. At the second trial, Mrs. Porter revealed that while Bess was in prison, he had sent three letters in which he asked her to get her son to lie under oath that he had seen Martha Martin riding with another man the day she was murdered. When Mrs. Porter visited Bess in jail, he made the same desperate request in person. The Commonwealth had possession of the letters and proved Mrs. Porter's statements were true. In the face of such evidence, it took the jury only twenty-seven minutes to reach a verdict: James Bess was found guilty and given the death sentence a second time. Judge Parker decreed that Bess would swing on May 27. Bess responded with a tirade in which he accused the Commonwealth's Attorney of "persecuting" him. He said nothing about the indefensible letters he had sent to Mrs. Porter, which had made the prosecutor's job so easy.

Bess's fight for life had only just begun. His attorneys made a motion for another new trial in March; they tried again in October. Their appeals bought some time for Bess, who tried to influence public opinion by cultivating the friendship of a local minister, Rev. W. H. Allen, to whom he proclaimed his innocence with eyes cast upward and hand on heart. "It is the consensus of opinion," remarked a newspaper correspondent, "that Bess is trying to impose upon the ministers, and through them arouse sympathy for himself. After vainly trying to deceive the officers by the insanity dodge and failing in this it is thought he is trying as a final resort to convince the ministers that he is innocent and truly repentant for any misdeed he may have committed in the past, and secure their influence for his release."

On October 27, the Appellate Court ruled that Bess had been given a fair trial—two, in fact. His attorneys then drew the last arrow in their legal quiver: a plea for the governor to commute the sentence to life in prison. Naturally, they tried to prove that the public's heart had a soft spot for James Bess by sending petitions, no doubt largely signed by folk who will sign anything just to know the joy of feeling important for a moment. However, Mrs. Bess was unable to collect more than forty-nine signatures for her husband's cause; Bess's own brother, Thomas, refused to sign. The petitions were a useless exercise anyway. Mr. Beckham was not one of those governors who takes lightly his duty to enforce the law, as he had proved when faced with similar demands from supporters of Claude O'Brien, Earl Whitney, and William McCarty.

Bess's motive for killing his mistress was never explained. Despite his wealth, most likely he murdered her for her money. She was known to have kept $1,500 hidden in her stocking and it was missing when her corpse was discovered. The reader will remember that Bess kept most of a $225 insurance payment made to Mrs. Martin when her house burned and the woman had appealed to the police to make him give it back. It is likely that Bess and Mrs. Martin committed arson for the insurance money and that he wanted to keep her from revealing his role in the fraud. In addition, Bess owed Mrs. Martin money. Whatever the motive, when Bess realized that the commutation was not forthcoming, he announced that he was satisfied and spent some time preparing a statement denying his guilt. He said he would "take his medicine like a man."

At last came the cold, dark morning of January 13, 1905, when the forty-eight-year-old widow-robber and strangler had to swallow that medicine. Jailer Wallace was surprised to find that Bess had been hiding a knife blade in his mouth. Bess confessed that he had intended to commit suicide with it but lost his nerve. After saying cheery goodbyes to officers, friends, and fellow prisoners, Bess walked with the guards to the gallows in the jail yard. (The same gallows had been used a week earlier to execute John Hathaway, the only professional jockey ever to be hanged for murder. I shall tell his story in a later volume.) Bess did not confess as he stood before what was reportedly one of the largest crowds ever seen in Lexington, but he made a speech cautioning his observers to stay away from whisky and bad company. Then came a short prayer. Bess took his quick and painless "medicine." All was over.

Perfect Monsters: _____
The Murders of Lillian Patrick and Mary Magdalene Pitts

We expect certain places to breed brutality and murder. No one was surprised when the poverty-stricken slums of Whitechapel, London, became the hunting grounds for Jack the Ripper; that the lawless American Wild West gave rise to killers such as John Wesley Hardin was only to be anticipated. Every now and then, however, a perfect monster will unexpectedly emerge from the most ordinary surroundings, leaving his law-abiding fellow citizens to wonder how such things can happen. Boyd County, KY, is as pleasant a place as one could imagine; yet for a time, it seemed to breed more than its share of authentic monsters. The details of the famous Ashland Tragedy are well-known and need not be repeated other than to state the barest facts of the case: on December 23, 1881, three citizens broke into a house where two teenage girls and a boy were staying alone. After sexually assaulting the girls, the men killed all three teenagers and set the house on fire. The men were soon apprehended and the events afterward—the successful lynching of one suspect, threatened lynchings for the other two, a state militia that ended up shooting several citizens in a mob, ridiculously protracted trials, and the eventual legal hangings of the two surviving killers— did little to improve Kentucky's national image. Memories of the Ashland Tragedy had not faded when, nearly twenty years later, the community again had to face the unfathomable.

In an eastern precinct of Catlettsburg called Hampton City there lived John Gibson, originally from Beaver Creek, Floyd County; his eighteen-year-old wife; her three-year-old daughter by a former marriage, name given as Lillian Patrick in some accounts and as

Lillian Rowern in others; Gibson's sixteen-year-old brother, Henry; and a baby just two weeks old. In late November 1900, an anonymous person informed the city health officer, Dr. J. D. Williams, that the Gibson stepdaughter seemed to be suffering from smallpox. When Dr. Williams went to the Gibson house to investigate, he found little Lillian dying, but not of smallpox. Her back was broken and she had been burned repeatedly for at least two months, which the doctor judged by the fact that some of the burns were nearly healed. She bore the marks of dozens of burns on her head, face, and body, some so severe that strips of flesh were gone. She had fresh burns around the nose and mouth. Looking about, Dr. Williams noticed a red hot poker on the hearth. He also saw Mrs. Gibson and young Henry Gibson, both of whom seemed too terrified to speak. One thing Dr. Williams did not see was John Gibson himself, who had fled the house just as the physician arrived, without even taking his hat and coat. Williams knew what had happened and who was to blame. He immediately informed the coroner and Chief of Police Yost, but it was too late. Gibson had fled into the chill autumn night for parts unknown. Before leaving town, he set fire to the home of a widow named Curtis who lived two houses away, most likely in an effort to create a distraction.

Yost immediately deputized thirty men who set out in all directions searching for Gibson. By the next day, no fewer than three posses were on the manhunt. They found no trace of him, but thought that he must have found a hiding place, since he had not had sufficient time to flee the county. It was imperative that the law find him before the lynch mobs did. At the same time that the child's funeral took place at Ceredo, heavily-armed Boyd Countians competed with the posses and the talk was that if the mob found Gibson first, it would burn him alive at the stake—a threat that not even the reviled perpetrators of the Ashland Tragedy had faced.

Gibson was an unusually good hider. Bulletins came day after day announcing that he had been caught, or almost had been caught, or had been spotted here or there, yet he never seemed to be captured.

The law searched in Floyd County, just in case he had managed to give them the slip. Gibson formerly had been a brakeman on the Norfolk and Western railroad and it was thought that he might have stolen a ride on a train. A Dr. J. M. Logan, who knew Gibson, was certain he had seen the man heading for Wilson Creek, Carter County, where relatives lived. When this news reached Rush, a town straddling Boyd and Carter Counties, 150 coal miners ceased work for the day in order to search for the fugitive. It can be stated with certainty that they would have shortened his existence in some miserable fashion had they found him.

Others searched for Gibson in Greenup County, since he was a former resident of the town of Alcorn. On December 1, rumor held that Gibson had been caught and was imprisoned at Catlettsburg; hundreds of furious people came to the jail, not to sing Yuletide carols, and left quietly when the rumor proved untrue. The next day, an embarrassing moment came when Gibson was caught at Rush and placed under guard at the house of a man named Lust; Chief Yost and Sheriff Fields hurried to the town and seized the prisoner, but a controversy broke out as to who should get the reward money. While the parties argued, Gibson escaped. Some people blamed the aforementioned Dr. Logan, claiming that he knew all along where Gibson had been hiding, but had kept mum until a reward was offered. Meanwhile, men who were unfortunate enough to either resemble the fugitive or share his name were arrested in Maysville and Valley View, KY, and Corydon, IN. Gibson's wife and brother Henry refused to speak to the authorities at first. They had been forced to witness the toddler's repeated torture and were afraid Gibson would do the same to them if he had the chance. The boy did loosen up enough to inform a reporter that on the last morning of Lillian Patrick's life, Gibson had burned her and thrown her to the floor, muttering, "Now I guess you'll die."

One reliable sighting took place on December 2 when Gibson, armed with a rifle and two pistols, took a Sunday morning breakfast at the home of his friend Henry Haywood, who lived near Grayson, Carter County. When other witnesses saw him skulking about the county that day, heading for some abandoned coal mines, it was clear that his capture was imminent. The event came on December 5, when Griffith and John Davis made a citizens' arrest at the Iron Hill furnace. The authorities whisked Gibson off to Maysville as quickly as possible. They knew what would happen to him if they paused anywhere. (As they rode through the cold night, the jailer could not resist turning to Gibson and quipping, "I'm freezing to keep you from roasting.") Once they had arrived at the jail, the other prisoners were not delighted with his company. They feared they might be lynched by accident when the anticipated crowd came to get Gibson. The lawmen spread a false rumor that he had been taken to Ashland and a mob of 300 went there—no doubt intending to offer him the keys to the city. The feeling in Catlettsburg was that Gibson would be soundly, thoroughly, and comprehensively lynched the moment he was brought back for trial.

While in the Maysville jail, Gibson was at first communicative, perhaps too much for his own good; a *Louisville Courier-Journal* reporter noted that "some one must have told him he was talking too much, for later in the morning he lost the use of his tongue and since then will hardly let a caller get a glimpse of him, much less have any conversation." He avoided onlookers by hiding under his blanket, not unlike a frightened child. He answered all questions by saying only that he wanted a fair trial. Given the mass of evidence against him, the cruelty of his crime, and his flight from justice, he more logically might have hoped for an unfair trial. In addition to all of the other reasons to dislike him, reporters discovered that Gibson had deserted from the Fourth Kentucky Regiment during the Spanish-American War. Today, a clever defense attorney might claim that the horrors of war had sparked a post-traumatic stress disorder in Gibson, causing him to mercilessly torment his stepdaughter—so, jury, let the poor, persecuted man go!—but an equally clever prosecutor would point out that it is doubtful Gibson ever saw battlefield action, having deserted at Anniston, AL.

Deep inside, we have a psychological need to believe that good people are naturally beautiful and evil people are correspondingly as hideous as the deeds they perform. It is nearly impossible to abandon this ingrained fairy-tale way of seeing the world despite real-life experience to the contrary—for if only all evil people were ugly, it would be a simple matter to avoid them and the snares they lay for us. No doubt people in the year 1900 were surprised and disappointed to find that John Gibson was a perfectly normal and even pleasant-looking fellow. Similarly, many persons—including law enforcement officials who should have known better—found it hard to believe, decades later, that Ted Bundy was a serial killer just because he didn't "look like a murderer."

By the second day of his imprisonment, Gibson no longer denied his identity, but refused to speak of his inhuman crime. When asked why he ran away from his house as the doctor examined Lillian Patrick's burned remains, he explained that he fled not because he was guilty, but because he thought it better to go into hiding until he could clear his name. Such logic would be appropriate for the stock character of the Innocent Man Accused so beloved to writers of fiction—i.e., the classic television show *The Fugitive*—but in real life, innocent persons accused of an atrocious crime seldom take it on the lam and do their own detective work.

When Gibson went to trial in Catlettsburg at the end of January 1901, County Attorney Frank Bruning confidently promised a conviction for first-degree murder. There was some debate as to whether Gibson should be brought to town with a military escort, but in the end it was decided that the mob spirit had diminished. Just to be safe, Judge Kinner vowed that if Gibson were lynched, he would indict every member of the mob "if he had to impanel a grand jury and continue court indefinitely." The warning had a salutary effect and Gibson was left alone.

Henry Gibson, who had been too scared to speak out before, was terrified no longer. Under oath, he told of witnessing John burning Lillian Patrick with a hot poker, kicking her outside, and hitting her head with firewood. "Why did you not tell this to someone before?" asked the defense attorney, who undoubtedly did not appreciate Henry's answer: "Because John told me he would kill me." Witnesses noticed that when Henry testified, the defendant looked scared for the first time.

When John Gibson took the stand, he shifted all the blame on others by saying that he had never done a moment's harm to the child, but instead had seen his wife beat her with a stick and his brother Henry slap her. He came up with a new reason for his sudden flight from the law: he had been afraid he would catch smallpox from the girl (who, of course, did not have smallpox at all). The fact that he had left just after Dr. Williams arrived and started examining the girl's injuries was just a wild coincidence. The defense brought in a character witness, John Gruber of Rush, who attested to the defendant's good public reputation—although the way a man behaves in public and the way he behaves in private may be two different matters.

On February 1, the jury announced a verdict so appallingly weak that many took it to be a final injury to Lillian Patrick: the members found Gibson guilty of one of the worst crimes in Boyd County history, and against a three-year-old child at that, but merely sentenced him to life in prison. "A murmur of disapproval of the verdict could be heard from the crowd which thronged the courtroom," wrote a reporter. "Gibson was hurried back to jail by the officers, and he was met on every side by dark looks and mutterings of dissent." The *Louisville Courier-Journal*'s editorial page captured the public's mood by calling the verdict "inexplicable," and remarking: "[T]he punishment of death would have inevitably followed had it not been for that sentiment which…encourages Governors to refuse to sign the death sentence of murderers. Few juries can be got together on which there are not two or three men of such wavering convictions as hardly to be persuaded to obey the plain letter of the law in any case." The editorial writer concluded that wimpy compromises were to be expected as long as juries, not judges, determined punishment as well as guilt.

The next day, the prison doors clanged shut behind Gibson— forever, in theory. I have been unable to find out if the sentence was carried out in fact, but it does not require much imagination to picture a soft-hearted judge, several years down the road, allowing an aging or sick Gibson a pardon due to exemplary behavior. The last statement the child-torturer and killer made before reporters was an invidious remark about the courage of the locals. Sheriff Fields remarked to Gibson that he was lucky he didn't get lynched, to which the convict said: "It takes nerve to lynch a man and the people of Catlettsburg have not got it." He said that as if it were a bad thing.

Gibson's motive for the dreadful abuse and murder was never fully understood. We are left with a fact, a theory, and a flaw: the fact is that he had insured the child for $100 a few days before the murder; the theory is that he thought if he burned the child, he could fool the medical authorities into thinking she had died of smallpox and then could collect the loot; the flaw in the theory is that Dr. Williams's examination proved that Gibson had burned Lillian Patrick for many, many weeks before he finished her off.

Perhaps the people in that section of eastern Kentucky thought that with the close of the Gibson trial, they had seen the ultimate in the horrors of child abuse. Then, a generation later and in a neighboring county, came the still-notorious case of Mary Magdalene Pitts.

The sordid story began with the heroic actions of Dr. George K. Woods, a country physician who lived in Greenup County. Four days after Christmas 1927, he was awakened by frantic pounding on the door of his cabin home. When Dr. Woods stepped outside, he found two boys from a neighboring family, Hernden and Hubert Pitts, crying that their little sister Mary was dead. The doctor followed them to their cabin near Argilite, on the McCoy branch of Culp Creek, where he found a tiny body covered with a sheet. Nearby stood Marie B. Frazier, the Pitts family's thirty-two-year-old housekeeper. Dr. Woods noted her lack of emotion.

In a moment eerily similar to the earlier Lillian Patrick case, when the physician removed the sheet, he found that the beautiful blonde child, three-year-old Mary Magdalene Pitts, was covered with scars, bruises, burns, and other injuries, including a hole in her head. She clearly had been dead for several hours. Dr. Woods turned to Marie

Frazier and demanded an explanation: "What happened to her?"

"I don't know," responded Frazier as nonchalantly as if the child merely had a cold. "But she wanted water a lot."

Dr. Woods, knowing a case of child abuse and neglect when he saw one, went to the authorities in Greenup town. The next day, the police and the coroner went to the Pitts house and arrested Marie Frazier just as the family was about to hold a funeral service for little Mary in their yard. "She wanted water all the time. We did all we could to save her," Frazier protested as the police led her away. She did not help her case when she vowed: "I'll kill that coroner before we get to Greenup!"

A few days later, the police also took into custody the girl's father, thirty-five-year-old Robert H. Pitts, a native of Estill County who was in the habit of disciplining his child with willow switches, pokers, razor strops, or whatever blunt objects happened to be handy. The coroner had by this time examined Mary's body and her death certificate did not mince words or fail to name names: "The cause of death was as follows: Probably shock resulting from burns, bruises and cuts administered by father and housekeeper, Marie Frazier. Probably homicide. Contributory [cause]: Exposure to cold without proper clothing."

The autopsy revealed that the small girl had received a hard blow to the kidney and apparently had been forced to eat pepper—which might have been the cause of the thirst noted by Marie Frazier. Rumor held that Mary also had been poisoned, but chemical analysts found no traces of deadly substances. She had received so many injuries that medical experts never determined the precise cause of death, though some thought it was a blow to the head. Funeral director L. G. Stapf wrote:

> I have been a licensed embalmer since 1913 and have never seen a body in such shape. To my mind this is the most brutal and horrible murder that could be committed. A helpless, defenseless baby murdered by the people to whom it should have looked for protection. No wonder the community is aroused. No wonder the people talk of lynching.

When Pitts and Frazier faced the grand jury, the judge refused the defense's motion to allow them bond. It might have been a suicidal act if the two defendants had been permitted to step out onto the street: citizens had been unaware of Mary's plight while she was alive and suffering, but now they were determined to make the perpetrators pay for their crimes, preferably not in a legal fashion. An infuriated crowd gathered outside the heavily guarded Greenup County jail. By January 5, 1928, the crowd had become so ugly that the police slipped Pitts and Frazier from the jail and took them far away to Winchester, Clark County. No doubt the prisoners wondered along the way what a merciless beating might feel like.

Once safely hidden in Winchester, Robert Pitts and Marie Frazier developed a mania for writing self-aggrandizing confessions in which they made blaming each other an art form. They also released so many different versions of "what had actually happened" to Mary Magdalene Pitts that one almost needs a scorecard to keep up. On January 9, Mrs. Frazier told a *Lexington Herald* reporter that she was guilty of nothing worse than holding poor little Mary in her arms as she died from the effects of a whipping her brutish father had administered. Pitts countered by saying that his daughter was already dead when he arrived home from his job at the American Rolling Mills in Ashland on December 29, "and that [she] showed signs of having received a severe beating"—the inference being that someone else must have done it.

Shortly thereafter, the Clark County jailer found a written confession in Pitts's pocket. Strangely, the varied penmanship on the paper suggested that two or three people had collaborated on it. Much of the confession was unprintable in family newspapers. In it, Pitts (or whoever actually wrote it) made his household sound like something out of the ravings of the Marquis de Sade. He claimed that Mrs. Frazier had killed Mary by rubbing her back with salt and turpentine after whipping her. He also accused her of trying to hang the little girl upside down by her feet and of being so jealous that she would not allow Mary to kiss her own father. And why had Robert Pitts stood aside and knowingly allowed the housekeeper to abuse his daughter? Well, he hadn't, according to the confession; in fact, just a couple of weeks ago, the noble father had slapped Marie Frazier and whipped her with a switch to give her a taste of her own violent medicine. Matters could not have been too bad between Pitts and his housekeeper, however, since a censored paragraph concerned "intimate relations between Pitts and the Frazier woman," according to the *Lexington Herald*. Both prisoners asked for, and received, stationery and pens so they could continue their literary war against each other.

Mrs. Frazier—who had called the child "Hellcat" and (sarcastically, one assumes) "the Queen of Sheba"—went on the defensive by writing a new confession in which she depicted herself as Mary's true friend and protector. She tried to explain away the burns on the girl's body by stating that her dress had caught fire not long before she died. Pitts replied that Frazier had poisoned the child with the disinfectant potassium permanganate, which had caused her to die of thirst. Mrs. Frazier admitted that Mary had been so thirsty just before her death that she had drunk cup after cup of creek water, but Pitts's charge was seemingly refuted by the autopsy, which had turned up no traces of poison. The two continued to scribble attacks upon each other by the hour, causing Assistant Jailer J. J. Hammond to remark to a reporter on January 10: "They might be through with the confessions by the morning, but I can't tell." By noon of the next day, the prolix jailbirds had stopped writing—for the time being—but said they would not hand over their newest confessions to the authorities yet, because they wanted to "finish them first."

In the meanwhile, reporters found Mary Magdalene Pitts's mother, Lucy Walker Green, who lived with her brother-in-law, Robert Estep, in a houseboat on the Kentucky River near Boonesborough, Madison County. (The press called her "Mrs. Pitts" and referred to her as being Robert Pitts's second wife, although in fact the two never had been legally married.) Mrs. Green accomplished the impossible by making Robert Pitts seem even more of an unsympathetic blackguard than ever before. She had left him in June 1927 after she could tolerate his abuse no longer. She had tried to take daughter Mary with her, but Robert demanded that the girl stay and emphasized his point by firing a few shots at his fleeing ex. The grieving mother believed that Robert Pitts had murdered their daughter out of spite, since she would not return to his loving arms. When Madison Countians realized that the mother of the abused child was in their midst, they took up a collection so she could travel to Greenup County and attend her daughter's funeral, which had not yet been held due to the outpouring of grief from the public when the details of the child's pitiable life and death were revealed. At least five thousand people—some say it was closer to ten thousand— paid their respects at the L. G. Stapf Funeral Home, where Mary's body lay in state for several days. Mourners came from as far away as Ohio, Virginia, West Virginia, Indiana, Pennsylvania, Tennessee, Michigan, and Illinois to pay tribute to the small victim. Her funeral was held on January 15 and so many people were present that services had to be held on the courthouse lawn. Even newsreel cameramen were present. Thousands solemnly passed the open casket—which was placed in a bandstand—to gaze for the last time upon the girl's calm features. In a searingly poignant touch, she held her only doll. At the end of the day, a group of small girls acted as her pallbearers at Riverview Cemetery. One account describes the scene: "Other children carried the array of floral tributes. Hundreds followed the line of march. Mary Magdalene, who knew only hardship and suffering, was borne to her grave like a modern Cinderella." Citizens purchased a burial plot and later erected a statue of a small angel. The base reads: "Cruelly Murdered."

The new confessions/accusations of Robert Pitts and Marie Frazier were released on January 13 to a skeptical audience and received scathing reviews from their many, many critics. The authors belabored themes they had already explored: both maintained their utter innocence—heroism, even—while blaming the other for the child's torturous death. This time, Mrs. Frazier added that Pitts had struck his daughter's head with a poker the night before she died. For his part, Pitts produced a statement in which he named twenty-four men who he claimed had been intimate with his decidedly unattractive and hatchet-faced housekeeper. Perhaps he was attempting to imply that any one of those two dozen men could have abused and murdered his daughter. Soon afterwards, he issued a statement in which he continued to pin the murder on his housekeeper, but said that he "had agreed to the crime" after the villainess got him doped up. Mrs. Frazier was not about to take that lying down and she released a hastily written statement in which she accused Pitts of a previously undetected second murder, that of a twenty-month-old son. She ended her fourth confession to date with a cry from the heart that she was "worried to death" and did not want "to be bothered with any more questions." (If that were the case, perhaps she should have ceased writing sensational confessions that were guaranteed to draw the attention of law enforcement officials and the media.) Nothing more was said of the charge, so we may assume it was vindictive nonsense.

Then, Pitts broke new ground by contradicting not Mrs. Frazier, but himself. He flatly denied the report that he had ever agreed to the housekeeper's plan to kill his daughter; he haughtily labeled the statement—which he had made himself—"fictitious." Pitts and Frazier had released so many conflicting stories that the authorities no longer placed credence in anything they said. Perhaps their strategy was to baffle everyone so badly that the legal system would acquit them out of sheer confusion. To give him the tiniest modicum of credit, Pitts finally did make a partial confession of his guilt. He affirmed that he had, on occasion, beaten his tiny daughter—but, he protested, never with anything larger than a switch "about fifteen inches long and not more than three at a time." You know, lest anyone get the wrong idea about him. In addition, he vowed that he had not thus reprimanded Mary since Christmas Day!

In mid-January, the grand jury in Greenup County adjourned after speaking with twenty-eight witnesses, including Mary Magdalene Pitts's four half-brothers and half-sisters. At last, far too late, Pitts and Frazier saw the wisdom in keeping their mouths shut and ceased writing their endless confessions and counter-confessions.

The damage had been done, not that there was much serious doubt about their guilt anyway. The grand jury indicted them jointly and on January 22, they were taken to the last place on earth they wanted to go: back to Greenup County, where they would have their examining trial. Mrs. Frazier begged the officers to save her from the howling mobs which she expected to deal with her in a manner not unlike the way she had treated Mary Pitts.

She had good reason to be worried. Sheriff Edward Tinsley stated that feelings were still running so high there that authorities considered whisking Pitts and Frazier back to Clark County after the examining trial. Defense attorneys asked for a change of venue on the grounds that their clients could not get an unbiased jury in Greenup—plus, they might end up with elongated necks and have to undergo the annoyance of purchasing new collars. To the relief of Pitts, Frazier, and their attorneys, Judge William C. Halbert decided to postpone the trial until the next term of court. As a compromise, the judge agreed to transfer the trial to Lewis County, the county adjoining Greenup.

Robert Pitts and Marie Frazier were to be tried separately. Frazier's trial came first, and began in Vanceburg on a Leap Year Day: February 29, 1928. A rumor spread that she was pregnant. Perhaps someone started the rumor to earn a shred of public sympathy for the baby-torturer, but a couple of doctors examined Frazier and revealed that the report was untrue. On March 1, Frazier pled guilty against the advice of her counsel and, though she was somewhat lacking in the quality of mercy, she threw herself on the mercy of the court. It is unclear whether her long-dormant conscience troubled her or she simply thought that by pleading guilty she could avoid a date with the electric chair. The jury took Frazier's word for it and found her guilty as charged.

Within minutes of Frazier's departure from the courtroom, the trial of Robert Pitts commenced. Unlike Frazier, Pitts pled not guilty, an extraordinary act since he had made a partial confession. No doubt he felt—as has many a murderer—that where there are soft-hearted juries, sentimental judges, and defense lawyers who excel at clouding issues, there is hope. Unfortunately for Pitts, he faced a wise jury and a fair judge, and his attorneys had an uphill battle since his partner-in-crime already had been convicted. Worse, Mrs. Frazier was brought in as a witness against him. One might wonder how anyone could believe a word she said since she had spun so many contradictory yarns in the past, but her testimony was corroborated by Pitts's sons. She told many horrifying tales of the father's abuse of his daughter. Sometimes, said Mrs. Frazier, Pitts would hit the girl so long and so hard with a razor strop that he would sink to the floor from exhaustion and continue beating her from a sitting position. She maintained that Pitts had administered the fatal wound by hitting Mary over the head with a poker and her word seemed to be confirmed by a poker placed on exhibit. It was curved, suggesting that it had struck something with such force that the handle bent. The crook of the poker fit in a wound in the girl's head. Dr. A. S. Brady testified that the child's head wound was sufficient to cause death.

The jury also saw photos of the girl's many injuries. Funeral director L. G. Stapf provided a life-size drawing depicting the wounds he noticed on the corpse of the child when it was brought to him. The letter-writing habit Pitts had exhibited while in jail came back to haunt him: the prosecution displayed letters he had written to Mrs. Frazier in which he expressed the fear—not groundless as it turned out—that she would turn State's evidence. He had written, "Baby, I will have two men testify that [Assistant Jailer] Hammond forced me to tell what I did," and, "I will confess to three little switches. What you tell will clear me or convict me."

When Pitts took the stand, he did what he always had done: he blamed everything on Mrs. Frazier and said she was just a big old liar. He could not explain why he had not troubled to call a doctor when he allegedly came home from work on December 29, 1927, and found his daughter dead. Then Pitts's sons, thirteen-year-old Herden and eleven-year-old Hubert, took the stand. They told the court of having witnessed both their father and Mrs. Frazier abuse their baby half-sister thoroughly and often, just as the law suspected all along. The Commonwealth's Attorney said to Pitts: "You have not shown as much interest in your baby as you would a hound dog. A hound dog would have known how to care for himself. A hound dog would have bitten you or run away."

Today, of course, anytime a lowlife commits an infamous crime he can count on celebrities with time on their hands and air in their heads taking up his cause and arguing his case before the public. Such was the case with jailbird author Jack Henry Abbott—who murdered a waiter soon after the writer Norman Mailer got him released from prison, where he had been sent for forgery and for committing a previous homicide—and Bob Dylan's cause célèbre "Hurricane" Carter, and Tookie Williams, Hollywood's favorite gang leader, cold-blooded killer and author of children's books, to name only three. It is a wonder that a gaggle of movie stars did not take an interest in Pitts's plight and show up in court to plead on his behalf and try to get him released back into society, but perhaps most celebrities of the Twenties, unlike the ones of today, did not make a hobby of attempting to use their fame to thwart justice.

On March 3, both Pitts and Frazier got life sentences from their respective juries. Pitts's attorneys said they would not appeal; Mrs. Frazier expressed the hope that she might get paroled someday if she were a model prisoner. They began their sentences in Frankfort the next day. Justice was served—for a little while, anyway. Robert Pitts served only thirteen years of his putative life sentence and Marie Frazier was likewise paroled. He moved to Kansas City and she moved to Michigan. They knew better than to go back to Greenup County.

Every year, December 29 is celebrated—but that is hardly the correct word—as Mary Magdalene Pitts Day in Greenup. Christmastime seems an appropriate time of year to contemplate the eternal struggle of good versus evil—as represented on the former side by Mary and the law, and on the latter side by an abominably cruel woman and one of the worst fathers in the history of parenting. As the decades roll by, let it be remembered that in this case, at least, evil was punished—but only temporarily.

Hanging of the Mystery Tramp

On September 22, 1900, there was a murder among hoboes near Terre Haute, IN. Two brethren of the road named Vandeveer and James Hogue had stolen a ride on a Big Four freight train. Their excursion was ruined when two other tramps, John Owen and William Daily, tried to rob them at gunpoint. Though they were on a locomotive traveling at twenty miles per hour, Hogue and Vandeveer decided to lam it. Vandeveer somehow managed to escape; Hogue made it as far as the top of a boxcar. Owen pursued Hogue and shot him twice atop the train, accidentally shooting himself in the hand in the process, after which he threw the corpse over the side.

Vandeveer went to the authorities and gave a description of the two tramps. Owen and Daily were captured the next day in Maxville, IN. They were suspected of being the perpetrators of a very similar crime that had occurred on a Northwestern freight train at Algona, Kossuth County, IA, three weeks before the Hogue murder: two tramps had killed two railroad workers, stripped them of clothing and valuables, and tossed their bodies from the train.

When they stood trial, Daily received a sentence of forty years in the penitentiary at Chester, IL, since the murder of Hogue had occurred on the Illinois side of the state line. Owen, who had pulled the trigger, received the death penalty. He laughed at the judge when the sentence was passed. Owen was taken to the jail at Paris, IL, to await his last day, December 21, which by cosmic irony happened to be the shortest day of the year.

That should have been the end of the story, but it wasn't. When first arrested, Owen had claimed to be John Radcliffe, son of Joseph

Radcliffe of Philadelphia. This was quickly exposed as a lie. When taken to Paris, he admitted that he was really named John Owen. Jailhouse officials discovered that this was also false. The prisoner flatly refused to reveal his true identity. Naturally, word got out about the condemned man with the dashing, romantic secret and he received much press coverage. A general description went out over the wires: he was about forty years old, above average in height, and his hair and moustache were dark red. He had scars all over his body—the remnants of gunshot wounds. For the sake of convenience, the newspapers and jail officials continued to call him John Owen.

In the days before mandatory birth certificates, Social Security numbers, computerized national fingerprint databases, and DNA testing, a person who wanted to keep his identity an enigma had a good chance of succeeding. Nevertheless, a few clues about Owen leaked out, mostly due to his own self-aggrandizing chatter. A former Kentuckian who spoke with him found that they had many mutual friends in Mt. Sterling and Louisville. Owen finally confessed that he was a Kentuckian. Owen was not his real surname, he said, but he was related to the Owen family of Kentucky. To one person, he claimed to be from Bell County and said that his parents lived in Middlesboro. He said that he had been disowned by his family due to his outlaw ways and that when he had last seen them in 1895, they had cheated him out of some property. Nevertheless, he declared that his reluctance to disgrace his prominent family was his motive for keeping his identity secret.

He dropped another tantalizing hint by declaring that he was a graduate of Centre College in Danville, Boyle County. He proved that he was more polished than the average drifter by speaking in fluent German with a jailhouse visitor. Owen professed to have no fear of his imminent execution, explaining that he had a fatal stomach disorder and would have died within a year or two anyway. He cavalierly sold one of the tickets to his execution for ten dollars and gave the money to a favored cellmate named John Meece, with whom he got along since Meece was also from Kentucky.

During jailhouse conversations Owen claimed to have traveled in Europe and South America, "showing an intimate knowledge of countries and peoples." In frustration, officials contacted Owen's partner in crime, William Daily, but he was of no help in uncovering the truth. From solitary confinement, he claimed that he barely knew Owen and in fact had only recently met him before they committed their robbery-murder. (Daily was to serve considerably less than his sentence of forty years; he committed suicide before the year 1900 came to a close.)

As late as December 19, with his execution only three days away, Owen refused to give his real name. Despite his rough looks, Owen's pretensions to having had a good education seemed confirmed by the fact that he breezily quoted from the classics—not just to fellow prisoners, but also to the men who were building the scaffold outside his cell window. Only two men in Paris knew Owen's true identity: his cellmate Meece and his attorney, J. E. Dyas. Owen teased everyone by saying that he might instruct Meece or Dyas to reveal his name after the hanging; he claimed he had been writing his autobiography and would authorize Meece to release it postmortem. Other biographical details that Owen did not mind releasing to the public were that he never had been married and that he was an "infidel." He refused to see ministers who came to call, but the night before his hanging he spoke with Father Lee, a Catholic priest. Owen was friendly, but would neither speak on religious topics nor reveal his name. When Father Lee asked if he should return the next morning, Owen replied with a smile and classic gallows wit: "I guess not, Father. Tomorrow will be my busy day." Owen was similarly lighthearted with his attorney, Dyas, to whom he said words that will puzzle anti-capital punishment zealots: "I am better off than [my partner] Daily with his forty years' sentence. While it is true that he can get out in twenty years, he will not live to be a free man. If what I hear about him since he was taken to the penitentiary is true, that is that he has been punished by being placed in solitary confinement, he will not live a year. As for me, why, it will be over like that."

So saying, Owen snapped his fingers.

John Owen walked unsupported to the gallows on December 21. He seemed bemused rather than fearful. One of his final actions was to shake the hand of the sheriff's small son, whom he had befriended. When standing on the gallows, Owen let the sheriff know when he was ready to die by dropping a handkerchief. After he paid the ultimate penalty for his crimes, he was buried in the Paris cemetery.

Owen never lost his nerve. He also kept his promise and did not reveal his identity—at least, not in a direct way. One of the last things he did was hand Sheriff Myers a card reading: "T. H. Wolsam, Middlesboro, Ky." The condemned man said to the sheriff, "My home is six miles southeast of Middlesboro; that explains all that is necessary." Some thought that Wolsam must be Owen's father.

However, Owen was full of lies and red herrings right to his last minute. There seemed to be no end of surprises from this surprising man. The only "T. H. Wolsam" who could be found lived not in Middlesboro, but near Wellsburg, TN. He was not related to Owen. The convict had also lied about never being married. Dr. L. Sproule of Williamsburg, Whitley County, stepped to the fore and related that Owen had married his sister-in-law in Pineville, Bell County, in 1888 but proved a less than ideal husband—abandoning her and robbing her of $1,000 only two months after the nuptials. The woman died in December 1892, some said of grief. Dr. Sproule related details about Owen's past that he had heard from the mystery man's own lips, details that were farfetched to the extreme and sounded as though they had come from a dime novel. They contradicted everything else that was thought to be known about Owen. According to the doctor, Owen claimed that he had been born in Missouri; that he had run away from an abusive stepmother while a youth; that he had gone to Mexico at age fourteen, where he had received his scars while fighting bandits; that he had been a member of a vigilance committee.

No answers were forthcoming from the prisoner's autobiographical manuscript, for he had ripped it up the day before his death. It was further discovered that Owen had had a cache of morphine capsules on his person and could have committed suicide at any time.

The unidentified tramp's identity was a matter of speculation in the nation's papers for a couple days more. For a while, it was thought that John Owen might have been the criminal's real name after all. There actually had been a mountain desperado by that name who had left Bell County years before and had become a professional felon.

Then the mystery died like a dog. The Chief of the Louisville Detective Department picked up his morning paper and saw a photograph of John Owen. The detective thought Owen looked awfully familiar and thumbed through a rogue's gallery of photographs to confirm his suspicions. He found that "John Owen" was identical to William Owen, alias "Shiner" Tom Sullivan, a crook who had formerly lived in the city and who had spent a considerable portion of his life in reform school, the Frankfort penitentiary, and the Louisville workhouse. His rap sheet was long and impressive; he had been arrested several times starting at age fifteen for crimes ranging from petty theft to highway robbery. He had come from Middlesboro, the place "John Owen" had claimed as a hometown. The bullet wound scars that adorned his body came not from Mexican bandits but were the fruits of a failed attempt to hold up an armed Louisville barkeeper. The Chief of Detectives noted to the press that years before he had tried to befriend Owen when the latter was sentenced to the workhouse; even then, Owen had been tight-lipped concerning his family, his background, and his place of origin. Owen had never been to college, so it appears he simply read a lot and was adept at faking a veneer of refinement and education. A certain poverty of imagination might be indicated by the fact that, when choosing an alias, he altered his first name but did not bother to change his last.

Although Owen destroyed his autobiography, he had allowed his cellmate John Meece to read it. Owen had also told his friend where he had buried about $800 in stolen money and Meece anxiously waited for his prison term to expire so he could go on a treasure hunt. He was released a week after Owen's hanging and made a beeline for Kossuth County, Iowa—evidence that Owen and Daily had indeed murdered the two train employees there.

As the year 1901 dawned, John Meece spilled the beans as to what his late cellmate had told him about his life story. John Owen, William Owen, and "Shiner" Tom Sullivan were in fact the same person, since the details revealed matched what was known of William Owen's life—for example, that he had lived in Louisville and had been a member of the Eleventh Street gang. There is no indication that Meece ever found Owen's hidden treasure. Perhaps Owen lied about that, as he had lied about so many things in his last days.

A Picnic Spoiled

William Zinsmeister's lot was not easy. At age thirty-five, he was divorced and had achieved no higher station in life than being a vendor of soft drinks at his stand located at Seventh and Magnolia Streets, Louisville. His former wife Mary, nearly twenty years his senior, had met a horrible death on November 19, 1922, when she had recklessly heated a container of gasoline on a stove with the intention of cleaning a coat. The gas exploded, setting her clothes aflame. Zinsmeister's brother Louis was in prison at Frankfort, serving a life term; on May 24, 1917, he had shot and killed a married couple, Lawrence and Elizabeth Reinhardt, right in front of their teenage daughter during an argument over Louis's digging on the Reinhardts' property. Yet, what really seemed to prey on William Zinsmeister's mind was his fifteen-year-old daughter Mamie. She had been showing an annoying independent streak lately. She had started keeping company with boys! What was to be done?

Relatives noted that Mr. Zinsmeister had had a fierce temper all his life and he had a Louisville police record to prove it. He had been arrested for violating Prohibition and for firing weapons. He also had a drinking problem, which had a volatile effect on his temper. His stepdaughter, Mrs. Chris Luckert, noted: "He never wanted his children to go anywhere or have any pleasure…. He did not care so much about boys, but some way he didn't believe that girls should have anything." His attitude made life miserable for his daughter Mamie. The aforementioned Mrs. Luckert said of her stepsister, "That child never went anywhere in peace." He was known to threaten boys who wanted to go out with Mamie and once physically removed her from the presence of a boy walking with her in a local park. Zinsmeister's neighbors thought he was crazy and dangerous, making him a textbook example of a man who should have been picked up by the law, examined by physicians and psychiatrists, and involuntarily committed if necessary. But nothing was done.

On Saturday, June 23, 1923, Mamie received a call from fifteen-year-old Edward "Pete" Crowley, inviting her to go to a picnic to be held the next day on the banks of the Ohio at Ed Senn's farm on Cane Run Road. The picnic was sponsored not by the wild youth of the Roaring Twenties but by St. William's Catholic Church. Nevertheless, Mr. Zinsmeister forbade her to go.

On Sunday, Zinsmeister came to his home at 1368 South Sixth Street and found that Mamie was missing. He asked his stepson-in-law, Mr. Luckert, where she had gone. Upon finding out that she was attending the picnic in defiance of his command, he wanted to know who had accompanied her. Luckert named a few of her acquaintances. In a sputtering fury, Zinsmeister hailed a cab at 1:20 p.m. and rode to the site of the picnic, coincidentally located near both his boyhood home and the spot where his brother Louis had killed the Reinhardt couple five years earlier. Just before Zinsmeister left, he said to Mr. Luckert: "I am going to kill five kids this afternoon." Luckert took him at his word and hurried to the picnic site to warn Mamie; by the time he arrived, the coming tragedy had already been enacted. He should have phoned the police instead.

After arriving at the river, Zinsmeister paid his fare and mingled among the estimated fifty-five picnickers. Eventually, he found Mamie—not drinking bootleg hooch, smoking cigarettes, playing jazz records on a portable Victrola, or flirting with a "sheik," but merely sitting on a log near the river's edge with two female friends, Bertha Hefferman and Gertrude Franconia. When she spotted her father approaching, Mamie said, "Hello, Daddy!"

"What are you doing out here, Mamie?" he demanded.

"I came for a good time."

"Well, I'm going to kill you."

He immediately drew a pistol from his pocket and started shooting. Two bullets entered Mamie's head, killing her instantly. However, the irate father was determined to take out his anger on all those who, in his somewhat less than rational judgment, had led his daughter so astray as to make her want to attend a church function. He shot Gertrude Franconia, eighteen, in the leg. Sixteen-year-old Sarah Connelly was swimming when one of Zinsmeister's bullets hit her in the back and exited through her neck. Her body crumpled and was carried away by the current in view of horrified spectators.

One victim, eighteen-year-old Thomas Mullaney, fought back heroically. When he saw that Zinsmeister was out of bullets, he came out of the river and grappled with the killer, who clouted him over the head with the empty revolver. When Mullaney succeeded in taking the gun, he threw it into the river. However, Zinsmeister had brought a second revolver as a backup weapon and he shot Mullaney in the shoulder. Zinsmeister continued firing randomly at swimmers and fleeing picnickers. Charles Eifler, sixteen, received a flesh wound in the face and a bullet in the left shoulder as he swam, Zinsmeister following along the bank and shooting at him. "I'll kill you for going with my daughter!" he shouted, mistaking Eifler for Edward "Pete" Crowley.

"I never went with your daughter," the terrified and bleeding Eifler responded. Showing compassion, Zinsmeister said, "I'll let you go if you promise to be a good boy." Eifler promised most fervently to be virtuous and Zinsmeister helped him out of the water. Then he walked away. (The real "Pete" Crowley was indeed among the picnickers, undoubtedly relieved that Zinsmeister did not recognize him.)

The carnage could have been much worse considering that the killer had brought ninety rounds of ammunition. For some reason he ceased the massacre after firing a total of eighteen shots and, perhaps in the mood to take a sentimental journey, walked toward the nearby home of his parents Peter and Ellen Zinsmeister on Camp Ground Road.

As Zinsmeister continued on the last stroll of his life, he wandered through a campground occupied by W. P. Fitzgerald and J. T. Kinberger. The two men found him standing noticeably drunk at a water pump, the gun still in his bloody hand. He told Fitzgerald, who happened to be an acquaintance, that he would shoot himself in five minutes. Fitzgerald and Kinberger, showing an admirable sense of social decorum, begged him to do it somewhere other than their camp as ladies were present. Zinsmeister mentioned by way of casual conversation that he had just killed his own daughter. After taking a drink from a water bucket he waved goodbye and recommenced his walk—to be more precise, he ran, aware that the police would soon be looking for him and time was running out. Minutes later, eyewitnesses saw him unsuccessfully attempting to open the gate at his parents' home. No one knows what grand finale he had been planning, but instead he walked to the neighboring Gocke farm and sat under an accommodating shade tree. There, only a hundred feet from the place where he had been born, he held his revolver to his head and blew out his whisky-soaked brains.

The victims of Zinsmeister's rampage were neither rich nor prominent and, therefore, the story dropped from the national papers almost immediately. It was forgotten by everyone except those most affected: the friends and relatives of the dead and survivors who spent the rest of their lives pondering how lucky they had been that day. The aftermath can be summed up in a few short sentences. Gertrude Franconia, Charles Eifler, and Thomas Mullaney were not seriously injured and soon recovered. The Coast Guard searched in vain for the body of Sarah Connelly on the evening of her death. Fishermen recovered it on the morning of June 25 and she was taken to St. Louis Cemetery for burial. William Zinsmeister was laid to rest in an unmarked grave in Cave Hill Cemetery, far from his daughter who was buried beside her mother's scorched remains in Calvary Cemetery.

When Zinsmeister's body was taken back to his house for the funeral, his twelve-year-old son William, Jr., took a look at the corpse. Then he excused himself and left for a playmate's house.

Bibliography

How Isaac Desha Escaped the Noose Five Times

Bussey, Charles J. "Joseph Desha (1824-1828)." In *Kentucky's Governors*. Ed. Lowell H. Harrison. Lexington: University Press of Kentucky,2004. (Updated edition.)

"The case of Isaac B. Desha…" *Kentucky Reporter* [Lexington] 20 June 1827: 3.

"A Celebrated Pardon." *Louisville Commercial* 15 Feb. 1885: 6.

Colangelo, Drema. E-mail to author. 27 Jan. 2006.

Coleman, J. Winston. "Kentucky's Most Unusual Criminal Case." *Kentucky Images* 1982: 14-16.

Craig, Berry. "Trial of Governor's Son Created Sensation." *Richmond* [KY] *Register* 26 Apr. 2004: A3.

Deming, W. C. "Not the First." *Louisville Courier-Journal* 12 May 1895, Section I: 7.

"Desha." *Kentucky Reporter* [Lexington] 27 June 1827: 3.

"Desha's Trial." *Kentucky Gazette* [Lexington] 3 Feb. 1825: 3.

"Desha's Trial." *Kentucky Reporter* [Lexington] 7 Feb. 1825: 2+.

"Desha's Trial." *Kentucky Gazette* [Lexington] 10 Feb. 1825: 3.

"Desha's Trial." *Kentucky Reporter* [Lexington] 10 Oct. 1825: 1.

"Domestic Items." *Kentucky Gazette* [Lexington] 22 June 1827: 2.

Hinds, Charles F. "Issue Was Disastrous for Eighth Kentucky Governor." *Lexington Herald* 12 Jan. 1958: 36.

"I. B. Desha." *Kentucky Reporter* [Lexington] 3 Oct. 1825: 3.

"Isaac B. Desha." *Gettysburg* [PA] *Adams Centinel* 23 Aug. 1826.

"Isaac B. Desha." *Kentucky Gazette* [Lexington] 6 July 1827: 2.

"Judge Shannon's Opinion." *Kentucky Gazette* [Lexington] 3 Mar. 1825: 3.

"Kentucky Justice." *Kentucky Reporter* [Lexington] 31 Oct. 1825: 3.

"The *Lexington Whig* furnishes…" *Gettysburg* [PA] *Compiler* 9 Aug. 1826.

"The motion to discharge…" *Kentucky Gazette* [Lexington] 30 Mar. 1827: 3.

Muir, Andrew Forest. "Isaac B. Desha, Fact and Fancy." *Filson Club History Quarterly* Oct. 1956: 319-23.

"A Murdered Man Found." *Kentucky Gazette* [Lexington] 11 Nov. 1824: 3.

"To the Editor." *Kentucky Reporter* [Lexington] 10 July 1826: 3.

"The trial of Isaac B. Desha…" *Kentucky Gazette* [Lexington] 20 Jan. 1825: 3.

Adventures of a Busy Young Man

Colangelo, Drema. E-mails to author. 18 Jan. 2006.

"Examination of a Murderer." *Louisville Daily Journal* 6 June 1857: 3.

Hawkins, Edward. *The Confession of Edward W. Hawkins, A Detail of Crimes Unparalleled in History, etc.* Winchester, KY: *Sun-Sentinel* Office, 1907.

"Lynch Law." *Louisville Daily Courier* 16 Apr. 1857: 3.

Wilson, Jess D. *The Sugar Pond and Fritter Tree.* Manchester, KY: Possum Trot University Press, 2003. (Reprint of 1981 edition.)

Gore in Garrard

The Wilmot Massacre:

"Butchered." *Louisville Courier-Journal* 19 Jan. 1882: 1.

Colangelo, Drema. E-mails to author. 6 Aug., 8 Aug. 2005.

Kentucky State death certificate for Benjamin Wilmot. Number 2915, Volume 1930.

"An Old Tragedy Recalled." *Louisville Courier-Journal* 18 Feb. 1898: 5.

"The Wilmot Horror." *Louisville Courier-Journal* 20 Jan. 1882: 1.

William Austin:

"Betsy Bland's Murderer." *Louisville Courier-Journal* 2 Mar. 1882: 5.

"The Bland Butchery." *Louisville Courier-Journal* 22 Jan. 1882: 4.

Calico, Forrest. *History of Garrard Co., Ky., and Its Churches.* New York: Hobson Book Press, 1947.

"Cheerful." *Kentucky Register* [Richmond] 23 June 1882: 3.

"The Commonwealth." *Louisville Courier-Journal* 28 Sep. 1882: 4.

"Home Harvest: Lancaster." *Louisville Courier-Journal* 13 Oct. 1882: 3.

"Kentucky Intelligence: Lancaster." *Louisville Courier-Journal* 14 Feb. 1882: 2.

"Kentucky: Lancaster." *Louisville Courier-Journal* 12 Oct. 1882: 3.

"Kentucky: the Austin Case." *Louisville Courier-Journal* 17 Feb. 1882: 2.

"Matters in Kentucky." *Louisville Courier-Journal* 16 Feb. 1882: 6.

"Matters in Kentucky: Betsy Bland's Blood." *Louisville Courier-Journal* 18 Feb. 1882: 3.

"Matters in Kentucky: Lancaster." *Louisville Courier-Journal* 16 June 1882: 2.

"Matters in Kentucky: Lancaster." *Louisville Courier-Journal* 17 June. 1882: 3.

"More Garrard Gore." *Louisville Courier-Journal* 21 Jan. 1882: 3.

"Off For Another World." *Kentucky Register* [Richmond] 13 Oct. 1882: 3.

"The Rope Route." *Louisville Courier-Journal* 14 Oct. 1882: 4.

"Swung Off." *Kentucky Register* [Richmond] 20 Oct. 1882: 3.

"William Austin Sentenced." *Louisville Courier-Journal* 20 Feb. 1882: 1.

Death of an Artist

"Clarence Boyd." *Louisville Courier-Journal* 12 June 1883: 3.

"Clarence Boyd Dead." *Louisville Courier-Journal* 9 June 1883: 6.

"Clarence Boyd's Funeral." *Louisville Courier-Journal* 10 June 1883: 8.
"Clarence Boyd's Pictures." *Louisville Courier-Journal* 15 June 1883: 8.
"Clarence Boyd's Pictures." *Louisville Courier-Journal* 20 June 1883: 6.
"Clarence Boyd's Pictures." *Louisville Courier-Journal* 23 June 1883: 5.
"Dismissed." *Louisville Courier-Journal* 16 June 1883: 8.
"In Society." *Louisville Courier-Journal* 8 Feb. 1891: 10.
"In the Courts." *Louisville Courier-Journal* 14 June 1883: 8.
"A Lost Leader." *Louisville Courier-Journal* 13 Mar. 1892: 7.
Price, W. T. "The Exposition Gallery." *Louisville Courier-Journal* 3 Nov. 1883: 5.
Thies, Julie. E-mail to author. 29 Nov. 2005.
"Two Pistol Shots." *Louisville Courier-Journal* 13 June 1883: 8.
"An Unfortunate Affair." *Louisville Courier-Journal* 7 June 1883: 6.

The Best-Looking Man Ever Hanged

"A Demon Meets His Dues." *Owensboro Messenger and Examiner* 20 Jan. 1887: 1.
"Expiated." *Louisville Courier-Journal* 13 Jan. 1887: 5.
"Ill-Health and Drink." *Louisville Courier-Journal* 28 Nov. 1886: 5.
Johnson, Augusta Phillips. *A Century of Wayne County, Kentucky 1800-1900.* Louisville: Standard Printing Co., 1939.
Montell, Lynwood. *Killings.* Lexington: University Press of Kentucky, 1986. (Mr. Montell gives Prewitt the pseudonym "Bronston Nesbitt.")
"Two Horrible Murders." *Louisville Courier-Journal* 31 Oct. 1886: 2.

The Murdered Maid

"Albert Turner's Ghost." *Louisville Courier-Journal* 20 Nov. 1887: 16.
"Alleged Confession." *Louisville Courier-Journal* 24 June 1887: 2.
"An Alibi." *Louisville Courier-Journal* 1 May 1887: 4.
"Another Season of Life." *Louisville Courier-Journal* 16 Feb. 1888: 2.
"At Bay." *Louisville Courier-Journal* 30 Apr. 1887: 1+.
"At Turner's Cell." *Louisville Courier-Journal* 12 June 1887: 7.
"At Turner's Cell." *Louisville Courier-Journal* 24 June 1887: 8.
"Awaiting Death." *Louisville Courier-Journal* 22 June 1888: 6.
"Awaiting Developments." *Louisville Courier-Journal* 3 May 1887: 6.
"Believe Him Innocent." *Louisville Courier-Journal* 24 June 1888: 4.
"Both Guilty." *Louisville Courier-Journal* 13 May 1887: 6.
"Bouquets for Turner." *Louisville Courier-Journal* 26 June 1887: 9.
"The Bowman Benefit." *Louisville Courier-Journal* 18 May 1887: 6.
"The Bowman Fund." *Louisville Courier-Journal* 3 July 1887: 6.

"Brought Back." *Louisville Courier-Journal* 28 Apr. 1887: 6.

"A Brutal Crime." *Louisville Courier-Journal* 22 Apr. 1887: 8.

Bugliosi, Vincent. *Outrage*. New York: Island Books, 1996.

"A Card from Dr. Converse." *Louisville Courier-Journal* 19 Apr. 1888: 8.

"The Criminals Caught." Editorial. *Louisville Courier-Journal* 25 Apr. 1887: 4.

"Daily Bulletin from Patterson." *Louisville Courier-Journal* 19 June 1888: 5.

"Death of Jennie Bowman." *Louisville Courier-Journal* 10 May 1887: 1.

"The Death Penalty." *Louisville Courier-Journal* 14 May 1887: 1.

Dominé, David. *Ghosts of Old Louisville*. Kuttawa, KY: McClanahan Publishing, 2005.

"Doomed." *Louisville Courier-Journal* 7 Oct. 1887: 6.

"Expiated." *Louisville Courier-Journal* 1 July 1887: 1+. (Late edition.)

"Fears of a Mob." *Louisville Courier-Journal* 28 Apr. 1887: 5.

"For His Life." *Louisville Courier-Journal* 19 May 1887: 6.

"Guilty As Charged." *Louisville Courier-Journal* 21 May 1887: 6.

"A Harmless Mob." *Louisville Courier-Journal* 29 Apr. 1887: 5.

"His Last Day." *Louisville Courier-Journal* 1 July 1887: 1.

"His Last Hope Gone." *Louisville Courier-Journal* 24 Nov. 1887: 3.

"Horrible!" *Louisville Courier-Journal* 25 Apr. 1887: 1.

"In and About." *Louisville Courier-Journal* 26 Apr. 1887: 4.

"In and About." *Louisville Courier-Journal* 22 May 1887: 12.

"In and About Kentucky." *Louisville Courier-Journal* 26 May 1888: 4.

"In Doubt." *Louisville Courier-Journal* 26 Apr. 1887: 1.

"In Honor of a Heroine." *Louisville Courier-Journal* 7 Oct. 1888: 8.

"It is reported that ladies are in the habit..." *Louisville Courier-Journal* 26 June 1887: 2.

"Jail-Bird Life." *Louisville Courier-Journal* 23 Oct. 1887: 11.

"Jennie Bowman Dying." *Louisville Courier-Journal* 9 May 1887: 3.

"The Jennie Bowman Fiend." Editorial. *Louisville Courier-Journal* 1 July 1887: 4.

"The Jennie Bowman Fund." *Louisville Courier-Journal* 2 July 1887: 1.

"The Jennie Bowman Monument." *Louisville Courier-Journal* 1 July 1887: 1.

"The Jennie Bowman Monument." *Louisville Courier-Journal* 5 Oct. 1887: 8.

"The Jennie Bowman Monument." *Louisville Courier-Journal* 20 Nov. 1887: 5.

"The Jennie Bowman Monument Fund." *Louisville Courier-Journal* 4 July 1887: 6.

"The last act in the sorrowful drama..." *Louisville Courier-Journal* 11 May 1887: 1.

"Latest News from Patterson." *Louisville Courier-Journal* 20 June 1888: 5.

"Miss Bowman Recovering." *Louisville Courier-Journal* 24 Apr. 1887: 8.

"Miss Bowman's Story." *Louisville Courier-Journal* 23 Apr. 1887: 2.

"More Life for Patterson." *Louisville Courier-Journal* 23 May 1888: 2.

"Mr. Turner's Guests." Editorial. *Louisville Courier-Journal* 2 July 1887: 4.

"A Murderer's Rage." *Louisville Courier-Journal* 23 June 1887: 5.

"Murder Must Be Punished." Editorial. *Louisville Courier-Journal* 23 Apr. 1887: 4.

"New Evidence." *Louisville Courier-Journal* 2 Feb. 1888: 8.

"No False Hopes Held Out." *Louisville Courier-Journal* 16 June 1888: 5.

"O'Doherty is Sanguine." *Louisville Courier-Journal* 27 Nov. 1887: 16.

"Of Tear-Drop Granite." *Louisville Courier-Journal* 4 Oct. 1888: 8.

"Our Colored People." *Louisville Courier-Journal* 3 July 1887: 11.

"Patterson Again." *Louisville Courier-Journal* 31 July 1888: 3.

"The Patterson Case." *Louisville Courier-Journal* 28 Nov. 1887: 8.

"The Patterson Case." *Louisville Courier-Journal* 11 Feb. 1888: 8.

"The Patterson Case." *Louisville Courier-Journal* 12 Feb. 1888: 7.

"The Patterson Case." *Louisville Courier-Journal* 18 Apr. 1888: 3.

"The Patterson Case." *Louisville Courier-Journal* 19 Apr. 1888: 8.

"The Patterson Case." *Louisville Courier-Journal* 15 May 1888: 6.

"Patterson is Happy." *Louisville Courier-Journal* 21 June 1888: 6.

"Patterson Must Die." *Louisville Courier-Journal* 15 June 1888: 1.

"Patterson Reprieved." *Louisville Courier-Journal* 25 Jan. 1888: 5.

"Patterson's Day." *Louisville Courier-Journal* 29 Nov. 1887: 6.

"Patterson's Funeral." *Louisville Courier-Journal* 9 July 1888: 6.

"Patterson's Last Days." *Louisville Courier-Journal* 19 Dec. 1887: 8.

"Patterson's Last Days." *Louisville Courier-Journal* 14 Jan. 1888: 8.

"Patterson's Last Hope." *Louisville Courier-Journal* 9 Oct. 1887: 12.

"Patterson's Reprieve." *Louisville Courier-Journal* 17 Feb. 1888: 6.

"The Proof and the Law." *Louisville Courier-Journal* 24 Jan. 1888: 1.

"Robert Crow's Story." *Louisville Courier-Journal* 10 Feb. 1888: 6.

"Safe in Jail." *Louisville Courier-Journal* 27 Apr. 1887: 2.

"Still On Trial." *Louisville Courier-Journal* 20 May 1887: 6.

"The Story is Told." Editorial. *Louisville Courier-Journal* 10 May 1887: 4.

"Strangled to Death." *Louisville Courier-Journal* 23 June 1888: 6.

"Those having in charge the matter…" *Louisville Courier-Journal* 19 June 1887: 1.

"Times of Peace." *Louisville Courier-Journal* 2 May 1887: 8.

"To Hang at Daybreak." *Louisville Courier-Journal* 28 June 1887: 8.

"To Jennie Bowman." *Louisville Courier-Journal* 3 Feb. 1888: 8.

"To Jennie Bowman's Memory." *Louisville Courier-Journal* 6 Oct. 1888: 8.

"To Save His Neck." *Louisville Courier-Journal* 21 Jan. 1888: 1.

"Turner Buried." *Louisville Courier-Journal* 3 July 1887: 8.

"Turner Hanged." *Louisville Courier-Journal* 2 July 1887: 6.

"Turner's Big Day." *Louisville Courier-Journal* 29 June 1887: 6.

"Turner's Five-Cent Show." *Louisville Courier-Journal* 3 July 1887: 4.

"Turner's Last Sunday." *Louisville Courier-Journal* 27 June 1887: 8.

"Twelve Days to Live." *Louisville Courier-Journal* 19 June 1887: 7.

"Under the Sod." *Louisville Courier-Journal* 11 May 1887: 8.

"Visiting the Murderer." *Louisville Courier-Journal* 5 June 1887: 10.

"Wants a Big Funeral." *Louisville Courier-Journal* 30 June 1887: 6.

"Will Die Game." *Louisville Courier-Journal* 25 June 1887: 6.

"Will Patterson Hang?" *Louisville Courier-Journal* 5 Sep. 1887: 8.

"William Patterson's Case." *Louisville Courier-Journal* 20 May 1888: 11.

"You Must Die." *Louisville Courier-Journal* 31 May 1887: 7.

Never Tease an Angry Sheriff

"Acquitted." *Louisville Courier-Journal* 24 Feb. 1895: 2.

"Back to Jail." *Louisville Courier-Journal* 17 Jan. 1895: 1.

"Bad for Vanarsdall." *Louisville Courier-Journal* 16 Jan. 1895: 2.

Colangelo, Drema. E-mail to author. 27 Feb. 2006.

"The Defense." *Louisville Courier-Journal* 19 Feb. 1895: 1.

"His Fate Will Soon Be Known…" *Louisville Courier-Journal* 23 Feb. 1895: 2.

"In and About Kentucky." *Louisville Courier-Journal* 28 Feb. 1895: 4.

"Jury Charged." *Louisville Courier-Journal* 22 Feb. 1895: 3.

Kentucky State death certificate for John VanArsdale. Number 18796, Volume 1943.

"Ruled Out." *Louisville Courier-Journal* 21 Feb. 1895: 2.

"Shot Down." *Louisville Courier-Journal* 5 Jan. 1895: 1.

"Threats." *Louisville Courier-Journal* 20 Feb. 1895: 1.

"Two Years for Murder! One Year for Theft." *Louisville Courier-Journal* 26 May 1895, Section II: 4.

"The Vanarsdall Acquittal." *Louisville Courier-Journal* 2 Mar. 1895: 6.

"Vanarsdall Indicted." *Louisville Courier-Journal* 8 Feb. 1895: 9.

"The Vanarsdall Verdict." *Louisville Courier-Journal* 1 Mar. 1895: 4.

"Vanarsdal's Trial." *Louisville Courier-Journal* 17 Feb. 1895: 3.

"Vanarsdall's Case Called." *Louisville Courier-Journal* 15 Feb. 1895: 1.

"Vanarsdall's Trial Set." *Louisville Courier-Journal* 12 Feb. 1895: 2.

"Vanarsdell Tells of His Crime." *Louisville Courier-Journal* 13 Jan. 1895, Section I: 5.

"Vanarsdell Was Waiting." *Louisville Courier-Journal* 12 Jan. 1895: 1.

"Was Shot From Behind." *Louisville Courier-Journal* 6 Jan. 1895: 2.

Webb, Donna Jean. *Mercer County, KY, Newspaper Extracts, Vol. One*. Lexington: Donna Jean Webb, 1996.

---. *Mercer County, KY, Newspaper Extracts, Vol. Two*. Lexington: Donna Jean Webb, 1996.

"Who Will Try It?" *Louisville Courier-Journal* 25 Jan. 1895: 1.

Sketches in Kentucky Murder

Tripped by His Big Toe:

"Betrayed by a Big Toe." *Louisville Courier-Journal* 20 Aug. 1885: 1.

"Crime's Punishment." *Louisville Courier-Journal* 24 Apr. 1886: 3.

"For the Murder of a Woman." *Louisville Courier-Journal* 19 Sep. 1885: 4.

History of Union County, Ky. Evansville, Ind.: Courier Co., 1886.

The Acid Assassin:

"Can Prove an Alibi." *Louisville Courier-Journal* 17 Nov. 1897: 3.

"Capt. Hoobler's Murderer." *Louisville Courier-Journal* 9 Nov. 1897: 3.

"Chase for a Murderer." *New York Times* 6 Nov. 1897: 3.

"Killed by Muriatic Acid." *Louisville Courier-Journal* 4 Nov. 1897: 3.

"May be Henry Halbert." *Louisville Courier-Journal* 18 Nov. 1897: 4.

Murder at the Revival:

Bailey, Jack Dalton. *Murders, Mischief, Mysteries, Mayhem, Madness, Misdemeanors and Downright Meanness in Mercer, Vol. One.* N.p.: Harrodsburg, KY, c. 2004.

"Dick Votaw Killed." *Louisville Courier-Journal* 8 July 1898: 5.

"Officers and a Posse Following Richard Votaw." *Louisville Courier-Journal* 5 July 1898: 5.

"Votaw Still at Large." *Louisville Courier-Journal* 6 July 1898: 5.

The Fatal Barnyard Fowl Impersonation:

Baldwin, Flora. Personal interview, circa 1980.

"The Fight at McKee." *Louisville Courier-Journal* 30 Aug. 1899: 1.

"Hand-To-Hand Fight." *Louisville Courier-Journal* 2 Nov. 1899: 2.

A Corpse in the Closet:

"He Dies, Too." *Louisville Courier-Journal* 24 June 1901: 5.

"Hid Body." *Louisville Courier-Journal* 23 June 1901, Section I: 7.

"Murderer and Suicide Buried in Frankfort." *Louisville Courier-Journal* 25 June 1901: 7.

"Trap Door Found." *Louisville Courier-Journal* 30 June 1901, Section I: 4.

Murder Near the Springhouse:

"Hundreds of Men are Searching..." *Louisville Courier-Journal* 22 Aug. 1902: 1.

"Murdered…" *Louisville Courier-Journal* 21 Aug. 1902: 1.

"Suicide was the Last Refuge…" *Louisville Courier-Journal* 23 Aug. 1902: 1.

At Least He Had a Good Motive:
"Killed Him in a Quarrel Over $1.50." *Louisville Courier-Journal* 13 Feb. 1903: 2.
"Sent Up for Eleven Years." *Louisville Courier-Journal* 20 June 1903: 4.
"Shot Down." *Louisville Courier-Journal* 12 Feb. 1903: 2.
"Waives Examining Trial." *Louisville Courier-Journal* 14 Feb. 1903: 3.

"Bad Tom" Smith Entertains 5,000 Spectators
"Assassinated." *Louisville Courier-Journal* 7 Feb. 1895: 1.
"'Bad Tom' Smith May Escape Execution." *Louisville Courier-Journal* 5 May 1895, Section I: 9.
"'Bad Tom' Smith's Case." *Louisville Courier-Journal* 9 June 1895, Section I: 5.
"Both Held in Heavy Bond." *Louisville Courier-Journal* 10 Feb. 1895, Section I: 3.
Colangelo, Drema. E-mail to author. 3 Apr. 2006.
"Confessed on the Scaffold." *Louisville Courier-Journal* 29 June 1895: 1+.
"Confession." *Louisville Courier-Journal* 27 Apr. 1900: 5.
"Dies To-Day." *Louisville Courier-Journal* 28 June 1895: 4.
"Found Guilty." *Hamilton* [O.] *Republican* 18 Mar. 1895: 1.
"Gets Off Light." *Louisville Courier-Journal* 17 Oct. 1893: 3.
"Guarding Tom Smith." *Louisville Courier-Journal* 26 June 1895: 7.
"Gossip from the State Papers." *Louisville Courier-Journal* 18 June 1895: 4.
Hayes, Charles. "The Hanging of Bad Tom Smith…" Part One. *Kentucky Explorer* Sep. 1994: 63-8.
---. "The Hanging of Bad Tom Smith…" Part Two. *Kentucky Explorer* Oct. 1994: 72-6.
"His Accomplice." *Louisville Courier-Journal* 15 Mar. 1895: 1.
"His Last Hope Gone." *Louisville Courier-Journal* 22 June 1895: 1.
"His Life Pays." *Louisville Courier-Journal* 14 Mar. 1895: 1.
"In and About Kentucky." *Louisville Courier-Journal* 17 May 1895: 4.
"It Is Safe." *Louisville Courier-Journal* 16 Aug. 1895: 7.
"Joseph Adkins." *Louisville Courier-Journal* 6 Dec. 1899: 2.
"Long Mountain Journey." *Louisville Courier-Journal* 30 June 1895, Section I: 2.
"Miscellany That Interests Kentuckians." *Louisville Courier-Journal* 17 June 1895: 4.
"Mrs. M'Quinn Also Guilty." *Louisville Courier-Journal* 17 Mar. 1895: 4.
"Neither Believes It." *Louisville Courier-Journal* 30 June 1895: 5.
"Nerve Failed." *Louisville Courier-Journal* 23 June 1895, Section I: 7.
"The Noose." *Louisville Courier-Journal* 14 Apr. 1895, Section II: 3.
"Oath-Bound." *Louisville Courier-Journal* 16 Mar. 1895: 3.

Pearce, John Ed. *Days of Darkness*. Lexington: University Press of Kentucky, 1994.

---. "Feuds." *The Kentucky Encyclopedia*. Ed. John E. Kleber. Lexington: University Press of Kentucky, 1992.

"A Remarkable Execution." Editorial. *Louisville Courier-Journal* 1 July 1895: 4.

"A Shocking Tragedy." *Louisville Courier-Journal* 1 Sep. 1898: 8.

"Tom Smith Must Hang." *Louisville Courier-Journal* 21 June 1895: 3.

"Tom Smith to Take an Appeal." *Louisville Courier-Journal* 14 May 1895: 1.

"Unmoved." *Louisville Courier-Journal* 20 Mar. 1895: 1.

"Wanted Vengeance." *Louisville Courier-Journal* 13 May 1893: 4.

"Weird Folk Songs of To-Day Among the Eastern Kentucky Highlands." *Louisville Courier-Journal* 7 May 1911, Section IV: 3.

"Will Be Respited." *Louisville Courier-Journal* 30 May 1895: 5.

Works Project Administration (WPA) Writers' Program. *In the Land of Breathitt*. New York: Bacon, Percy and Daggett, 1941.

What Came of Stealing Some Quilts

"All Ready." *Louisville Courier-Journal* 4 Oct. 1896, Section II: 8.

"Buford Overton." *Louisville Courier-Journal* 11 Oct. 1896, Section I: 2.

"Date of Execution." *Louisville Courier-Journal* 12 Sep. 1896: 10.

"Flight for Life." *Louisville Courier-Journal* 15 Sep. 1895, Section I: 6.

"For the Loeb Murder." *Louisville Courier-Journal* 27 Aug. 1895: 3.

"Hope for Clemency." *Louisville Courier-Journal* 29 Sep. 1896: 3.

Kentucky State death certificate for John Scott. Number 19828, Volume 1922.

"Murderer Overton Caught." *Louisville Courier-Journal* 2 Sep. 1896: 9.

"Murderers Run Down." *Louisville Courier-Journal* 26 June 1895: 6.

"One Is Dead." *Louisville Courier-Journal* 27 June 1895: 9.

"Overton." *Louisville Courier-Journal* 13 Oct. 1896: 7.

"Overton Still At Liberty." *Louisville Courier-Journal* 18 Sep. 1895: 6.

"Overton's Last Night." *Louisville Courier-Journal* 12 Oct. 1896: 3.

"Peddler and Wife Murdered." *Louisville Courier-Journal* 24 June 1895: 2.

"Reward for an Escaped Murderer." *Louisville Courier-Journal* 17 Sep. 1895: 5.

RootsWeb.com. Messageboard posts, circa Oct. 2002. <http://archiver.rootsweb.com/th/read/KYHARLAN/2002-10/1035907779>.

"To Hang." *Louisville Courier-Journal* 20 Aug. 1895: 6.

"Told It All." *Louisville Courier-Journal* 28 Aug. 1895: 7.

The Fictitious and Real Ordeals of Robert Laughlin

"Arrested." *Louisville Courier-Journal* 17 Feb. 1896: 1.

"Arrested All the Mob." *Louisville Courier-Journal* 26 Feb. 1896: 5.

"Cremated." *Louisville Courier-Journal* 16 Feb. 1896, Section I: 4.

"Disguised." *Louisville Courier-Journal* 19 Feb. 1896: 2.

"Evidence." *Louisville Courier-Journal* 14 July 1896: 5.

"The Evidence All Heard." *Louisville Courier-Journal* 16 July 1896: 5.

"Five Murder Cases." *Louisville Courier-Journal* 17 Feb. 1896: 1.

"Good Counsel Prevailing." *Louisville Courier-Journal* 7 Mar. 1896: 4.

"Hiding." *Louisville Courier-Journal* 18 Feb. 1896: 1.

"In and About Kentucky." *Louisville Courier-Journal* 24 Feb. 1896: 4.

"A Jailer's Happy Thought." *Louisville Courier-Journal* 24 Feb. 1896: 2.

"Last Day." *Louisville Courier-Journal* 9 Jan. 1897: 1.

"Laughlin." *Louisville Courier-Journal* 12 Mar. 1896: 6.

"Laughlin." *Louisville Courier-Journal* 17 Mar. 1896: 7.

"Laughlin In Danger Once More…" *Louisville Courier-Journal* 15 July 1896: 3.

"Laughlin, the Double Murderer…" *Louisville Courier-Journal* 10 July 1896: 7.

"Laughlin's Last Letters." *Louisville Courier-Journal* 13 Jan. 1897: 5.

"The Law in the Case." *Louisville Courier-Journal* 31 Dec. 1896: 2.

"Neck Broken." *Louisville Courier-Journal* 10 Jan. 1897, Section I: 2.

"No Further Dangers of a Mob." *Louisville Courier-Journal* 22 Feb. 1896: 2.

"No Hope." *Louisville Courier-Journal* 7 Jan. 1897: 1.

"On Trial." *Louisville Courier-Journal* 11 July 1896: 7.

"Postponed." *Louisville Courier-Journal* 18 Mar. 1896: 4.

"Prayed Aloud." *Louisville Courier-Journal* 20 Feb. 1896: 6.

"Returned to Brooksville." *Louisville Courier-Journal* 8 Jan. 1897: 1.

"Says He Is Innocent." *Louisville Courier-Journal* 28 Apr. 1896: 7.

"Sentenced." *Louisville Courier-Journal* 18 July 1896: 5.

"Sheriff Backs Down." *Louisville Courier-Journal* 3 Jan. 1897, Section II: 6.

"Some Unfounded Reports." *Louisville Courier-Journal* 19 Nov. 1896: 1.

"Verdict." *Louisville Courier-Journal* 17 July 1896: 5.

"Wife-Murderer Laughlin." *Louisville Courier-Journal* 15 Nov. 1896, Section I: 2.

In Which Mr. Dever and Mrs. West Lose Their Social Standing

"Adding to Kentucky's Bad Name." *Louisville Courier-Journal* 2 Jan. 1896: 4.

"After the Assassins." *Louisville Courier-Journal* 6 Feb. 1896: 6.

"Boyle to Be Tried." *Louisville Courier-Journal* 28 Apr. 1896: 8.

Colangelo, Drema. E-mail to author. 6 Feb. 2007.

"Condemned." *Louisville Courier-Journal* 31 Dec. 1895: 1.

"Had Talked Too Freely." *Louisville Courier-Journal* 10 Jan. 1896: 7.

"In the Jury's Hands." *Louisville Courier-Journal* 14 May 1896: 1.

"Is Alma Dever Dead?" *Louisville Courier-Journal* 8 Sep. 1898: 5.

"John Boyle." *Louisville Courier-Journal* 13 Feb. 1896: 8.

"The Jury Failed to Agree." *Louisville Courier-Journal* 15 May 1896: 2.

"Lee Boyle." *Louisville Courier-Journal* 23 Feb. 1896, Section I: 7.

"Lee Boyle's Trial Begun." *Louisville Courier-Journal* 12 May 1896: 5.

"The Marion County Outrage." *Louisville Courier-Journal* 1 Jan. 1896: 4.

"May Soon Be Captured." *Louisville Courier-Journal* 1 Jan. 1896: 2.

"May Yet Indict All." *Louisville Courier-Journal* 16 Feb. 1896, Section I: 3.

"One Hundred Witnesses." *Louisville Courier-Journal* 28 Apr. 1896: 8.

"Phillips in More Hot Water." *Louisville Courier-Journal* 11 Jan. 1896: 2.

"Phillips Shifts the Blame." *Louisville Courier-Journal* 10 Jan. 1896: 4.

"Prompted by Revenge." *Louisville Courier-Journal* 7 Jan. 1896: 9.

"Quickly Denounced." *Louisville Courier-Journal* 9 Jan. 1896: 1.

"Shocking Assassination." *Louisville Courier-Journal* 30 Dec. 1895: 1.

"Trial of Lee Boyle." *Louisville Courier-Journal* 13 May 1896: 8.

"Two Indictments Found." *Louisville Courier-Journal* 9 Feb. 1896, Section I: 9.

"The Voice of Marion." Editorial. *Louisville Courier-Journal* 1 Jan. 1896: 4.

"Warned From the County." *Louisville Courier-Journal* 8 Jan. 1896: 2.

The Case of the Killer Coroner

"Bail Fixed." *Louisville Courier-Journal* 28 Sep. 1900: 5.

"Blow on the Head." *Louisville Courier-Journal* 12 Nov. 1900: 2.

"Coroner Being Investigated by Grand Jury." *Louisville Courier-Journal* 17 Oct. 1900: 6.

"Coroner McCullough's Trial Set." *Louisville Courier-Journal* 24 Oct. 1900: 10.

"Did Not Die of a Blow." *Louisville Courier-Journal* 2 Dec. 1900, Section I: 10.

"Dr. McCullough Indicted." *Louisville Courier-Journal* 23 Oct. 1900: 7.

"Goes Free." *Louisville Courier-Journal* 24 Nov. 1900: 1+.

"His Story." *Louisville Courier-Journal* 22 Nov. 1900: 1+.

"In Custody." *Louisville Courier-Journal* 18 Oct. 1904: 10.

"In Death Wm. M. Owen Finds Relief…" *Louisville Courier-Journal* 8 Oct. 1904: 2.

"In the Net." *Louisville Courier-Journal* 30 Oct. 1900: 6.

"Indicted." *Louisville Courier-Journal* 30 Oct. 1900: 7.

"Indictment Bill Against Mrs. McCullough Also." *Louisville Courier-Journal* 25 Oct. 1900: 6.

"More Witnesses." *Louisville Courier-Journal* 17 Oct. 1904: 10.

"Mrs. McCullough Pleads Not Guilty." *Louisville Courier-Journal* 26 Oct. 1900: 6.

"Murder?" *Louisville Courier-Journal* 16 Oct. 1904, Section III: 1.

"No Reason to Hold Mrs. Owen..." *Louisville Courier-Journal* 21 Oct. 1904: 5.

"On Thursday." *Louisville Courier-Journal* 26 Sep. 1900: 5.

"On $2,500 Bond." *Louisville Courier-Journal* 19 Oct. 1904: 5.

"One Shy." *Louisville Courier-Journal* 21 Nov. 1900: 5.

"Shot Dead." *Louisville Courier-Journal* 25 Sep. 1900: 1+.

"To Be Heard Today." *Louisville Courier-Journal* 27 Sep. 1900: 10.

"Tripped." *Louisville Courier-Journal* 23 Nov. 1900: 5.

"Was Hit With a Brick." *Louisville Courier-Journal* 1 Dec. 1900: 3.

Four Murderers

William McCarty:

"Another Witness Found." *Louisville Courier-Journal* 4 May 1902, Section I: 9.

"The Case Appealed." *Louisville Courier-Journal* 24 Aug. 1902, Section III: 1.

"Clemency Refused..." *Louisville Courier-Journal* 12 May 1902: 5.

"Damaging Testimony..." *Lexington Morning Herald* 4 May 1902: 3.

"Death Penalty..." *Louisville Courier-Journal* 26 June 1902: 3.

"Doctor Called..." *Lexington Morning Herald* 5 May 1902: 4.

"Driven Insane by M'Carty Tragedy." *Louisville Courier-Journal* 26 Apr. 1902: 4.

"Evaded Death on Gallows...." *Louisville Courier-Journal* 16 May 1903: 4.

"Execution of M'Carty." *Louisville Courier-Journal* 27 Mar. 1903: 3.

"Four Men are in Lexington Jail..." *Louisville Courier-Journal* 15 May 1903: 1.

"Four of a Kind." *Louisville Courier-Journal* 4 Apr. 1903: 10.

"Grand Jury Takes M'Carty Case Today." *Lexington Morning Herald* 22 Apr. 1902: 1.

"Huber the Maiden Name..." *Lexington Morning Herald* 4 May 1902: 1.

"Interference Not Probable." *Louisville Courier-Journal* 10 May 1903, Section I: 5.

"Investigating the M'Carty Poisoning." *Louisville Courier-Journal* 19 May 1903: 4.

"Love for His Wife..." *Louisville Courier-Journal* 24 Apr. 1902: 1.

"May 15 Date for Execution..." *Louisville Courier-Journal* 2 Apr. 1903: 5.

"McCarty Barely Able to Walk." *Louisville Courier-Journal* 13 Apr. 1903: 2.

"McCarty Breaking Down." *Louisville Courier-Journal* 21 Apr. 1902: 7.

"M'Carty Breaks Down..." *Lexington Morning Herald* 21 Apr. 1902: 1+.

"M'Carty Has Another Grievance..." *Lexington Morning Herald* 25 Apr. 1902: 1.

"M'Carty Makes Statement to the Public." *Lexington Morning Herald* 24 Apr. 1902: 1+.

"McCarty Preparing for Death." *Louisville Courier-Journal* 9 May 1903: 3.

"M'Carty Sentenced." *Louisville Courier-Journal* 1 July 1902: 5.

"McCarty's Trial Begun." *Louisville Courier-Journal* 25 June 1902: 6.

"M'Keever Still Absent." *Louisville Courier-Journal* 21 May 1903: 4.

"Morphine and Cocaine..." *Louisville Courier-Journal* 28 May 1903: 4.

"Mother Dies Without Knowing Son's Fate." *Louisville Courier-Journal* 10 May 1903, Section I: 5.

"No New Trial…" *Louisville Courier-Journal* 26 Mar. 1903: 2.

"The Penalty for Wife's Murder…" *Louisville Courier-Journal* 15 May 1903: 1.

"Raving Maniac's Mind Was Deranged…" *Lexington Morning Herald* 26 Apr. 1902: 5.

"Refuses to Interfere…" *Louisville Courier-Journal* 14 May 1903: 5.

"Several Theories as to M'Carty's Suicide." *Louisville Courier-Journal* 17 May 1903, Section I: 2.

"To Grand Jury William M'Carty Held…" *Louisville Courier-Journal* 22 Apr. 1902: 5.

"Two Shots Ended the Life…" *Louisville Courier-Journal* 20 Apr. 1902, Section I: 2.

"Was Married Under an Assumed Name." *Louisville Courier-Journal* 4 May 1902, Section I: 9.

"Will Be Buried To-day." *Louisville Courier-Journal* 23 Apr. 1902: 5.

"Young Wife Foully Murdered…" *Lexington Morning Herald* 20 Apr. 1902: 1+.

O'Brien and Whitney:

"Appeal to Gov. Beckham…" *Louisville Courier-Journal* 10 July 1903: 1.

"Arguing for New Trial…" *Louisville Courier-Journal* 17 Apr. 1903: 10.

"Asa Chinn Able to Walk About Hospital." *Louisville Courier-Journal* 22 Oct. 1902: 9.

"Asa Chinn Tells of the Awful Tragedy…" *Louisville Courier-Journal* 3 Nov. 1902: 4.

"Ask for New Trial." *Louisville Courier-Journal* 12 Dec. 1902: 3.

"Brother of O'Brien Arrives…" *Louisville Courier-Journal* 1 July 1903: 4.

"Circulating a Petition." *Louisville Courier-Journal* 24 June 1903: 9.

"Claude O'Brien Ill." *Louisville Courier-Journal* 18 May 1903: 2.

"Clinging to Faint Hope…" *Louisville Courier-Journal* 29 June 1903: 2.

"Coils Are Tightening…" *Louisville Courier-Journal* 13 Oct. 1902: 1+.

"Death is the Verdict…" *Louisville Courier-Journal* 5 Dec. 1902: 1.

"Death Watch on Whitney and O'Brien." *Louisville Courier-Journal* 11 July 1903: 6.

"Each Declares He is Innocent." *Louisville Courier-Journal* 8 July 1903: 3.

"Excused the Jury…" *Louisville Courier-Journal* 6 Dec. 1902: 2.

"February 13 Named as Date…" *Louisville Courier-Journal* 14 Dec. 1902, Section III: 1.

"Feigning Ignorance of the Saw…" *Louisville Courier-Journal* 14 Feb. 1903: 3.

"For Trial." *Louisville Courier-Journal* 25 Nov. 1902: 3.

"Forbids Inoculation of Claude O'Brien." *Louisville Courier-Journal* 4 Mar. 1903: 2.

"Four Men are in Lexington Jail…" *Louisville Courier-Journal* 15 May 1903: 1.

"Four of a Kind." *Louisville Courier-Journal* 4 Apr. 1903: 10.

"Fund to Bring Back…O'Brien's Body." *Louisville Courier-Journal* 18 July 1903: 6.

"Governor Will Hear Plea of Mrs. O'Brien." *Louisville Courier-Journal* 26 June 1903: 2.

"Hundreds of People View Whitney's Body." *Louisville Courier-Journal* 26 July 1903, Section I: 4.

"Identified Fully..." *Louisville Courier-Journal* 15 Oct. 1902: 6.

"Indicted by Special Jury." *Louisville Courier-Journal* 24 Oct. 1902: 2.

"Insanity Will be the Plea..." *Louisville Courier-Journal* 7 July 1903: 10.

"Jailer Relents..." *Louisville Courier-Journal* 17 June 1903: 10.

"Jailer Will Allow No Experimenting." *Louisville Courier-Journal* 1 Mar. 1903, Section II: 1.

"Losing Their Nerve..." *Louisville Courier-Journal* 22 July 1903: 4.

"More Saws are Found..." *Louisville Courier-Journal* 9 July 1903: 5.

"Mrs. O'Brien Broken-Heated." *Louisville Courier-Journal* 11 July 1903: 2.

"Mrs. O'Brien Calls at Chinn Residence." *Louisville Courier-Journal* 2 July 1903: 6.

"Mrs. O'Brien Coming to Lexington..." *Louisville Courier-Journal* 14 June 1903, Section I: 5.

"Murder Mystery at Lexington Solved." *Louisville Courier-Journal* 16 Oct. 1902: 1+.

"No Error is Found..." *Louisville Courier-Journal* 21 May 1903: 2.

"No Relief." *Louisville Courier-Journal* 7 July 1903: 6.

"O'Brien and Whitney to Hang July 24." *Louisville Courier-Journal* 27 June 1903: 1.

"O'Brien's Mother Arrives in Lexington." *Louisville Courier-Journal* 16 June 1903: 3.

"Pathetic." *Louisville Courier-Journal* 30 June 1903: 5.

"Petition for Clemency..." *Louisville Courier-Journal* 10 June 1903: 3.

"Petition for Pardon." *Louisville Courier-Journal* 27 May 1903: 5.

"Preparing to Hang..." *Louisville Courier-Journal* 23 July 1903: 7.

"Records Filed..." *Louisville Courier-Journal* 7 Feb. 1903: 9.

"Rehearing... Is Refused." *Louisville Courier-Journal* 21 June 1903, Section I: 5.

"Reward... Goes to Foster." *Louisville Courier-Journal* 9 Mar. 1903: 2.

"Saws Sent to Claude O'Brien..." *Louisville Courier-Journal* 13 Feb. 1903: 1.

"Separate Trials." *Louisville Courier-Journal* 3 Dec. 1902: 9.

"Sheriff Ordered to Summon Special Grand Jury." *Louisville Courier-Journal* 19 Oct. 1902, Section I: 5.

"Shot Down in Cold Blood..." *Louisville Courier-Journal* 12 Oct. 1902, Section IV: 1.

"Smiling to the Last..." *Louisville Courier-Journal* 25 July 1903: 2.

"Sorrowing Mother to Visit Condemned Son." *Louisville Courier-Journal* 4 June 1903: 9.

"Suspects May Have Been Under Arrest in Louisville..." *Louisville Courier-Journal* 14 Oct. 1902: 1.

"Sympathy for Them." *Louisville Courier-Journal* 15 Jan. 1903: 5.

"Tack Chosen by Claude O'Brien..." *Louisville Courier-Journal* 17 Oct. 1902: 2.

"Thinks Her Husband is the One Condemned." *Louisville Courier-Journal* 15 July 1903: 2.

"Wants Revenge." *Louisville Courier-Journal* 26 July 1903, Section VI: 1.

"Whitney Did It." *Louisville Courier-Journal* 7 Dec. 1902, Section I: 9.

"Whitney Will Testify..." *Louisville Courier-Journal* 4 Dec. 1902: 4.

"Will Expiate Their Crime To-Day on the Scaffold." *Louisville Courier-Journal* 24 July 1903: 3.

"Will Let the Law Take Its Course." *Louisville Courier-Journal* 23 July 1903: 2.

James Bess:

"Absence of Witnesses…" *Louisville Courier-Journal* 13 Mar. 1903: 5.

"Bess Murder Case Argued." *Louisville Courier-Journal* 1 Oct. 1904: 2.

"Bess Will Not Confess." *Louisville Courier-Journal* 16 July 1904: 3.

"Bess Will Plead Insanity." *Louisville Courier-Journal* 21 Mar. 1903: 2.

"Body Will Not Be Exhumed." *Louisville Courier-Journal* 17 Mar. 1903: 5.

"A Death Sentence for Second Time." *Louisville Courier-Journal* 16 Mar. 1904: 3.

"Death the Penalty." *Lexington Morning Herald* 2 Apr. 1903: 1+.

"Death Verdict Returned…" *Louisville Courier-Journal* 2 Apr. 1903: 7.

"Decoy Letter." *Louisville Courier-Journal* 1 Apr. 1903: 1.

"Defendant Testified For Himself." *Lexington Morning Herald* 1 Apr. 1903: 1+.

"Doctor Who Examined Bess Found Nothing the Matter…" *Lexington Morning Herald* 21 May 1903: 5.

"Evidence Was Damaging to Bess." *Lexington Morning Herald* 29 Mar. 1903: 1+.

"Executed." *Louisville Courier-Journal* 14 Jan. 1905: 3.

"Fair Trial Was Given J. W. Bess…" *Louisville Courier-Journal* 28 Oct. 1904: 2.

"Four Men are in Lexington Jail…" *Louisville Courier-Journal* 15 May 1903: 1.

"Four of a Kind." *Louisville Courier-Journal* 4 Apr. 1903: 10.

"Hope for Commutation… Still Lingers." *Louisville Courier-Journal* 30 Dec. 1904: 3.

"Important Testimony..." *Louisville Courier-Journal* 29 Mar. 1903, Section I: 4.

"In a Pond…" *Louisville Courier-Journal* 11 Mar. 1903: 8.

"In Prayer Bess Spends Last Day…" *Louisville Courier-Journal* 13 Jan. 1905: 3.

"James W. Bess on Trial." *Louisville Courier-Journal* 28 Mar. 1903: 3.

"June 12 Fixed as Date…" *Louisville Courier-Journal* 11 Apr. 1903: 3.

"Lexington Murder Case." *Louisville Courier-Journal* 16 Mar. 1903: 5.

"Lexington Notes." *Louisville Courier-Journal* 2 Mar. 1904: 8.

"Lexington Notes." *Louisville Courier-Journal* 9 Mar. 1904: 8.

"Lexington Notes." *Louisville Courier-Journal* 11 Mar. 1904: 2.

"Lexington Notes." *Louisville Courier-Journal* 13 Mar. 1904, Section I: 4.

"Lexington Notes." *Louisville Courier-Journal* 17 Mar. 1904: 2.

"Lexington Notes." *Louisville Courier-Journal* 18 Mar. 1904: 2.

"Lexington Notes." *Louisville Courier-Journal* 26 Mar. 1904: 2.

"New Trial Asked For." *Louisville Courier-Journal* 30 Sep. 1904: 2.

"New Trial for Bess…" *Louisville Courier-Journal* 3 Dec. 1903: 1.
"New Trial Will Be Asked…" *Louisville Courier-Journal* 6 Apr. 1903: 2.
"Notes Written to Mrs. Porter." *Lexington Morning Herald* 31 Mar. 1903: 1+.
"One More Day…" *Louisville Courier-Journal* 12 Jan. 1905: 5.
"Petition for Commutation…" *Louisville Courier-Journal* 26 Dec. 1904: 3.
"Plea of Not Guilty." *Louisville Courier-Journal* 19 Mar. 1903: 1.
"Resigned to His Fate…" *Louisville Courier-Journal* 11 Jan. 1905: 5.
"Restless." *Louisville Courier-Journal* 12 Mar. 1903: 4.
"To Save Neck Attorneys… Will Appeal…" *Louisville Courier-Journal* 19 Dec. 1904: 3.
"Two Letters from Bess…" *Louisville Courier-Journal* 31 Mar. 1903: 1.
"Violent Outbreak from Bess…" *Louisville Courier-Journal* 21 May 1903: 4.
"Visit Paid Hess…by Minister Allen." *Louisville Courier-Journal* 18 July 1904: 3.
"Will Try to Prove Alibi." *Louisville Courier-Journal* 23 Mar. 1903: 2.

Perfect Monsters:
The Murders of Lillian Patrick and Mary Magdalene Pitts

Lillian Patrick:
"Burning at the Stake…" *Louisville Courier-Journal* 30 Nov. 1900: 2.
"The Case of Gibson." *Louisville Courier-Journal* 26 Jan. 1901: 3.
"Child Tortured With Red-Hot Iron." *Louisville Courier-Journal* 29 Nov. 1900: 1.
"Denies His Guilt." *Louisville Courier-Journal* 31 Jan. 1901: 1.
"The Elusive Gibson." *Louisville Courier-Journal* 5 Dec. 1900: 6.
"Escaped…" *Louisville Courier-Journal* 3 Dec. 1900: 2.
"Gibson Before the Court." *Louisville Courier-Journal* 30 Jan. 1901: 1.
"Gibson… Captured…" *Louisville Courier-Journal* 6 Dec. 1900: 6.
"Halbert is Real Name…" *Louisville Courier-Journal* 2 Dec. 1900, Section I: 8.
"His Right Name is John." *Louisville Courier-Journal* 11 Dec. 1900: 6.
"Judge Kinner's Warning." *Louisville Courier-Journal* 29 Jan. 1901: 1.
"Juries Shirk Responsibility." Editorial. *Louisville Courier-Journal* 3 Feb. 1901, Section II: 4.
"No Verdict Reached Yesterday…" *Louisville Courier-Journal* 1 Feb. 1901: 1.
"Officers Still Making Active Search…" *Louisville Courier-Journal* 1 Dec. 1900: 7.
"Prison Doors Close on John Gibson..." *Louisville Courier-Journal* 3 Feb. 1901, Section I: 13.
"Refuses to Relate the Details…" *Louisville Courier-Journal* 8 Dec. 1900: 3.
"Still in Carter County." *Louisville Courier-Journal* 4 Dec. 1900: 2.
"Talkative at First…" *Louisville Courier-Journal* 7 Dec. 1900: 1.

"Verdict of Life Imprisonment..." *Louisville Courier-Journal* 2 Feb. 1901: 1.

Mary Magdalene Pitts:

"Accused Pair Silent." *Lexington Herald* 19 Jan. 1928: 1.

"Accused Pair Still Writing." *Lexington Herald* 13 Jan. 1928: 5.

"Greenup Mob Foiled." *Lexington Herald* 6 Jan. 1928: 1.

"Jury May Decide Pitts' Fate Today." *Lexington Herald* 3 Mar. 1928: 1.

Kentucky State death certificate for Mary Magdalene Pitts. Number 27764, Volume 1927.

"Mother of Slain Baby is Found." *Lexington Herald* 12 Jan. 1928: 1+.

"Mrs. Frazier, Pitts Taken to Greenup." *Lexington Herald* 23 Jan. 1928: 1.

"Mrs. Frazier Pleads Guilty, Gets Life Term." *Lexington Herald* 2 Mar. 1928: 1.

"Neglect Charged." *Lexington Herald* 1 Jan. 1928, Section I: 1.

"New Confessions Begun by Pitts and Mrs. Frazier." *Lexington Herald* 11 Jan. 1928: 1+.

"Officers Fear Mob Violence." *Lexington Herald* 5 Jan. 1928: 1.

"Pitts Denies...That He Was Doped by Mrs. Frazier." *Lexington Herald* 17 Jan. 1928: 1.

"Pitts-Frazier Trial Transferred to Vanceburg..." *Lexington Herald* 29 Jan. 1928, Section I: 1.

"Pitts Hearing Friday." *Lexington Herald* 25 Jan. 1928: 1.

"Pitts is Accused of Second Murder." *Lexington Herald* 16 Jan. 1928: 1.

"Pitts is Given Life Sentence." *Lexington Herald* 4 Mar. 1928: 1.

"Pitts Jury Called." *Lexington Herald* 15 Jan. 1928, Section I: 2.

"Pitts, Woman End Reports." *Lexington Herald* 14 Jan. 1928: 1+.

"Pitts, Woman Not to Face Trial This Term." *Lexington Herald* 28 Jan. 1928: 5.

Richards, Marmon, and David P. Spencer. *Another Time and Place*. N.p.: Schuerholz Graphics, 2000.

"Trial of Mrs. Frazier Begun at Vanceburg." *Lexington Herald* 1 Mar. 1928: 1.

"Woman Accuses Pitts of Causing Child's Death." *Lexington Herald* 10 Jan. 1928: 1+.

Woods, Carrie, and Carrie Rogers. "Hill Doctor of Greenup County Discovered Uncommon Murder." *Kentucky Explorer* Sep. 2007: 36-7.

Hanging of the Mystery Tramp

"College Bred." *Louisville Courier-Journal* 21 Dec. 1900: 1.

"His Silence Was Golden." *Louisville Courier-Journal* 29 Dec. 1900: 5.

"John Owen." *Louisville Courier-Journal* 2 Jan. 1901: 7.

"Light on Mystery." *Louisville Courier-Journal* 26 Dec. 1900: 2.

"Near to Death." *Louisville Courier-Journal* 20 Dec. 1900: 3.

"Owen Kept His Word." *Louisville Courier-Journal* 22 Dec. 1900: 1.

"'Shiner' Tom." *Louisville Courier-Journal* 23 Dec. 1900, Section II: 2.

"Sure Now That He Was 'Shiner John.'" *Louisville Courier-Journal* 4 Jan. 1901: 4.

A Picnic Spoiled

"Body of Picnic Massacre Third Victim is Found." *Louisville Times* 25 June 1923: 1+.

Kentucky State death certificate for Mamie Zinsmeister. Number 15921, Volume 1923.

Kentucky State death certificate for Mary Zinsmeister. Number 24454, Volume 1922.

Kentucky State death certificate for William Zinsmeister. Number 15920, Volume 1923.

"Maniac Kills Daughter, Chum, Self." *Louisville Courier-Journal* 25 June 1923: 1.

"Mrs. Zinsmeister Dies from Gasoline Burns." *Louisville Courier-Journal* 20 Nov. 1922: 8.

"Two Killed, Climax to Ill Feeling." *Louisville Courier-Journal* 25 May 1917: 1.

"Uncontrolled Temper Blamed by Kin for Zinsmeister's Deed." *Louisville Times*
26 June 1923: 1+.

About the Author

Keven McQueen is an instructor in the Department of English and Theater at Eastern Kentucky University and is the author of six books on Kentucky history, including the *Offbeat Kentuckians* series and the true crime book *Murder in Old Kentucky*. He lives in Berea and currently is working on several projects. He is married to his work, but his work is demanding a trial separation.

LET'S ALL GIVE A ROUND OF APPLAUSE TO

Geneta Chumley, Drema Colangelo, Jackie Couture, Paula Cunningham, David Dominé, Eastern Kentucky University's Department of English and Theatre, Eastern Kentucky University Special Archives and Collections, Megan Fairchild, Lee Feathers, Jennifer Gibbs, Dr. James Gifford, Jeff Gray, Rosie Grimm, Florence Huffman, Laura James, The Jesse Stuart Foundation, Rene McGuire, Kyle and Bonnie McQueen, the Darrell McQueen family, Brett Nance, Pat New, Deonna Pinson, Gaile Sheppard, J. B. Speed Art Museum, Michelle Steele, Michelle Stone, Mia Temple, Julie Thies, University of Kentucky Art Museum, Deborah Whalen…and the Architect.

This book was edited by Lee Feathers and Megan Fairchild.